HERE FOR GENEI

The Story of a Maine Ban

HERE FOR GENERATIONS:
The Story of a Maine Bank and its City

Dean Lawrence Lunt

ISLANDPORT PRESS • FRENCHBORO, MAINE

Other Maine books from Islandport Press
Hauling by Hand: The Life and Times of a Maine Island
In Maine
The Story of Mount Desert Island
A History of Little Cranberry Island, Maine

Islandport Press Inc.
22 Lunt Harbor
Frenchboro, Maine 04635
www.islandportpress.com

ISBN: 0-9671662-6-8
Library of Congress Number: 2002101951

First edition published June 2002

This edition published by Islandport Press Inc. in cooperation with
Bangor Savings Bank

Book design: Islandport Press/ Frenchboro and Yarmouth
Book jacket design: CDM Communications/ Portland
Cover photograph courtesy of the *Bangor Daily News*
Printing by: J.S. McCarthy Inc./ Augusta

Dedication

To our customers and employees — past, present and future.
They are the story.

Acknowledgements

It is a cliché to say that a book such as this is a collaborative effort. But it is certainly true. First, as lead author, let me thank Bangor Savings Bank and President P. James Dowe Jr., for the interest, vision and self-assurance to develop a book that is more than corporate history, instead one that truly offers something back to the community through the retelling of Bangor's history, the bank's history and banking history.

Katherine I. Hoving, who also wrote some of the sidebar stories that appear in this book, provided dogged research assistance and much appreciated manuscript and historical critique. Katherine is now at the Adirondack Museum in New York. The bank's 150th Anniversary Book Team of Joyce Sarnacki, Timothy Cropley and David Zelz were crucial in shepherding this book through the development process and in providing important insight and critique. David wrote several sidebar stories for this book, while his interest in bank history and his knowledge of the city as a Bangor native were invaluable.

As for the manuscript, Amy Canfield and Deena Maniscalchi helped edit it, along with Michelle Lunt, Ann Parrish and Jeff Clark. Richard Judd of the University of Maine, Richard Shaw of the *Bangor Daily News*, Arthur Johnson, former vice chair of the Bangor Savings Bank board of trustees and former president of the University of Maine, and Christopher Pinkham, president of the Maine Association of Community Banks, provided important critiques on all or parts of the manuscript. Dick Shaw is a valuable authority on local history and also helped identify photographs. Dana Lippitt at the Bangor Historical Society, Earle G. Shettleworth Jr. at the Maine Historic Preservation Commission, William Cook at the Bangor Public Library, Charlie Campo at the *Bangor Daily News*, Elizabeth Paradis at Fogler Library Special Collections and Marcia Bond and Margaret Cote at Bangor Savings Bank all provided valuable assistance.

We also owe thanks to: Mal Jones, Alice McInnis, and G. Clifton Eames as well as to all those who granted interviews.

Also, thanks to the Bangor Public Library, the Maine Archives, the Maine Historical Society, Everett L. Parker at Moosehead Historical

Society, University of Maine Special Collections, Ann McDonald at the Hamlin Memorial Library and Museum in Paris Hill, The Ruggles House Society in Columbia Falls, the Maine State Library and the Portland Public Library. Special thanks to Stephen King.

And I never close without thanking historians who have gone before and those still producing, upon whose knowledge and experience writers must draw, especially when writing a history book as broad and sweeping as this one. They include Bangor historians John Godfrey of the nineteenth century and James Vickery of the twentieth century as well as Walter Chadbourne who ably chronicled general nineteenth and early twentieth century banking history. Please read our bibliography, and recognize that all those books are not only good sources of information, but many of them are wonderful, if sometimes forgotten, reads.

— D.L.L.

Table of Contents

Introduction

I've done my share of introductions during the thirty-plus years I've been a professional writer, but most of them have been for anthologies or collections of short stories. I never expected to be writing one for the history of a banking institution, especially one prepared by the institution in question, and there's a good story as to how that came about. What makes the story good, I think, is the light it casts on how our business lives and institutions may enrich our personal community lives.

My wife and I came to Bangor in 1979, bought a house, enrolled our three children in the local schools, and put down roots. To us that means community involvement, and community involvement means community service. My wife has worked on a number of boards, including that of the Bangor Public Library, Shaw House (a resource for troubled adolescents), and the Maine Public Broadcasting Network (where she met Jim Dowe of Bangor Savings).

At the same time I got involved in some of the city sports programs at the coaching level and was eventually asked to serve on the Bangor YMCA's board of directors. (This was an especially touching vote of confidence after my spectacular losing record as a Middlers' League coach.)

During my tour of duty on the YMCA board, I became interested in Camp Jordan, the Y's coed sleepaway camp. I had attended camp myself as a kid (on a church scholarship; my mother could never have afforded a week of camp on her own) and had good memories of the experience. The best part, for me, was the way one's relationships with the other kids started, right there, at camp. You didn't have to drag a lot of baggage along with you — how much money your Dad made, where you went to school, what kind of social standing (if any) your family might have. When you throw a bunch of kids together, especially out in the woods, they more often than not learn first to play together and then work together. These are priceless socialization skills that can last a lifetime.

Great as it was, Camp Jordan had some serious problems when I came on the Y's board in the mid-'90s. The septic system was in dire need of an overhaul. The boys' and girls' bathroom and toilet facilities were nearly as bad. Many of the cabins stood on rotting sills, and some of the mattresses had been overrun by mold colonies that, well, let's just say that some of those mattresses looked like something out of a Stephen King novel. Worst of all, the dining hall was in dire danger of falling down and the roof had been covered by a giant blue tarp to keep the rain from flooding the common room below.

The total cost of the necessary renovations and refurbishments ran into the millions. After the sober discussion such a sum warranted (folks may speak lightly of millions in New York, but not in Bangor where the average annual salary is twenty-seven thousand dollars), the Y's board of directors agreed to take on the Camp Jordan Renewal Project. I was teamed with a Bangor businessman (and personal friend) named Paul Means. Our first job was to make a list of potential big contributors — everyone from noted Maine philanthropist Harold Alfond to Portland's extraordinarily generous Libra Foundation — and then brace them for the contributions in the five-, six-, and even the seven-figure range. Eventually, of course, this brought us to the Bangor Savings Bank and the office of Jim Dowe.

You might be forgiven for believing the point of this story is, "We asked, we got, and God bless Bangor Savings Bank!" Well, we did in fact get a contribution a few weeks after we made our pitch, and it was a good one, but that is not the point I have set out to make here. The point is that Paul Means and I found ourselves in a rare and fortunate position, one you can only gain when dealing with a business institution from one's hometown.

Paul Means needed no formal introduction to Jim; they have known each other for years (have probably golfed together, for all I know). Nor did I need one. Jim knew me from the YMCA, he knew my wife from their work together on the MPBN Board, and he may even have read one or two of my books. More importantly, our friends at Bangor Savings Bank needed no introduction to either the YMCA or to Camp Jordan. If you were a stranger in need of directions, most of these ladies and gentlemen could tell you what road to take to get out there and just where to turn.

This sort of knowledge is good for business. Beyond that, though, good is too mild. Once you move into the community sphere, the word is invaluable. Probably the only cities that don't know how wonderful it is to have a strong banking institution that is owned and operated by local people are those not fortunate enough to have such a thing. With Bangor Savings Bank, this sort of commitment to and knowledge of local affairs and needs began a hundred and fifty years ago, in 1852, when Samuel Hersey and Elijah Hamlin (the first president) opened the bank's doors. The truest fact of community life — and the reason, it seems to me, that communities exist in the first place — is that it always puts a higher priority on giving back than on taking out. Employees of Bangor Savings Bank are encouraged to take part in the affairs of their various communities. They are encouraged to serve on various boards — the YMCA, the YWCA, the school board, Eastern Maine Technical College, to mention just a few — and use their banking skills to help the community grow. When I asked Jim how many business loans the bank wrote in the course of a year, the answer was hundreds. When asked how many mortgages the bank had approved, the answer was thousands. Many of these are starter-home mortgages, written for people who are buying their first homes.

Any bank will do the deal if the deal looks good, but all of a banking concern's vital services — from investment management to lending to deposit services — gain a dimension when the people doing the work are the people you see when you go to lunch or maybe to a basketball game at the William S. Cohen School. Bangor Savings has been this sort of hometown resource for a long time, as this remarkable book shows. It also illustrates a long-held belief of mine: a living, vital community has two hearts. One is cultural. The other is the heart that drives business and commerce. Bangor, I think, is in good shape in both spheres. We have a wonderful library, a wonderful symphony orchestra, and a lively community of the mind. We also have a thriving, community-oriented business community, and of this there is no better example than the Bangor Savings Bank.

— Stephen King
March 2002

Prologue

Bangor.

Few city or town names conjure an image and true sense of place — a feeling of being firmly and squarely rooted in the heart of traditional Maine — as does Bangor.

Much like the Eastern and Northern Maine region it has always represented, and like the state of Maine itself, there is a real texture to the name and the city.

For 150 years and even longer if you consider the contributions made to Bangor — not to mention the state — by the bank's founders, Bangor Savings Bank has helped define that sense of place. It is difficult to imagine a more remarkable era or collection of people than Bangor circa 1852. During their active lives, the bank founders built an economy, fought a war, developed entirely new industries, established cultural and communal organizations, and in the process created modern Bangor.

Chief amongst their legacies, of course, is Bangor Savings Bank, the oldest incorporated business still active in Bangor. Mutual banks such as Bangor Savings were born of religiously-inspired social conscience. In the mid-nineteenth century leaders still believed that thrift and industry were the best means by which to lift the poor, protect the growing working class against disaster and old age, and help society by producing better citizens. Until mutual banks were established, most citizens did not have a place or the means to save.

In that vein, Elijah Livermore Hamlin led a group of twenty-four men to start Bangor Savings Bank as a part-philanthropic, part-community-minded effort. Unlike existing commercial banks, which focused on business, investment and return to shareholders, mutual bank trustees at the time received no pay and largely no benefit. Given their public-spirited mission, savings banks were afforded a special place and protection by the state. As Joshua Lawrence Chamberlain (a Brewer native) said as governor in 1870, "These banks are the special depositories of the poor; treasuries of pittances which could in no other way be so well guarded and made profitable. If not kept here many of them would not be kept at all."

Of course, times changed and laws changed and Bangor Savings Bank rose from humble roots to become ever more infused in the city's workaday life. It became not only a place to save money, but a place that provided money to buy a home, a place that offered support to community organizations and finally a place that provided the capital to help Maine businesses. And along the way, the institution's definition of community has expanded to include all of Maine from Aroostook County to York County and from Washington County to Oxford County.

Throughout its history, Bangor Savings Bank has been a common thread running throughout the life of the community, its people and Maine banking. Some of today's bank trustees can trace the involvement of their ancestors back for generations.

Presidents and trustees since the earliest days have been forces in the community, from Elijah Hamlin and lumber baron Samuel F. Hersey to G. Clifton Eames and David Carlisle. Eames, former chairman, retired in the 1990s from N.H. Bragg & Sons, a company started by his great great grandfather in the mid-1800s, while Carlisle, current chairman, still chairs the board at Prentiss & Carlisle, a company started by his grandfather in the early 1900s.

Clearly, a lot of history has passed by the banks of the Kenduskeag Stream, a spot where Bangor Savings Bank has kept its main office for 113 years. The bank has watched not just one or two, but four easily identifiable banking revolutions and seen no less than thirty-one local banks come and go in Bangor. It has survived and helped people through depressions and recessions, floods, fires, wars and social change. And it has watched the life of Bangor as it rose to dizzying heights of grandeur in the mid-1800s when it was, without exaggeration, the "Lumber Capital of the World" and stood as an epicenter of culture, business and dreams. Governors and vice presidents and other leaders rose to power from its streets. The Queen City was a combination of rowdy and refined, its Broadway mansions and majestic church steeples sharing a riverbank with the brothels and bars that catered to the legions of woodsmen and sailors. It was not for tourism purposes that Maine was nicknamed, "The Pine Tree State." It was because of its economic power.

Eventually, the lumber boom died, but like Bangor Savings Bank, the city didn't. It adapted and changed and still stands as the commercial and service hub of the region.

The bank's history, along with the history of Bangor, banking and Maine, are inextricably entwined and provide a remarkable view of how we developed as a people and a place. To know history you must know its texture and its context and its people. We hope you will find this in *Here for Generations: The Story of a Maine Bank and its City.*

There is value in a rich legacy, value in history and value in a proud name as we look to the future.

Bangor.

What could be more "Maine" than that?

— Dean Lawrence Lunt
April 2002

.

Chapter One

The Birth of Bangor

In the sixteenth and seventeenth centuries the Penobscot was a river of dreams, a golden highway said to lead from fish-rich Penobscot Bay to Norumbega, a walled city of gold at the head of the tidewater. Explorers regaled listeners with wondrous tales of an unparalleled land of milk and honey. Such stories of riches to be found in the river valley and in Maine helped lure more explorers across the Atlantic searching for Norumbega, a city said to sit near present-day Bangor.

Of course, there was no gold and no great city, only a beautiful but harsh and remote land, lush in the summer but besieged in winter as the river froze solid, cutting off the inland towns. Even into the mid-1700s, the Penobscot River valley and the lands east remained a vast, mostly untamed wilderness, inhabited by a few thousand Wabanaki who never actively cultivated the land. And the European settlers who finally sought a new life and freedom on those river banks enjoyed not the luxuries of wealth, but struggled through a hardscrabble existence.

The entire Province of Maine also remained mostly unsettled, a sprawling, war-battered buffer sitting between the French strongholds in Canada and the English Massachusetts Bay Colony. Maine's southern coast saw some growth as settlements such as Saco, Kittery and York haltingly evolved from outposts to stable towns, but their expansion was invariably slowed by war and fear. Some settlements were abandoned altogether.

During nearly one hundred years of warfare from the 1670s to the 1760s, the English established no permanent settlement east of Castine on Penobscot Bay. But then the mid-1700s marked a watershed in the settlement of Eastern Maine. In short order, the British vanquished arch-enemy France in North America and made a permanent peace with the remaining Wabanaki tribes.

In those post-war days, even as revolutionary sentiment took root in the Colonies, a tough-minded band of settlers braved the general isolation and lack of basic needs such as money, food and clothing and began building the bleak little riverside settlement of Kenduskeag into the city of Bangor. It was a long haul, but by the mid-1800s, writer Henry David Thoreau proclaimed the city "a star on the edge of night," and its residents were convinced that Bangor would rival New York as a great city of the East.

It all happened so quickly, but it was a long time coming.

The Wabanaki

Wabanaki (Algonquian for "people of the dawn") was the umbrella name for several American Indian tribes who lived in northern New England and Maritime Canada and spoke variations of the Algonquian language. The Wabanaki primarily included the Western Abenaki of Vermont; the Eastern Abenaki, including the Penobscot, Kennebec and Androscoggin tribes; and the Maliseet, Passamaquoddy and Micmac tribes.[1]

The Wabanaki typically gathered along major rivers and drainage basins, which by English convention produced their tribal names. For the Wabanaki, rivers provided both a food source and a crucial transportation system to the coast and inland.

The principal Eastern Abenaki tribe in the Penobscot Valley was the Penobscot, eventually the state's most powerful tribe and one that maintains a presence in the river valley today. In the early 1600s, historian Dean Snow estimates the entire Eastern Abenaki population in Maine was perhaps ten thousand, roughly equal to one-third the population of Bangor in 2002.

The Eastern Abenaki sometimes battled other northeastern tribes. Relationships were particularly hostile with the Micmacs to the east and the Mohawks to the west.

In the early 1600s, war with the Micmacs, who were often supplied by the French, featured alternating village raids and kidnappings. In one incident, Micmac attacked a village, killing several Abenaki warriors and kidnapping Abenaki women who were put to death at Mount Desert Island.

In revenge, a Micmac trader was killed on Penobscot Bay in the summer of 1607. The war essentially ended in victory for the Micmac in 1615 when the great leader Bessabez (a.k.a. Bashabes and Bashaba) was killed by a Micmac raiding party at his village, perhaps on the Penobscot River.

This was a powerful blow. Bessabez possessed great power and was said to rule over at least twenty-two tribes from Saco Bay to Mount Desert Island in a territory known as Mawooshen. Upon Bessabez's death, the coalition he oversaw collapsed.

During the same period Wabanaki relations with the Mohawks and the Iroquois frequently turned into violence. In the 1630s, Wabanaki tribes took part in the so-called Beaver Wars, a particularly violent and deadly conflict that engulfed nearly every tribe from Canada to the Chesapeake to the Great Lakes.

The Wabanaki east of the Kennebec, unlike those in southern New England and Southern Maine, were not significant farmers, given the rugged, tree covered territory and the cold weather. Instead, Eastern Abenaki lived by hunting and gathering. They often spent spring along the coast catching fish, seals and other coastal animals, supplementing their catches with berries and other wild fruit. They spent colder months inland hunting moose, deer and bear and trapping beaver, muskrat and other fur-bearing animals. After contact with Europeans, fur trading emerged as a significant enterprise for the Wabanaki. Beaver fur was the rage in Europe, and was especially popular for fashionable felt hats. The Wabanaki quickly came to covet and depend on European trade goods.

Above all else in the Wabanaki world, the early 1600s were marked by a tragic, near-apocalyptic pandemic — The Great Dying — that devastated tribes in Maine. Estimates vary, but the diseases that whipped through Maine Wabanaki villages in the early 1600s killed perhaps 50 percent of the local population. The diseases, such as smallpox, were unknowingly brought to the New World by explorers, and the Wabanaki possessed no natural resistance. Following the outbreaks, many villages in Maine were abandoned. Some historians believe the disruptions caused by the massive epidemics led to the disorders and violence of the post-contact period, as everything — society, tribal and family alliances and traditions — was destroyed.

The Explorers

European explorers began visiting Maine as early as the 1500s. The first European definitively known to have sailed the coast of Maine was Giovanni da Verrazano in 1524. Verrazano, an Italian sailing for the king of France, struck what is now Cape Fear, South Carolina, then sailed northward along the Atlantic seaboard and eventually reached the coast of Maine. Estevan Gomez (also known as Estevao Gomes or Estaban Gomez), a Portuguese sailor in service to Spain, crossed Penobscot Bay in 1525 during his search for a strait to the Pacific and the Orient. He named Casco Bay in Southern Maine and ventured up the Penobscot River to modern-day Bangor. Other explorers also reached North America during the 1500s, visiting Maine and its outer islands, which served as seasonal fishing ports.

Early European visitors found the fishing off the Maine coast and Canada superb. Gulf of Maine fisheries and the plethora of islands that served as critical fishing stations played a significant role in bringing European vessels to Maine — along with the search for the fabled Northwest Passage to the Orient — and encouraged continued exploration. Certainly by the early 1600s, widespread knowledge existed in Europe of the great Norumbega (Penobscot) River.

Perhaps the most significant early explorer of Eastern Maine, and unquestionably one of history's great explorers, was Samuel de Champlain.[2] Champlain, who eventually founded Quebec and gave his name to Lake Champlain, provided the outside world with perhaps its first authentic, detailed glimpse of the Penobscot River and the beautiful oak grove that came to be Bangor.

In 1604, Champlain worked as a pilot and guide serving the Sieur de Monts, a Huguenot nobleman who possessed a grant to "La Cadie" from Henry IV, King of France. La Cadie (translated Acadia) covered France's North American claim to the territory that at the time extended roughly from what is now Philadelphia to Montreal. The Sieur de Monts sought to establish a French foothold on the continent with a permanent settlement.

As his first order of business, de Monts built a trading post and settled on an island in the St. Croix River not far from what is now Calais. The settlement survived only one severe winter, during which about half the seventy-nine men died, many from scurvy.

However, while settling on the St. Croix that fall, de Monts sent Champlain westward to explore the coast. Champlain, like so many explorers, also searched for Norumbega, the wealthy city believed to sit on the banks of the Norumbega River. The myth of Norumbega grew through the great exaggerations of explorers boasting of their adventures. Norumbega was said to be filled with furs and ivory and chunks of gold as big as a fist. The houses, some claimed, sat on pillars of gold, silver and crystal and the city was inhabited by an advanced civilization. It was a creative and powerful lure, even if completely false.

In early September 1604, Champlain sailed from St. Croix in an eighteen-ton pinnace with twelve sailors and two Indian guides. On September 6, with calm seas and a light breeze, Champlain reached Frenchman Bay and sailed toward smoke he saw rising from the south side of an island he named l'isle des Monts-deserts, or isle of the desert mountains, now know as Mount Desert Island. As he approached the island, his pinnace struck a ledge, forcing him to land for repairs. The Wabanaki who summered at Mount Desert Island greeted him and agreed to provide him with a guide to the Norumbega (Penobscot) River where their own sagamore (a sagamore was an important Wabanaki leader) resided.

The guides led Champlain to the mouth of the Norumbega (which natives called Peimtegouet and the French called Pentagoet) River. Then on a September day, Champlain sailed up the great river past unbroken wilderness, seeing no signs of civilization save for a few abandoned wigwams covered with tree bark. Champlain looked in vain for Norumbega, eventually concluding it was a myth, and said, "I am convinced that the majority of those who mention it never saw it, and speak of it only by hearsay from people who had no more knowledge of it than themselves."[3]

He anchored near the confluence of the Kenduskeag and Penobscot, only a short distance from what is now Treats Falls. From the deck of his pinnace he gazed toward the beautiful stand of oaks on ground that more than 160 years later would become Bangor. The grove was so beautiful it appeared as if the great trees were planted by design. While Champlain went ashore to hunt, the Penobscot guides left to get Bessabez, the same great leader who was later killed by a rival tribe. Bessabez, accompanied by six canoes, paddled up the Norumbega to visit Champlain. Upon seeing Bessabez, the Penobscots on shore began to sing and dance and leap until he landed.

Champlain, two companions, and his interpreters then came ashore to meet with the great chief. So there, perhaps on the spit of land between the Penobscot and the Kenduskeag, Champlain met with Bessabez, who presented Champlain with venison and waterfowl. Champlain in turn presented him with hatchets, rosaries, caps, knives and various trade goods.

Champlain told Bessabez that the Sieur de Monts wished to become friends and teach his people to cultivate the land, help improve their living conditions, and help them reconcile with enemy tribes to the east. Bessabez was receptive. Champlain stayed a short while longer and bartered for a few beaver furs before sailing back down Norumbega to the sea, ending perhaps the first modern-style business meeting in Bangor.

Outposts

Fishing and fur continued to lure the adventurous to Maine. In the early 1600s, fishing stations existed on islands such as Damariscove and Monhegan and on the mainland at Pemaquid. The Jamestown Colony in Virginia regularly sent fishing vessels into Maine waters, and Europeans sponsored annual fishing trips into the Gulf of Maine. Meanwhile, fur-trading stations began popping up on the coast, including at Pejepscot sometime between 1625 and 1630 and at Castine in 1630.

The French seized control of the region in about 1632 and Charles d'Aulnay built Fort Pentagoet in 1635 on the site of a former Pilgrim post that had been used to supplement the Plymouth Colony. Fort Pentagoet (Castine) became an important post on the Penobscot, allowing the French to conduct trade with area tribes and serving as a key outpost for French interests. Because of its location, Castine was recognized as the region's key site, allowing control of the Penobscot River and Penobscot Bay. Control of the Castine region alternated between the French and English until 1759 when Massachusetts established a key post at Fort Pownal (Stockton Springs) that helped open up Eastern Maine for settlement.

Despite the trading posts of the seventeenth century, Eastern Maine remained a frontier. The small number of settlers struggled with isolation, poor or nonexistent overland transportation, food shortages and lack of clothing.

Meanwhile in Southern Maine, fledgling local governments along with active Protestant churches played a key role in bringing stability and a rule of law to the English frontier. Perhaps most critically for English settlers, some land titles were established. English settlers saw land titles as essential to provide the security, stability and foundation of an organized society.

In 1670, on the eve of warfare that would last more than a century, perhaps thirty-five hundred European settlers lived in Maine, nine hundred of them in Kittery alone.

War

The development of Maine, New England and much of North America was influenced by the nearly continuous global warfare waged between France and England throughout the seventeenth and early eighteenth centuries. Essentially, all but one of the Colonial wars on American soil from 1675 to 1763 were to some degree extensions of conflicts in such places as India and Europe.

During the Colonial wars, the Wabanaki aligned with the French, who had maintained more friendly relations with them. The French frequently incited the Wabanaki to strike against English settlements. The English relationship with the Wabanaki was damaged by certain early explorers who had kidnapped a number of natives and by the growth of English permanent settlements. The English aligned with the New York-based Iroquois, who had hostile relations with the French and Wabanaki.

The first New England war, King Philip's War, started in 1675 and is considered the most violent and devastating of the Colonial wars. It was marked by widespread destruction, massacres and terror on both sides and led to a sweeping withdrawal of settlers from the western frontier of New England and the end of significant tribal influence in southern New England.

In Maine, Wabanaki raids on Brunswick, Falmouth, Saco, Scarborough and other towns killed more than fifty English settlers between the Piscataqua and the Kennebec. In the summer of 1676, the Wabanaki destroyed all but the southernmost English settlements in Maine. The English retaliated in kind against Wabanaki villages. Before a peace treaty was signed in 1678, hundreds of Maine settlers and Indians were killed.

After King Philip's War, began the group of five Colonial wars known collectively as the French and Indian Wars (1689–1763). In Maine, by the end of King William's War (the first war), Maine settlers had abandoned all settlements east of Wells. These wars, which ultimately engulfed all the Colonies in America and spread to the western frontier and Canada, finally drew to a close in the mid-1700s and definitively settled the issue of control in the eastern region of North America.

In 1758, Lord Jeffrey Amherst captured the French fortress of Louisburg in Canada. In 1759 General James Wolfe dramatically defeated the Marquis de Montcalm on the Plains of Abraham to capture Quebec, and the British captured Montreal the following year. French power crumbled, and the Treaty of Paris in 1763 officially eliminated France as a power in the region.

With the defeat of France, Wabanaki in Eastern Maine, already weakened by decades of war and the ravages of disease, either continued their retreat into Canada or made permanent peace with Maine settlers. In the mid-1700s, the Penobscots had distanced themselves from other Wabanaki tribes and sought to make their own peace with the European factions. (During the Revolutionary War, the Penobscots fought on the American side while many of their former Wabanaki allies fought for the British.) Although unsuccessful, the Penobscots ultimately remained on the Penobscot River.[4]

While peace following the Colonial wars in Maine provided only a brief respite before Revolutionary conflict arose, it opened a small window for settlement of the eastern frontier.

Conduskeag Plantation

Along the coast and great rivers of Eastern Maine, the wilderness slowly broke down, giving way to log homes, saw mills, gristmills and the steady advance of settlers and their ambitions. On the Penobscot River, Fort Pownal, built in 1759 at what is now Fort Point in Stockton Springs, served as an important trading post and helped establish the English in the region. Once the French and Indian Wars ended, settlers streamed into Maine and the Penobscot Valley. The population of Maine in 1765 was twenty-three thousand; ten years later it had more than doubled to forty-seven thousand.

In 1761, Abraham Somes and James Richardson arrived at Mount Desert Island to settle Somesville; in 1764, Jonathan Buck settled what is now Bucksport; Benjamin Wheeler settled Wheelersborough (now Hampden), and John and Josiah Brewer settled New Worcester (now Orrington and Brewer) in 1767.

In the autumn of 1769, the fingers of settlement finally reached up the Penobscot to Kenduskeag Stream. Jacob Buswell, a former soldier, cooper, hunter, fisherman and boat builder from Salisbury, Massachusetts, brought his wife and nine children to settle at Conduskeag (The name Conduskeag was later altered to Kenduskeag. Both names are derived from the Wabanaki word Kadesquit meaning "eel weir place").

Buswell, a relatively poor man perhaps looking to escape as much as to build a new village, reached the tidal headwaters and built a log cabin before the gracious stands of oak that had so impressed Champlain. Buswell built his cabin beside a spring located near the present-day intersection of York and Boyd streets, not far from today's St. John's Catholic Church, where he enjoyed a view that extended a couple of miles down the river. That winter, the Buswell family dwelt in solitude — miles from the nearest settlement. Regardless, Bangor was born.

Buswell, once called by a fellow settler an "old damn grey-headed bugger of hell," and his family were not alone for long.[5] They were joined the following year by Buswell's newlywed son, Stephen, and his wife, Lucy Grant, and by Caleb Goodwin and his wife and family of eight children. The three families comprised the entire village in the winter of 1770. Other families soon followed, building log cabins or huts along the Kenduskeag or the Penobscot, and slowly carving out a small community and bringing important skills to the village.

By the end of 1771, twelve families lived in what some described as a "bleak" little community with little money or signs of prosperity. The heads of those households included: Thomas Howard, Jacob Dennet, Simon Crosby, Thomas, John and Hugh Smart, Andrew Webster, Joseph Rose, David Rowell, Soloman and Silas Harthorn and Joseph Mansel. All the settlers confronted harsh conditions with long winters and poor soil. To compensate for inferior soil, they dug small holes in the ground into which they placed alewives. They planted seed potatoes or other vegetables into the fish and covered the hole. The rotting fish provided warmth to help germinate the seeds and was a fertilizer, necessary given the dearth of manure, to help the garden grow.

Some progress did occur in the area that would eventually become Kenduskeag Plantation. In 1772, Joseph Mansel built a small sawmill for Silas and Soloman Harthorn on the easterly side of the Penjejawock Stream and the first settlers' child, Mary Howard, was born. Robert Treat, later a Revolutionary War soldier, opened the Plantation's first store, also near the Penjejawock.

Treat played an important role in Bangor's fledgling economy through his store and trading post.* Other important businessmen included: James Budge, who developed the first small lumber business to grow beyond supplying strictly local needs; Thomas Howard, who made barrels; and Jacob Dennet, who built a few small fishing vessels. Kenduskeag remained a barter economy and most goods were exchanged for food and other basic needs. No sufficient wealth existed to establish any significant economic activity or make lucrative use of skills.

As a budding businessman, storeowner Treat recognized the great distance — more than twenty-five miles — between Fort Pownal and the Penobscot Indians to the north, and saw an opportunity. Treat decided to build a post closer to the Penobscots and intercept some of their business. He built a cabin just below Penjejawock Brook, about two miles above Bangor's "City Point." He converted all available goods into articles for trade with the Penobscots and locals when possible, although locals worked mainly to fill personal needs and did not trap for trade. His business increased when Fort Pownal was dismantled.

In his unpublished sketch of early Bangor history written in 1860, Jacob McGaw wrote: "By much effort and peril, he [Treat] succeeded in obtaining at Boston and removing to Bangor, powder, shot and some other merchandise in small quantities to supply their wants. He also furnished goods to such of his neighbors as, like Indians, brought furs to barter with for them."[6]

However, the settlement's growth remained stunted in large part because of the distance to markets. Furthermore, Kenduskeag, like many

---

* By the 1790s, Treat had built enough wealth to hire a handful of neighbors — Dennet, the boatbuilder, William Boyd, a shipwright, and Nathaniel Harlow, a pump and block maker — to build the first boat in Bangor larger than a yawl.

parts of Maine, remained captive to Boston merchants and financiers. Lack of local capital and financing would plague Bangor well into the 1800s, even beyond. Assessing the situation in 1775, Elihu Hewes of Hampden wrote: "We are here in a deplorable condition ..."[7]

Unfortunately, it would only get worse.

Revolution

For Maine pioneers, the respite from fear after the French and Indian Wars proved relatively brief. By the early 1770s, barely a decade after those wars ended, patriots made noises of rebellion.

In the revolutionary hotbeds of Boston and Philadelphia tensions already ran high. During the wars against France, the colonies were largely self-governed. Once those wars ended, Britain exerted more control. In part, the king sought to raise monies from the colonies to help pay for the additional cost of defending the newly expanded borders. The imposition of a series of taxes and other inflammatory acts by the British fueled patriot fever in Maine and the colonies. In response, the first Continental Congress met in Philadelphia during September and October of 1774. And finally, the Revolutionary War erupted when British soldiers and American patriots clashed at Lexington and Concord on April 19, 1775. The colonies adopted the Declaration of Independence on July 4, 1776.

Unlike its experience in the Colonial wars, the district of Maine largely escaped significant bloodshed during the Revolutionary War. Certain Maine towns became Tory strongholds, but significant rebel sentiment existed and Maine patriots carried out acts of vandalism and protest against British customs officials, tax collectors and other loyalists.

In Kenduskeag, patriots threatened to execute a sea captain named David Rogers who refused to swear allegiance to the rebel cause. They trimmed a tall oak by the river and slung a rope over a branch to hang him. Apparently, with the noose in the waiting, the men enjoyed some rum, after which Rogers took the oath and earned a stay of execution.

The shooting war came to the Penobscot River in 1779. That year, the British Navy, with strongholds in Canada, moved on Penobscot Bay and seized Castine. With a fortified post at the mouth of the Penobscot River, the British shut down all trade along the river and seized the towns along

11

its banks. This was unacceptable to the Americans, so soon a Continental naval force under the command of Admiral Dudley Saltonstall of Connecticut sailed for Penobscot Bay to drive the British out. The so-called Penobscot Expedition began in glory, but ended as one of most embarrassing naval defeats in United States history.

The Continental forces included nineteen armed vessels with 334 guns and more than one thousand men — firepower superior to the British holding the fort. American ground forces quickly seized a high bluff and the onshore commanders urged Saltonstall to strike. But Saltonstall didn't act. He waited for two weeks. Taking advantage of the delay, the British brought up naval reinforcements. The Continental fleet initially turned to face its advancing foe, but then turned and fled up the Penobscot. Patriots watching from shore said they could barely stomach the sight of British warships chasing down the larger American armada. During their flight, the Colonials scuttled and burned their ships to prevent capture, torching perhaps ten in Kenduskeag alone. Once ashore, soldiers fled through the woods to escape. Saltonstall was later court-martialed for his decisions in battle.

With Saltonstall's failure, the British sat entrenched in Castine. They blocked the river and raided coastal towns and islands, only increasing the isolation for Kenduskeag settlers. The village was surrounded on three sides by wilderness and on the fourth by the British. While the British didn't care much about the small community, their presence on the river did prevent most shipping and communications. More than ever, villagers lacked food, money and clothing.

The British did visit Kenduskeag. According to Joseph Mansel, "A British officer came [to Kenduskeg] … and [ordered] the men to come down and take the oath [of allegiance to Britain]; the most of them went; but some of them as would not go down, had their houses burnt."[8]

Elsewhere the war raged on until, at long last, Gen. George Washington pinned the main British forces against the sea and a waiting French Navy at Yorktown, Virginia, forcing Cornwallis to surrender his troops in 1781.

The war officially ended with the Treaty of Paris in 1783 and finally the river flowed freely once again, though life at Kenduskeag remained difficult. According to McGaw, "Pine trees suitable to be manufactured into boards could not be hauled in plentiful quantities to saw mills because sufficient teams could not be obtained. Fisheries could not be improved to limits much exceeding domestic requirements by reason of deficiency in number of laborers, and for want of means to procure salt.

"So also, in regard to furs, men could not be spared from their homes long enough to accomplish much systematically or profitably."[9]

The New Migration

The end of the Revolutionary War effectively ignited perhaps the greatest eastern migration in United States history. Former soldiers flooded into Maine seeking land.

After the war, Massachusetts opened up Maine lands to help settle war debts. Massachusetts provided land to soldiers and continued to sell vast tracts to land speculators or proprietors who then established towns. The population of Maine in 1777 was 42,300; by 1784 it hit 56,000 and by 1800 it soared to 151,719. In just sixteen years the population had tripled.

The key draw, of course, was land, the most valuable and most prestigious asset in eighteenth century America and crucial to stability. In many areas, the understanding was that if a person agreed to settle a piece of land, clear a set portion of it, work it, build a house, and stay for an agreed period of time, they would eventually receive title.

Unfortunately at Kenduskeag, settlers did not receive land titles until 1801 — thirty-two years after Buswell built his log cabin — when the General Court of Massachusetts finally agreed that each settler who arrived prior to 1784 and each settler who arrived between 1784 and 1798 should have one hundred acres of land and title for $5 and $100, respectively. While settlers there waited for clear title to land, Kenduskeag struggled. By 1780, more than ten years after Buswell first settled, Kenduskeag Plantation had grown to only 169 residents and offered its citizens neither a school building nor a chapel.

In 1789, Kenduskeag settlers seeking a tax abatement told the General Court of Massachusetts that surely none other was as needy as their community. "Could your honors come into our huts, fare as we do, and look upon our half naked children, we should need no other petition to have [our] taxes postponed."[10]

Likewise, European visitors to the backcountry of Maine in the late

1700s described the frontier region as "inhabited by poor people, whose cottages could not be exceeded in miserable appearance by any of the most miserable in Europe."[11] By 1790, the population of Kenduskeag still had reached only 279.

While the village had no church in 1780, its first minister, Rev. Seth Noble, had lived in town for seven years. Noble, a powerful speaker and also a man prone to drink and intemperate remarks, ignited a religious revival. That revival later waned as the village began to question his fitness to occupy the pulpit. The concern grew more intense after Noble, a widower, delayed marrying his housekeeper until she was visibly pregnant.[12]

Despite his eventual disfavor, Noble is forever entwined in the early history of Bangor, most notably through the oft-repeated story of how the town of Bangor was named. According to legend, villagers sent Noble to Massachusetts in 1790 to incorporate Kenduskeag Plantation as the town of Sunbury. While waiting at the clerk's office, Noble whistled his favorite hymn, Bangor. When the clerk asked Noble what the name of the new town was going to be, Noble mistakenly thought the clerk had inquired about the name of the hymn.

"Bangor," Noble replied.

And so it was.

A New Century

While Bangor's struggle to escape both isolation and poverty would not end with the dawn of a new century, signs of prosperity did begin to emerge. Late in the 1700s, James Budge had moved to City Point, where he owned one hundred acres, and established a new, larger sawmill. For the first time, his mill produced more lumber than was needed by settlers. Budge also began the practice of felling trees and lashing them together for transport down the river for use as masts.[13]

The seeds of a woods-based economy were slowly starting to sprout. Furthermore, a few vessels from Newburyport, Massachusetts, and other ports began venturing up the Penobscot for fish, especially alewives. These vessels paid $1.00 to $1.25 per bushel and hauled the fish to markets in southern states and the West Indies. Outside money was finally being injected into the local economy.

This didn't mean that the prospects of success were always obvious.

William Crosby had little use for Bangor after visiting in 1801: "I went to Bangor, but to my astonishment I could see no village, now the city. I tied my horse to a bush fence, and descended the precipice just above the present Hatch House, which was then a mere frame, where I found one James Thomas. Mr. Thomas was kind enough to pull a piece of paper out of his pocket, on which he shewed [sic] me the great-to-be city of Bangor. I was so disappointed and mortified that I made up my mind to return home in the most direct way, immediately."[14]

Two years later, Deacon Eliashib Adams was equally as disgusted with the town, "Soon after I came to Buckport, which was July 5, 1803, I walked to Bangor. From its being the head of navigation and safe for ships, I had no doubt it would be the most important place on the river. I should have remained here had it not been that there were no religious privileges. It was a mere Sodom, with Lot dwelling in it by the name of William Boyd, afterwards one of the first deacons of the First church. I was so disgusted with the character of the place, that, for several years when my business made it necessary to remain over night, I used to cross the river to Orrington, now Brewer, and put up at Dr. Skinner's, who and his wife were both pious and intelligent."[15]

While lacking some refinements, Bangor slowly pieced together an infrastructure necessary for successful growth throughout the early 1800s. The town soon built its first schoolhouse and opened its first post office. Isaac Hatch built the Hatch House to accommodate visitors and finally a toll bridge connected the two sides of the Kenduskeag Stream. The town at last hired a settled Congregationalist minister and the church quickly became a powerful force in Bangor.

But ominously, the town still had no bank and little money and was set to enter another dark period caused by larger outside events — epidemics, natural disasters and another conflict with the Mother country.

War — Again

In the late 1700s and early 1800s, the fledgling nation watched as Great Britain and France continued their animosity, first during the French Revolution and then when a British-led coalition moved to stop expansion-minded Napoleon. Napoleon was not finally defeated until Waterloo in June of 1815.

During the early 1800s, Great Britain and France disrupted America's shipping interests by stopping American ships and seizing goods. Great Britain asserted its right to stop American ships and seize British subjects trying to escape military duty. However, they also seized American sailors for British service. This practice, known as impressment, outraged America. Furthermore, the United States was angry that the two countries failed to recognize her neutrality.

In response, President Thomas Jefferson pushed through the ill-conceived Embargo Act of 1807, prohibiting the export of any goods from the United States. The Embargo Act effectively shut down American ports. Merchants and sailors watched helplessly as ships swayed uselessly at anchor or rotted at port.

"It fell upon the business operations of Bangor with the like suddenness, and produced the like effect upon it, that a paralytic shock would have produced on the persons of its inhabitants. ... Business of every kind was in a ruinous condition; dwelling houses were so far advanced in the process of erection as to supply shelter to families in most cases, but remained in such unfinished state as to indicate poverty, or great embarrassment to the owners."[16]

The businessmen of Bangor, already in debt to Boston merchants, found it difficult or impossible to maintain good standing or credit.

Some men made money by smuggling, especially in places like Castine, but even that grew tougher when the United States cracked down on the practice. Jefferson rescinded the embargo in 1809, but the animosities did not end. France and Britain continued to disrespect America's neutrality and the British continued to impress American sailors into service.

President James Madison declared war on Great Britain June 18, 1812. The United States was ill prepared to fight a war and was perhaps fortunate that the Royal Navy, the most powerful fleet in the world, was preoccupied with France. Furthermore, Great Britain was America's chief trade partner. Thus when war interrupted its crucial trade and damaged ports, New England was again enraged. New England leaders actually put in motion a plan to dissolve the Union should the war persist.

Following the outbreak of war, American vessels were allowed to arm themselves and act as privateers harassing and capturing British vessels.

By 1814, the British had had enough of these privateers, and the Royal Navy launched an offensive against Maine.

In September of 1814, the Royal Navy left Canada and bore down on the Maine coast. One target was the privateer *Adams*. The *Adams* ran ashore on Isle au Haut in a storm and after relaunching, sailed for the Penobscot River to make repairs. Not far behind, the British headed for the Penobscot to cut her down.

British forces easily captured Castine and then swept up the Penobscot River, capturing all towns on their way and facing only a brief skirmish against overmatched Americans at Hampden. British troops marched into defenseless Bangor on September 3. Bangor selectmen quickly surrendered the town.

British troops looted parts of the city, forced residents to slaughter animals to feed them, broke open barrels of liquor in the streets and requisitioned houses for troops. They also rounded up local men as prisoners of war and then paroled them with the stipulation that if any of them ever defied the Crown, troops would return and torch the village. Even with that, the British moved whatever vessels were afloat into the river and, as owners and settlers watched, set them ablaze.

The capture of Castine and the effortless march into Bangor caused much alarm in the United States and increased popular sentiment in New England against the war. While American efforts proved more successful elsewhere, both sides were anxious for peace by the fall of 1814. The Treaty of Ghent ended the war in December of 1814, but word did not reach Maine until February and the British did not leave Castine until April. This time, after more than 150 years of regular warfare, lasting peace finally came to Maine soil.

Unfortunately, British occupation was not the only hardship suffered in Bangor during the early years of the 1800s.

From 1808 to 1810, Bangor was hit by an epidemic that killed scores of residents. Rev. John Sawyer, a missionary from New Hampshire, reported attending about a hundred funerals during one year of this period, all victims of what locals called "the black death."[17]

The epidemic was described as "a plague as rapid and fatal as the cholera, and if possible, more terrible from the condition in which it left the dead." From one point in Hampden, an observer claimed he could count eighteen houses, each containing the dead body of at least one victim of the disease.[18]

Starting in 1813, severe weather gripped the area and lasted for several years. In 1815, the corn crop was a near total failure. In 1816, wheat, oats and other vegetables froze in the fields because hard frosts hit all of Maine each month. The year 1816 was known for decades as "eighteen hundred and froze to death." During this time, "Ohio Fever" prompted many farmers to bolt for the better climes and soil of the Midwest to escape the ruinous weather. The Treaty of Ghent had also opened up western lands by forcing the British to leave such places as Fort Detroit and Fort Wayne.

Yet, as the teens wore down, Bangor's fortunes, stunted by more than a century of warfare, disease and general isolation, seemed to brighten. A little justified optimism was finally at hand.

"Against all obstacles, all calamities and not withstanding all evil auguries, [Bangor] kept on its way."[19]

At the Cusp of Greatness

Indeed, despite the epidemics, the natural disasters and the war, Bangor methodically, albeit slowly, established critical community foundations.

In 1812, the town built a new building at Hammond and Columbia Streets facing West Market Square to serve as town hall, court house and Congregational Church. The town's first bank, Bangor Bank, opened in 1817 and the first newspaper, the *Bangor Weekly Register*, was published in 1815. The Bangor Theological Seminary, founded as the Maine Charity School in Hampden, came to town in 1819.

By 1820, the year Maine separated from Massachusetts to become a state, the population of Bangor hit 1,221. A stage line opened to Augusta in 1821, the first steamship arrived, and the Bangor Mechanic Association, an organization dedicated to the general improvement of artisans, began to meet. River traffic grew ever busier.

By the dawn of the 1830s, Bangor's population had swelled to 2,867, more than double that of a decade earlier. The small base of sawmills continued to expand, more lumber floated in the river, and more ships arrived in port. The very forest that deepened Bangor's isolation for so long now offered up its white pine to build her wealth.

Courtesy of Bangor Public Library

Bangor's first courthouse also served as a meeting hall for the Congregational Church and as city hall. It was built in 1812–1813 on the corner of Hammond and Columbia Streets, facing West Market Square. It was remodeled and turned to face Columbia Street in 1849–1850. It was torn down in 1901–1902.

The 1830s were a decade of runaway growth, pausing only temporarily for the financial panic of 1837.

There was the sense that the town possessed a great future, that it was a place to succeed and grow. Its location at the head of the tidewater was paying off. Long gone was the rugged frontier town of spartan life, hardships and deprivation. The pioneers who struggled so mightily had paved the way and now Bangor attracted energetic people from about the countryside.

These were men and women whose families had survived wars, who had wrested independence from the greatest military power on earth, and who had struggled with little in frontier settlements, but came infused with a Yankee spirit of thrift, industry and enterprise. They made these ideals a mantra in the Golden Age of Bangor. Bangor natives like George W. Pickering came of age in the city in this era, while young men like Elijah L. Hamlin, Joseph S. Wheelwright, Samuel F. Hersey, Amos M.

Courtesy of Maine Historic Photograph Collection, University of Maine, Orono
A view of the developing city of Bangor, looking across the Penobscot River from Brewer, in the mid-1830s.

Roberts, Charles Hayward and Franklin Muzzy came bags in hand from other parts of Maine and New England seeking opportunity.

In the first four years of the 1830s the population of Bangor exploded, roaring past eight thousand. During the 1830s, the town would become a city and by the mid-1800s the city would rise politically, economically and culturally to its nineteenth century zenith as the self-proclaimed "Queen City of the East."

Chapter Two

The Rise of American Banking

If there was one thing many working men and women of eighteenth and nineteenth century Maine didn't trust, it was a bank. And not without reason.

Founded by wealthy businessmen or pure speculators, banks were sometimes corrupt, almost always risky and largely unregulated. They were also prone to failure. The landscape of the nation and Maine was littered with the corpses of dead banks, which meant people lost money.

It wasn't just banks, either. The nation struggled to fine-tune its new and developing capitalist system and shift from gold and coin to a paper currency economy. Early banks designed, created and issued their own currency through bank notes. As a result, the currency's value was tied to the soundness of the issuing bank and redemption was uncertain or costly as one traveled farther from home.

Some viewed the developing financial institutions, or certain offshoots of those institutions, not just as flawed, but *evil*. The *Eastern Argus*, the Portland-based organ of the Democratic Party, routinely savaged banks in its columns. It directed particular fire at the First Bank of the United States and its successor, the Second Bank of the United States, which operated a branch in Portland. In 1835, it assailed the national bank nearly every day as a tool of the moneyed class.

Yet, capital and investment as well as adequate currency were crucial as the nation developed beyond a subsistence, commodity-trading and barter existence. No capitalist economy could properly develop, let alone thrive, using a barter system without legitimate currency or the lure of investment opportunities. Lack of capital stymied growth. The banking system, however flawed, served as a critical source of capital for investment in Maine.

Still, the political bickering, newspaper vitriol, bank failures, scandals and recurring financial panics that plagued the United States and Maine in the nineteenth century certainly sowed the seeds of distrust of banks, especially among farmers, laborers and other wage earners of Maine. This distrust was almost certainly heightened when workers could look upon the mansions of lumber barons on Bangor hillsides and know those same men ran the banks.

It was this distrust that would ultimately help set the stage for a new type of banking concept aimed directly at the poor and the workingman — mutual banks like Bangor Savings Bank.

Colonial America

There were no banks per se in Colonial America. No checking accounts. No savings accounts. No passbooks. No American-based currency. The economic system was based largely upon private money such as IOUs, bills of exchange and, of course, gold, silver and foreign coin.

In the early days of the nation, the economy relied upon the barter of such items as work, furs, food and even lumber. The Bangor economy remained dependent upon trade and barter into the 1800s.

For coin (hard money), the British sterling pound was found in some places, but the dominant coin was the Spanish milled silver dollar, equal to eight Spanish reales, more commonly known as "Pieces of Eight." The coins were brought back by traders from the Spanish colonies. To make smaller denominations, colonists cut the Spanish coin in half or in quarters. Half a coin was known as "four bits" and a quarter of a coin was known as "two bits."

Massachusetts produced a pine tree shilling in a Boston mint in the 1600s, but the mint was quickly put down by the British Crown. In 1690, Massachusetts issued the first paper money to soldiers returning from the failed siege of Quebec, but the money soon became worthless. Other colonies attempted to issue paper money as well, but most issued far too much and the paper became worth only a fraction of face value.

In 1751, the Crown issued the Currency Act that forbade the creation of land banks, forbade making paper money a legal tender and demanded that all bills be withdrawn from circulation. The King did not want any new or independent financial system springing up in his colonies.

The nation's next attempt at paper currency came with the notes issued by the Continental Congress to fight the Revolutionary War. Like prior attempts, this money also became worthless, giving rise to the old saying "not worth a Continental."

To address its fiscal woes, the new nation established the First Bank of the United States in 1791, giving it a twenty-year charter. The bank was a private corporation and issued its own notes backed by its gold and silver. It served as the main depository of the U.S. Treasury and, to some extent, the bank's operating methods served to limit the amount of paper currency that state-chartered banks could issue beyond their specie reserves.

However, while the bank clearly provided some stability to the nation's finances, it also became a divisive and bitter political issue between the great men of the day.

On one side stood Alexander Hamilton, the first secretary of the treasury. He wanted to develop an industrial economy and believed large banks were essential. Furthermore, he felt a strong federal role, with the power to charter and supervise banks, was essential to create an effective fiscal policy. Thomas Jefferson, the first secretary of state and future president, thought the nation should remain mostly agricultural and he opposed the establishment of large banks. Those against a national bank also felt it infringed on states' rights and granted too much power to a central government. Bank opponents successfully killed the First Bank of the United States by refusing to renew its charter. It closed in 1811.

Then, during the War of 1812, state banks alone could not provide enough financial support to help the government pay for the war nor deal with the war's financial consequences. This problem prompted Congress to authorize the Second Bank of the United States, and it too became a bitter topic of dispute.

President Andrew Jackson, who believed hard money was the only legitimate currency, waged a vicious war against the Second Bank and its powerful leader, Nicholas Biddle, whom Jackson saw as a puppet of the rich. Jackson, ever the populist, insisted that a national bank infringed upon states' rights and was a dangerous monopoly that oppressed the workers and farmers of America.

The so-called Bank War helped give rise to the Whig Party, born almost exclusively to oppose Jackson's various policies. The Whigs were a descendent of Hamilton's Federalist Party (of which both George Washington and John Adams were members) and favored the Second Bank.

"Old Hickory" Jackson won the battle and vetoed a bill to recharter the Second Bank in 1832. The bank closed in 1836. The Portland branch, which had opened in 1828, was also closed.

There would not be another central bank in the United States until the Federal Reserve System was established in 1913. However, even at that time, the potential power of a national bank remained a concern, so a system was created rather than a single bank. The government established twelve geographic districts, each with its own reserve bank.

The lack of a central bank in the 1800s left the United States with no means to control money supply nor affect the economy. The nation suffered a string of financial panics, often caused or exacerbated by a fluctuating money supply, into the 1900s.

One panic occurred in 1837 in the days after the Second United States Bank shut down and the unprecedented speculation bubble finally burst. The two political parties sparred over who was to blame.

In 1837, the *Eastern Argus* attacked the whole banking system: "The whole tendency of the present banking system, and of grants of exclusive privileges in every shape and form, is in direct opposition to democracy. The system, too, on which the balance of bankers do business, is calculated to grind the faces of the common people, and to build up petty aristocrats on the strength of borrowed capital. In times of plenty or scarcity, the overgrown capitalist, or even the bankrupt on a large scale, will obtain loans of thousands of dollars on security which will not command as many hundreds for mechanics in middling circumstances — and when the latter do obtain assistance, they are taught to consider it as a great favor, to be obtained only by dancing attendance on the President and Directors."[1]

That same month, the *Bangor Daily Whig and Courier*, a supporter of the Second Bank of the United States, offered this tirade against the Democrats who helped kill the bank: "An Experiment has been forced upon the country, which has enriched the few, while it has beggared the many — which has paralyzed the arm of industry, and laid at the feet of usurers and extortioners, the enterprising and vigorous businessman — which has taken the means of support from thousands, who, had the reign of the Experiment never commenced, would have been enjoying a comfortable competency."[2]

The "Experiment" was closing the Second Bank and using certain state or "pet" banks to handle the nation's money supply and deposits. The decision unquestionably led to an explosion of state-chartered banks, and opened an era that would last nearly thirty years as the issuance and control of currency remained solely in the hands of the states and their numerous individual banks.

The State Banks

In 1784, seven years before the creation of the First Bank of the United States and five years before the U.S. Constitution, the state-chartered Massachusetts Bank was established in Boston. It was the second such bank in the United States and the first in New England. The Massachusetts Bank issued notes in various denominations and those notes circulated in the District of Maine and throughout New England.

The Massachusetts Bank opened fifteen years after Jacob Buswell settled in Bangor. Condeskeag Plantation and all settlements of Maine struggled not only for want of necessities, but also for want of money to effectively buy goods. There was no way to procure goods except through trade — the reason fur, a valuable trade commodity, was so crucial to Maine.

In 1799, the Portland Bank, the first bank in the district of Maine, was chartered by the Massachusetts General Court and opened with capital of one hundred thousand dollars. A handful of other Maine banks were soon chartered, including the Maine Bank of Portland in 1802, Lincoln and Kennebec Bank of Wiscasset in 1802, and the Penobscot Bank of Buckstown (Bucksport) in 1806.[3] By 1820, the year Maine became a state, nineteen banks had opened in Maine, but only eleven of them remained open. Six either voluntarily closed or failed and two let their charters expire. The original Portland Bank suffered a serious financial blow in 1808 and closed shortly thereafter, with investors suffering a loss of about 25 percent.

The Castine Bank also failed in 1815, due to outside manipulation. Bank historian Everett B. Stackpole used the bank to illustrate the developing problems of corruption and lack of oversight. "The Castine Bank appears to have been bought by speculators in Boston and conducted by them for their private advantage. ... The capital was mostly fictitious."[4]

Early banks differed in fundamental ways from modern banks. The banks existed to issue currency and raise capital and were viewed as a means for investors to make money. There was no real attempt to serve customers with a place to save or keep money in a safe and convenient place. Rich people could open their own bank and basically run it as they saw fit for the benefit of themselves and a few friends if they were so inclined. Some banks were run out of people's houses.

Early state banking was sometimes experimental — the period is sometimes known as the "Wildcat" era — and was fraught with fraud and systematic problems as a young nation and a young state tried to establish a viable and credible financial system.

The fact that each bank issued its own bank notes caused problems. If there were nine banks in Bangor, there might be nine different kinds of paper currency on the streets, not including currency from other Maine or out-of-state banks.

In addition, each bank note was issued with the promise that it could be redeemed for specie (or coin money, usually made of precious metals). It was generally considered risky to issue currency that far exceeded reserves and capital, and sound banking would require each bank to keep on reserve an adequate supply of specie to meet basic obligations. Yet, numerous times in the 1800s, specie payments were suspended. This caused economic distress, but helped keep some banks from failing.

There were also logistical problems.

Since each bank issued its own notes, they were often redeemed only at discount at other banks. Generally, the greater the distance someone traveled from the issuing bank, the greater the discount. In fact, there was no guarantee that the bills would even be accepted.

As notes circulated to other regions, they eventually needed to be brought back to the issuing bank for specie payment. However, even the redemption system was fraught with problems, especially in the minds of Maine bankers. Redemption can generally be broken into two distinct

Courtesy of Maine Historical Society

Examples of currency produced by nineteenth century Bangor banks. The Eastern Bank (top) was run by Amos M. Roberts, Exchange Bank (middle) was run by John B. Foster, and Maritime Bank (bottom) was run by George R. Smith. All three were also founders of Bangor Savings Bank.

eras, the pre-Suffolk Bank era and the Suffolk Bank era that began in 1819 and ended in the 1850s.

Prior to 1819, responsibility for redemption of bills in Boston rested with individual banks and was a constant source of trouble. Traders, merchants, and travelers carried bank notes from individual Maine banks to Boston, the primary financial and trade center of New England. Because they paid for goods with notes from Maine banks, these Maine notes eventually found their way into Boston banks.

The Massachusetts banks needed to redeem the notes at the Maine banks, which were at a considerable distance. They would gather all the Maine bank notes they had and a collector or team of collectors would travel to Maine by stagecoach to return the bills and demand specie payment to cover them. This collector might carry barrels that he had filled with the specie collected and used dogs to guard the valuable cargo. The Boston banks considered this method very costly and in 1809 decided not to accept bills from so-called country banks.

In 1819, the Suffolk Bank of Boston, seeing a chance to profit from the Maine banks, devised a new scheme to handle collection and obtained an agreement from other Boston banks, derisively called the "Boston Alliance" in Maine.[5]

Under the Suffolk system, arrangements were made with New England banks to redeem Maine bills at the Suffolk Bank. Each Maine bank was required to permanently deposit at least two thousand dollars in the Suffolk Bank — interest free. The Suffolk bank would keep Maine bills and return them after they reached a fixed sum, so long as the bank kept a sufficient deposit, independent of the permanent deposit. If the excess should become significantly larger than the permanent deposit, the Suffolk Bank would go to each bank and demand specie payment. Any bank that didn't join the system was forced to redeem all notes for specie upon demand.

Some financial historians maintain that Suffolk made the local economy more efficient, helped temper local bank excesses and brought order to general banking chaos. But in Maine, local banks and politicians despised the Suffolk system. They felt the powerful Boston banks were using their might to force Maine banks to pay what amounted to tribute money. It was just another conflict with Boston, a city many in Maine already considered self-important and egotistical.

This system became so despised in Maine that some banks eventually pulled out in the 1850s and created a rival system called the Bank of Mutual Redemption. Maine banks didn't like having their currency tied up in Boston rather than circulating, nor did they like the Suffolk Bank getting their assets, interest free.

Beyond the logistical problems and Boston issues, certain other flaws caused alarm. Banks were crucial to economic development, but lack of oversight and unsound practices caused significant problems and fueled popular distrust.

At one point in the 1830s, the *Whig and Courier* felt it necessary to defend bankers, saying all of them were not bad, despite attempts by some to arouse public denunciation.

"That some of the banks, in some things, have done wrong, and that some of the directors as individuals, have been guilty of improper practices, may or may not be true. But that all the banks, and bank directors, and brokers, are wicked and corrupt men — so greedy of gain as to be wholly indifferent to their own characters, and to the sufferings of their fellow citizens, we do not believe. Who are the directors of our banks? Are they, one and all, gamblers, cut-throat pirates? Nay, are they not for the most part merchants — men of honor and character — as deeply interested in the welfare of their class, and in the general prosperity of the city, as any other individuals whatever? So it strikes us, and we are therefore incredulous in regard to most of the sweeping charges brought in such wild fury against them."[6]

The *Whig and Courier*, of course, blamed the Democrats and their successful war against the United States Bank, "the great money regulator," for the problems.

In general, these were the major problems afflicting the banking world during this time:

- Insider lending. Banks were organized by investors and some were used largely for their own purposes. Investors lent largely to themselves, thus destructive insider lending became a major problem.
- Inadequate reserves. Some banks, especially during periods of rapid growth, opened with significantly inadequate reserves. When difficult financial times came, they simply couldn't survive due to lack of reserves and capital. One problem was that organizers might invest one day to start a bank and then borrow it all back the next, thus leaving the bank with little in capital reserve. Bankers sometimes used this trick to fool examiners.

- Risky loans. Banks during times of great growth made extraordinarily risky loans in terms of projects, soundness of borrowers, and issued notes far in excess of safe reserve levels.
- Counterfeiting. With so many different bank notes, it was easy to create counterfeit notes. This problem was largely solved in 1808 when Jacob Perkins invented a printing method using stereotype steel plates.
- Fraud. Some banks were started largely by outsiders to simply skirt laws and make money through shady means. The true "Wildcat" banks were those banks started in remote locations, making redemption of bills for specie difficult. They hoped to flood the market with bills and when it came time for redemption, simply disappear.
- Too many banks. The state had little control over the number of banks that opened. Many opened with too little capital or opened for no sound economic reason. Failure was inevitable.

With all the contributing problems, there existed an unpredictable and constantly fluctuating money supply as banks might lend money freely and issue large amounts of bank notes at one time, and at another time restrict the money supply and make few loans.

Bangor Banks

In Bangor, banking developed slowly. The first bank, Bangor Bank, opened in 1817 with a capital limit of one hundred thousand dollars. This opening came fifty years after Bangor was founded and nearly twenty years after the first bank opened in Portland. Before Bangor Bank opened, the closest bank to Bangor was Wiscasset Bank, which opened in 1815.

Bangor had operated in tough economic straits since it was founded and only as the 1820s approached did it begin to emerge from isolation caused by war, poor weather, location and lack of money.

With Bangor Bank chartered, the city finally had its own source of investment capital beyond the handful of local merchants and the hated Boston financiers. Like some other banks, Bangor Bank experienced some problems and was investigated in the early 1820s. It suspended specie payments, always a cause for community alarm, and during hearings in Boston rumors ran rampant. The alleged plight of Bangor was described

Courtesy of Maine Historic Preservation Commission
Hammond Street, downtown Bangor, in the 1860s or 1870s. Mercantile Bank office located
at far right.

at one hearing in which "representations were made of the distress of poor laborers who held the bills and could get rid of them only at a large discount, while their families were crying for bread."[7]

The investigation also prompted a Boston newspaper to attack the town of Bangor claiming, "Bangor was a little village of about twenty buildings, scattered on the banks of the Penobscot River, in the same manner that we would suppose a parcel of frogs would collect around a mud-puddle in spring."[8]

Commenting on the bank's dealings, the newspaper wrote: "One would think to judge from the quantity of bills in circulation, that all the specie in the United States was deposited in Bangor."[9]

31

But the Bangor Bank survived and remained the town's only bank until its charter expired in 1831 and was not renewed. It was replaced by Bangor Commercial Bank in 1831. When Kenduskeag Bank opened in 1832, Bangor had two commercial banks for the first time.

This launched the first boom in Bangor banking, coinciding with the city's rapid commercial and industrial development and the rampant land speculation that ended with collapse in the financial panic of 1837.

Starting with Kenduskeag Bank, eight banks opened in five years, with three banks opening in 1836 alone. The collective capital of Bangor banks rose from fifty thousand dollars in 1831 to eight hundred thousand in 1836. Unfortunately, not all the banks opened for legitimate reasons. It was a painful lesson when it all crumbled.

All banks suspended their specie payments during the panic of 1837 to prevent failure, causing great distress in Bangor. For years, Portland interests blamed "Bangor speculators" and banks for the economic problems of the late 1830s.

Of the nine banks operating in Bangor by the end of 1836, five were gone by 1841, either failing or liquidating all assets.

In 1838, in wake of the panic of 1837, the nine Bangor banks collectively had immediate liabilities of $420,098 and immediate assets of $106,141, according to the *Whig and Courier*. The worst offender in this regard was George W. Pickering's Kenduskeag Bank, with immediate liabilities of $48,264 and immediate assets of $3,698. On average, Bangor banks were in worse shape than their contemporaries. State banks collectively had a liabilities to assets ratio of 2–1 while the banks in Bangor had a ratio of nearly 4–1.

At one point during the crisis, the state legislature passed the soon-to-be hated "Small Bill Law," outlawing the circulation by Maine banks of any bills smaller than five dollars. The *Eastern Argus* argued that it would be best to drive all bills smaller than twenty dollars from circulation, thus bringing hard money or specie back into common use. The law failed miserably and only exacerbated the problems.

The banking shakeout led to a banking lull. No new banks opened in Bangor again until Samuel Veazie opened his self-named Veazie Bank in 1848. This triggered another banking wave that saw nine more banks open in the next six years. As before, the boom would end in another panic, this one in 1857.

Another feature of Bangor banks was how tightly they were controlled by a small group of local businessmen, mostly lumber merchants and producers, as well as Boston investors.

"Bangor banks were forced to secure Bay State capital in the 1840s ... As a result, Bay State capital accounted for 25 to 30 percent of the capital in most of the city's banks with the exception of Eastern Bank of Bangor, where Bay State capital accounted for 50 percent."[10]

That control increased in the 1850s, when "Massachusetts investors held no less than one-third of the bank stock in any one Bangor bank and as much as 100 percent of the capital stock in one Queen City bank. Approximately 45 percent of Bangor's total bank stock was held by Massachusetts investors."[11]

Mutual Savings Banks

As the state banks alternated between flush and failure, another type of bank that originated in the British Isles — the mutual savings bank — was making slow inroads into New England.

The mutual savings bank concept is generally considered to have been advanced by Hugues Delestre in 1610 when he offered an idea to combat pauperism and poverty. He suggested a place for the "Wage worker who might deposit his savings and withdraw them again in part or in whole as he might require, with interest according to the time they had been on deposit; and this institution was designed to take the place of alms giving."[12]

The concept also was tested in various forms in Europe, most notably Germany. The institution most akin to a modern savings bank or "society" was started by The Rev. Henry Duncan in Ruthwell, Scotland, in 1810. The savings bank by this time was seen as a potential tool to help elevate the poor and working classes, thus its significant religious ties. Duncan worked hard to publicize his bank and encourage imitators to help alleviate pauperism. Similar institutions or societies spread throughout Europe, "nurtured by the Philanthropic sense of Christendom and princely patronage."[13]

The first mutual savings bank in the United States was the Philadelphia Saving Fund Society, opening in December of 1816. The first mutual savings bank to receive a formal charter was the Provident Institution for Savings in Boston on Dec. 18, 1816. Early mutual savings banks sought to avoid the word *bank* in their title because the word carried such negative connotations to farmers, wage earners and many politicians.

It was believed that savings and hard work would lift the poor out of poverty and help wage earners achieve a degree of security. In the United States this idea was put forth in December 1816 by the *Christian Disciple* while commenting on the opening of the Boston savings institution: "It is not by the alms of the wealthy, that the good of the lower class can be generally promoted. By such donations, encouragement is far oftener given to idleness and hypocrisy, than aid to suffering worth. He is the most effective benefactor to the poor, who encourages them in habits of industry, sobriety and frugality."[14]

This was similar to the old Yankee values imbedded in most Bangor leaders of the nineteenth century, many of whom had achieved their stations through diligence, hard work and thrift.

The one fundamental difference between the mutual savings bank and the commercial bank was ownership. Mutual savings banks had no investors, only depositors who also owned the bank. All bank profits above expenses and reserve requirements were to be returned to depositors as dividends. Trustees were not to be paid nor receive any special financial benefit. In contrast, those investing in a commercial bank expected a handsome return.

Mutual savings banks experienced quick initial growth in the United States, arriving in Maine, then still of part of Massachusetts, in 1819. This first savings bank was the Institution for Savings for the Town of Portland and its Vicinity, incorporated June 11, 1819. Among its incorporators were Prentiss Mellen, who would become Maine's first chief justice, and Stephen Longfellow, father of poet Henry Wadsworth Longfellow.

The Portland savings bank failed following the panic of 1837 and was liquidated — the first failed savings bank in the United States. It failed because it had invested largely in the stock of Portland banks, which stumbled into severe problems when their stock plunged, subsequently taking the savings bank down with them. The closing left the largest city in Maine without a savings bank for more than a decade.

Its failure also led to an early savings bank statute, designed not to regulate banks in operation, but to outline rules for winding down a savings bank after it failed. The key part of the law required savings banks to spread their losses equally among all depositors, thus preventing those depositors who were most active or connected from losing less money than others. Despite that legislation and the growing presence of savings banks, no legislation was passed requiring a state examination of savings banks until 1855.

The state's second savings bank was the Saco and Biddeford Savings Institution which opened in 1827, followed in 1829 by Eastport Savings Bank.* Bangor business leaders organized the Bangor Savings Institution in 1833, the first savings bank in Bangor. However, it was liquidated in 1840.

By 1851, the economic woes of the late 1830s and early 1840s were past and the city and state were growing again. There was also a growing maturity in the economy and a burgeoning industrialization that in turn produced increasing class distinctions with more wage earners, factory workers, journeymen, domestic servants and poor, as well as more factory owners and businessmen. In general, money was replacing other sorts of economic activity such as barter and subsistence farming.

Great reforms were also sweeping the state and Bangor paid increasing attention to its cultural and social organizations as well as the relief needs of its poorer residents and working classes. Yet at mid-century, the city's financial institutions remained detached from those workers, leaving them with no significant access to banking. They remained distrustful of banks anyway.

What was needed was a group of public-spirited businessmen looking to use their experience and expertise to lift up the people through the mutual bank concept. Luckily, Bangor had them.

*Eastport Savings Bank was acquired in 1977 by Bangor Savings Bank.

Chapter Three

Elijah Livermore Hamlin

Among those enterprising young men who arrived in Bangor during the 1830s was Elijah Livermore Hamlin, a bright man whose varied interests, from business to history to public service, were melding into an eclectic mixture of lifetime achievement.

Elijah, although overshadowed in history by younger brother Hannibal Hamlin, was steeped in politics and public service as a youth in Oxford County. He cut his teeth as a young lawyer in Washington County and spent the balance of his life as a dynamic figure and leader notable not only in nineteenth-century Bangor but also nineteenth-century Maine.

During his life, Elijah served as a state senator, state representative, executive councilor, mayor, entrepreneur, businessman, banker and non-profit leader. He dedicated himself to such cultural and literary institutions as the Bangor Historical Society and Maine Historical Society. He was described at different times as the best mineralogist in Maine, the best antiquarian in Maine and the leading historian in Maine. The young man who discovered the first gem mine in the United States also founded Bangor Savings Bank, perhaps his most lasting legacy.

He also ran unsuccessfully for governor, negotiated the purchase of public lands from Massachusetts, helped define the fishery limits between the United States and Great Britain, and provided counsel to the state's Whig Party and its successor, the Republican Party.

In the midst of all this activity, he formed important friendships and influential partnerships that aided his success. It was this collection of businessmen, often with common interests and common goals, that helped shepherd the city through its growth and built the city's economy and its cultural institutions. It was not by accident that twenty-four of these men collectively started Bangor Savings Bank. However, while Elijah pursued business interests, he also pursued public-spirited ventures and personal interests that diverted him from great wealth. It is not easy to get rich as the "best antiquarian in the state." Perhaps as a result, while Elijah reached a comfortable station in life, he never achieved the wealth of some friends nor acquired the political power of his brother.

Elijah was hailed as bright, witty, and handsome and a man full of fun and humorous stories. He stood tall for the era and had a dark complexion with bushy eyebrows and piercing black eyes that twinkled with humor, a twinkle that saved his countenance from a stern look. Later in life, after Hannibal became vice president, it was said that at an important Washington, D.C., social function, Elijah "divided the honor for good looks with Secretary Chase of Ohio."[1]

Even to his death in 1872, the affable Elijah L. Hamlin took a daily walk whenever possible from his home on Court Street down to West Market Square and, despite failing health, maintained that twinkle in his eye that made him "a welcome visitant at any place where he chose to call, as he had a boundless fund of wit and humor that sickness or suffering did not crush."[2]

Elijah originally arrived in Bangor when it was nothing if not a hotbed of entrepreneurial activity. The best and brightest were coming to the banks of the Penobscot River and helping the Queen City rise to cultural, economic and political prominence. Such dedication and community involvement, you might say, were in Elijah's blood. The Hamlins, after all, had been helping shape New England since the 1630s.

The Hamlin Family

The Hamlin family left Devonshire, England, and landed on a windswept and mostly barren Cape Cod in 1639. Led by James Hamlin, the Hamlin family helped establish the town of Barnstable. Decades later, Hamlin men fought in King Philip's War and the French and Indian Wars, those bloody tests that hardened American patriots for the coming revolution.

Dr. Cyrus Hamlin, Elijah's father, was born a twin on the South Shore of

Boston in the small village of Pembroke on July 21, 1769. In those turbulent days, the Hamlin house served as a center of revolutionary passion. Eleazer Hamlin, Elijah's grandfather, was an early advocate of independence from Great Britain and fought in the Revolutionary War as a captain under Gen. George Washington. Some of his children with his first wife, Lydia Bonney, also fought in the war.

After the war, the Hamlins received a grant of land in Maine as reward for loyal service. Eleazer, after traveling into the backcountry to view his property, declared it fit only for bears. However, he offered parcels to his sons if they wanted to settle in Maine. They did and his sons Africa, America (Merrick), Eleazer Jr., and Hannibal (the future vice president's uncle) were among the early settlers of Waterford.

Meanwhile, a younger son, Cyrus, studied medicine at Harvard College and taught school. He eventually became a doctor and headed north himself. His timing was good. In 1795, the growing town of Livermore, located near Waterford, needed a doctor, and residents appealed to Cyrus, now in his twenties, to fill the position. (Doctors were commonly elected at a town meeting.)

In Livermore, Deacon Elijah Livermore essentially organized, built and controlled the town for years. It was said that for many years he *was* Livermore. For some reason, the deacon supported a rival physician over Cyrus. But in what may be a tribute to Cyrus' political skills, the town selected Cyrus despite the deacon's opinion. The town agreed to provide free board for Cyrus and his horse for one year. Cyrus was soon welcomed and supported by Deacon Livermore as well, perhaps because Elijah began courting Anna, the deacon's daughter. Anna and Cyrus married December 4, 1797.

For a few years, the family lived in Livermore. Cyrus bought a farm in the center of town, built a two-story house and planted a long row of elms along the road. Among other political positions, Cyrus served as a representative to the Massachusetts legislature in 1803. Elijah was born there in 1800 and grew up playing with the Washburn children, members of a future political dynasty.

Shortly after Paris became the county seat of the new Oxford County in 1805, Cyrus and Anna moved their growing family to Paris Hill, home of the new county offices. Cyrus bought land on Paris Hill for about $450 and built his house on the town common. The Hamlin house soon became a center for local social gatherings.

At Paris Hill, Cyrus served as the original clerk of the Court of Common Pleas that met in the Baptist church. Visiting judges often boarded with the Hamlins and were escorted across the town common to court by a fifer and drummer.

Cyrus also served as high sheriff, which led one town poet to pen these lines: "Of Sheriffs, Hamlin led the van, A doctor skilled, a noble man; Whose gates and doors were all ajar, to welcome strangers from afar. The children's friend, as known by many, for whom he always had a penny. The memory of his virtue still, is full of fragrance on the 'Hill.'"[3]

Anna Livermore, born April 6, 1775, in Waltham, Massachusetts, could easily match Cyrus' patriotic lineage. A descendent of Pilgrims, her mother was Hannah Clark, a close relative of Jonas Clark, the pastor whose parishioners were killed during the first battle of the Revolution at Lexington. When John Hancock and Samuel Adams asked Clark if his parishioners were ready to fight, Clark replied, "I have trained them for this very hour; they will fight, and, if need be, die, too, under the shadow of the house of God."[4] Then, after the battle, he looked over the bodies at Lexington and proclaimed, "From this day will be dated the liberty of the world."[5]

Bred from that stock, Anna grew up in the wilderness town of Port Royal (Livermore), founded and developed by her father, Deacon Livermore. Deacon Livermore had been sent into Maine in 1771 to explore the region and survey the proposed settlement as granted by the General Court of Massachusetts, but the war interrupted his plans.

After the war, Livermore took his family up the Kennebec River and through the forest in April 1779 to settle Port Royal. Anna was four years old.

One of Anna's earliest memories was seeing the frozen body of her father's friend, Major Thomas Fish. Fish had set out in a snowstorm to walk sixteen miles from Winthrop to Livermore's house in Port Royal. During what became a blinding snowstorm, Fish got lost and froze to death, about a mile from safety.

Anna later wrote: "I was a very little girl when Maj. Fish froze to death, and slept in the trundle bed. It was in the evening when they got Maj. Fish to our house; he was crooked, as he died, and they laid him upon the hearth before the fire to thaw him. Several times I looked out over the headboard of my trundle bed and saw them thawing Maj. Fish so that they could lay him out."[6]

As an adult, Anna, as described by her great-grandson Charles E. Hamlin, possessed New England's religious and domestic ideals. She was "patient and devoted, always energetic, yet not given to talking," he said.[7] She was imbued with the devoutness of many early New England Protestants and while her children lived with her, she required them to memorize biblical passages and recite them each day at family prayers.

And as befit her pioneer spirit, she could also handle an emergency. The local jail sat near the Hamlin's home. One day, when Cyrus, then the high sheriff, was away, inmates plotted an escape. According to legend, Anna heard a noise and rushed to the jail just as a prisoner tried to squeeze out the door. Anna seized the man's throat, choked him into submission and thrust him into the corner before fastening the door shut.

Anna gave birth to her first of twelve children on December 30, 1798, but the infant, Elijah Livermore Hamlin, died barely three months later. She would eventually watch five more children die in infancy. Her second son was born on March 29, 1800, and Anna gave him the same name as her first son, Elijah.

Elijah Hamlin Comes of Age

By the time he turned six, Elijah's family was ensconced at Paris Hill. The region surrounding the town, the Androscoggin Valley to the west and vast forest to the north, was prime country for young Elijah. He roamed the countryside, developing an avid interest in the outdoors and a fascination with history.

He sometimes ventured into a local Indian village to spend the night (he later became an avid collector of Indian artifacts). As a young man he hunted and fished in the Rangeley Lakes area with the famous Wabanaki guide Metallak, who eventually sketched a map of the Rangeley Lakes on birch bark for Elijah.[8]

While wandering in the area on a late fall day in 1820, Elijah and his cousin, Ezekial Holmes, stumbled upon tourmaline deposits on a nearby hillside. Their discovery, dubbed Mount Mica, was the first gem mine discovered in the United States.

At the Hamlin home, the culture and passion of politics and a spirit of public service permeated the household, clearly influencing Elijah and Hannibal. From the Paris Hill/Livermore region of the nineteenth century came such great politicians as Israel Washburn, Enoch Lincoln, Gov. Albion K. Parris, Stephen A. Emery and Deacon Livermore. A parade of judges and politicians also passed through the Hamlin homestead.

However, despite growing up in the same household with exposure to the same people and influences, Hannibal and Elijah pursued different political paths that wouldn't intersect for decades. Their father took both the *Portland Gazette* and the *Eastern Argus* newspapers. The *Gazette* was a leading Federalist and later Whig paper, while the *Argus* served as the leading organ of the Democratic Party. Cyrus, an ardent Federalist and Whig, and Elijah, who also became a diehard Whig, both read the *Gazette*. But Hannibal, the youngest, either waited his turn for the *Gazette* or read the *Argus* first. He was influenced by the Democratic organ, which matched his developing political outlook. Hannibal was enthralled with "Old Hickory" Andrew Jackson and the greatness of Thomas Jefferson, "the sage of Monticello."

As adults, Hannibal became the state's leading Democrat, Maine's dominant political party during the pre-Civil War era, while Elijah operated successfully, but more obscurely, in the state's minority party.

Elijah passed his teen years in Paris Hill, graduated first from Brown University and then from Waterville College (now Colby) in 1823. At Brown, Elijah became friends with Samuel Gridley Howe, later director of the Perkins Institute for the Blind in Boston, as well as a noted reformer and transcendentalist. Howe's wife, Julia Ward Howe, a well-known suffragist, wrote *The Battle Hymn of the Republic*. Also at Brown, Elijah helped found the Philophusian Society, dedicated to the investigation of scientific subjects.

Elijah also enjoyed the role of prankster. At Brown, one night he led a group of students who carried away the doors and furniture from the dining hall, seats and pulpit from the chapel, and the gates and bars from the college yard.

In advance of the mischief, Elijah posted a notice to students that read, "Hell fire rummaging club at half past twelve this night." When Brown officials discovered Elijah's role, he was "'sent away' for a few

Courtesy of Bangor Savings Bank
Elijah Livermore Hamlin (1800–1872), founding president of Bangor Savings Bank and noted Bangor politician, businessman and historian, probably in his twenties or thirties. One of only two known portraits of Hamlin.

weeks into the country to contemplate the enormity of his offense."[9]

Importantly for the brothers, Enoch Lincoln, future congressman and Maine governor, boarded at the Hamlin home in 1819 and remained there until 1826 when he moved to Augusta to serve the first of three one-year terms as governor. Lincoln, a poet, lawyer and antislavery advocate, kept one of the largest private libraries in the state, especially notable because books were expensive and somewhat rare. Both Elijah and Hannibal availed themselves of Lincoln's knowledge and his library. Lincoln's small law office in Paris Hill, originally built by Albion K. Parris, became a small classroom for young men studying law. Elijah read law with Lincoln before his admission to the bar. Lincoln died in 1829, at the age of forty.

In the early 1820s, Elijah left the comforts of Paris Hill to start a practice and teach school in South Waterford, the village his uncles helped build in the 1780s. He opened his first law practice in the village, but to make ends meet, the young lawyer also taught in the village school of this Oxford County town that sits in the shadow of the White Mountains.

Elijah's pupils sometimes sought him outside the classroom for advice. One pupil frequently visited Elijah at his small village law office and Elijah gave the boy books to read. He sometimes quizzed the boy to check his progress. One time he gave the boy *Robinson Crusoe*, which recounts the tale of an Englishman who spent twenty-eight years stranded on a tropical island. When the boy reached the chapter in which Crusoe spends weeks laboriously carving a boat from a large tree only to discover the boat is too big and too heavy to drag into the water, Elijah drew a life lesson for him.

"Now remember, my boy," Elijah said. "Never build any boats that you cannot get into the water. Lots of folks in this world do it; they start in without looking to see where they will bring up. Look ahead, my boy, and see what the end will be."[10]

Elijah may not have always known how things would end, but he always had a plan. And unlike his ancestors, Elijah's plan was not to stay in Western Maine.

Around 1825, Elijah headed east to Washington County, where he started a law practice in the village of Columbia Falls. The small village sat on the Pleasant River, not far from the head of Pleasant Bay, and was a well-known Federalist stronghold.

In Columbia, Elijah made a name for himself as both a lawyer and politician. He served the towns of Columbia, Addison, Jonesborough and Plantation No. 23 as a state representative from 1830 to 1832 and served as state senator in 1833. In the 1850s, years after Elijah left Columbia, the town erected a two-story Greek Revival building to serve as a schoolhouse and meeting hall. They named it Hamlin School House or Hamlin Hall in honor of Elijah.

Elijah married Eliza Choate of Ipswich, Massachusetts, on September 3, 1825. His four children, Adeline, Elizabeth, Augustus Choate and Julia, were all born in Columbia Falls.

While living in Down East Maine, Elijah's younger brother Hannibal came to live with him during the winter of 1829. Hannibal had attended Hebron Academy in 1826, but after another brother left for college he postponed his own dream of higher education to once again run the family farm in Paris Hill. In 1827, Hannibal spent a short time in Boston working as a clerk at a fruit store to earn money for school. He returned home after briefly entertaining notions of

Courtesy of John T. Alexander

A second portrait of Elijah L. Hamlin.

becoming an actor. Both Hannibal and Elijah were noted actors in South Paris, sometimes turning the house into a makeshift theater for the local Thespian Club. However, upon learning of Hannibal's interest in acting in 1827, his father admonished, "If you want to be a fool, and give up opportunities for a promising career, you can go on the stage; but if you want to be sensible, and make use of your talents in a sensible calling, come home."[11]

By winter of 1829, Hannibal had decided to become a lawyer and headed for Columbia to teach school and study law with his oldest brother at night. The brothers passed the days together, but their mentor-student relationship was interrupted in February 1829 by the unexpected death of their father from complications due to pneumonia.

Cyrus' will, which divided a family estate valued at about seventy-five hundred dollars, left Hannibal $250 and stipulated that he live with his mother until he was twenty-one. Elijah, despite being the eldest son,

45

received a token inheritance of five dollars. In making his will, Cyrus considered the cost and value of helping Elijah with a college education.

While Hannibal returned to the Oxford hills, Elijah remained in Columbia, continuing to build his practice, raise a family and launch a political career. Despite his success and prominence in Columbia, Elijah's eyes turned back westward within a decade of arriving in Washington County; this time he looked toward Bangor, roughly sixty miles away on the banks of the Penobscot.

The Queen City

By 1835, the once struggling town of Bangor had emerged as a city with a bright future, a lumber boomtown city where an ambitious man could quickly make a name for himself. Upon Bangor's incorporation as a city in 1834, Charles P. Roberts wrote: "The town came forth like a star in the forehead of the morning as the Queen City of the East."[12]

Historian Charles E. Clark painted this picture of the city: "All Maine was looking ahead in those years, but in Bangor, the mood was especially intense and high-spirited. The streets were crowded with speculators, gamblers, sailors, builders, salesmen, opportunists and adventurous men and women looking for each other. The waterfront was lined with grog shops, and they with seamen, and, in the spring, loggers seeking satiation of appetites built up during the winter in the woods and then climaxed by the dangerous drive down the Penobscot."[13]

Speculation in timberlands ran rampant, driven by easy capital and overly-generous banks. Land turned over and over, often on the same day. Land that originally sold for cents per acre might sell for dollars per acre a short time later. One tall tale about speculation in Bangor holds that two paupers escaped from the Bangor almshouse (the city's poor house) and were caught the next morning, but not before they had made more than eighteen hundred dollars speculating on timberlands.

Another tale claims that a traveler to Bangor could not find a hotel room in the crowded city, so he paid seventy-five cents for the right to lean against a lamppost for one night. The next night, he rented out his space for one dollar an hour and made ten dollars.

The tales are tall, but rooted in truth. The town was thriving as ambitious men and women looked to build a city of distinction and as a rowdy

Courtesy of Maine Historic Preservation Commission
Rafting lumber on the Bangor waterfront, 1800s

frontier town with hard-drinking sailors and lumbermen and enterprising ladies, some who opened well-known brothels (see page 110).

It was also an era in which the first foundry was established in the city in 1831 and steamship service began in 1834. Mount Hope Cemetery opened in 1836 and the city's first railroad came that same year as well.

Among those arriving on the outskirts of Bangor in 1834 was Hannibal Hamlin, now a lawyer himself, who set up a practice in the farming and shipbuilding town of Hampden, just down the mighty Penobscot from Bangor. Elijah Hamlin moved to neighboring Bangor in late 1835.

Starting in early January 1836, Elijah began announcing his arrival in the Queen City with small advertisements in the *Bangor Daily Whig and*

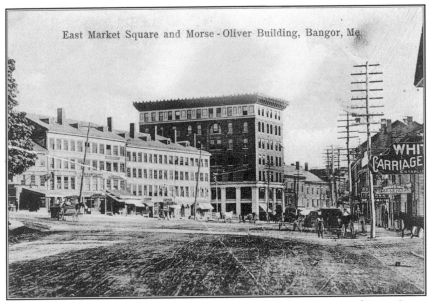

East Market Square and Morse-Oliver Building, Bangor, Me.

Courtesy of Maine Historic Photograph Collection, University of Maine, Orono
East Market Square, 1880s. Elijah Hamlin opened his first law practice here in 1835
after moving to Bangor from Columbia.

Courier that read: "Elijah L. Hamlin, Counselor at Law, has removed from Columbia, Washington County, and opened an office in Wadleigh's building, East Market Square."

Elijah quickly made headlines, not because of any great success or failure, but because of a feud. During the summer of 1836, his fight with the new Globe Bank became something of a cause célèbre in Bangor.

Newspapers of the era covered mostly politics, the sport of the era, and some ran business stories in their pages. All newspapers were partisan and existed largely as organs of a particular political party. Newspapers sometimes ran letters to the editor, but most letters were anonymous. Not so with Elijah. He took to the pages of the *Whig and Courier* with full disclosure, attacking his foes with flourish and rapier-like wit.

Elijah was an original corporator of the Globe Bank; he helped seek the bank charter in 1836. However, Elijah got a whiff of something he didn't like. He decided the bank was a mere front for outside or out-of-state interests seeking to circumvent state banking laws. He believed an agreement existed between certain local corporators to sell their interests to an outside person and name him president as soon as the state approved the bank.

48

That person was Samuel Smith, a notorious merchant and bold specu-
lator in Bangor who, along with his brother, made and lost several fortunes. Historian John Arndt offers this tale of the Smith brothers: "In
addition to this overabundance of banking facilities in the city, some
individuals even issued their own currency! In July 1835, at the height
of the frenzy, Edward and Samuel Smith ignored state law and issued
their own one dollar bills. When an individual questioned this practice,
one of the brothers threatened to flog the gentlemen."[14]

Elijah not only denounced the bank but demanded an investigation,
while fellow former corporators claimed Elijah was simply angry that
their actions thwarted his personal ambition to control the bank.

To such accusations, Elijah wrote in August 1836: "The assertions that I
used any influence against the Globe Bank while a petitioner for the same,
or that I ever wished to be President of the bank, Mr. Towle and his associates know to be untrue, and without the least foundation or shadow of
truth. However, I find no fault with this. As they have a hard case to make
out, they have my free permission to utter as many untruths as they please,
with all the personal abuse their ingenuity can contrive. Having embarked
in a rotton and fraudulent enterprise, I wish not to deprive them of the use
of any dirty weapon which they may think useful in their common cause."[15]

He also offered this advice: "I therefore advise these gentlemen, for
whom I have much respect, instead of quarreling with me through the
newspapers about undisputed facts, quietly to withdraw themselves from
this concern, like so many rats from a sinking ship, and save themselves
and their reputation before it is too late."[16]

Elijah was not alone in his distrust of the Globe Bank. Some other
Bangor banks also quarreled with it and helped delay its opening. The
Globe Bank never prospered. It struggled financially, undertook questionable business practices and possibly even committed fraud before failing in
1841. Bank historian Everett Birney Stackpole said of the bank that near
its end it was "evident that the bank was being conducted solely in the
interests of the New York parties." When it failed, he concluded, "The
only redeeming feature in this very bad situation was that the most of the
circulation was in the hands of the New York debtors or their associates."[17]

Elijah no doubt felt some vindication, but probably didn't have much
time to gloat: he was too busy.

Courtesy of Bangor Historical Society

The Smith Block at the corner of Hammond and Central Streets, about 1885. The block was built in about 1835. Elijah Hamlin kept a law office in this block for many years. Note Norombega Hall at upper left.

Maine Politics

From the 1830s to 1850s, the Whig Party was one of the nation's two major political parties, though generally weaker than the more established Democratic Party.

The Whig Party's antecedent was the National Republican Party, organized to support President John Quincy Adams in the 1820s. It also had roots in the old Federalist Party. The Whig Party was organized to oppose the policies of Andrew Jackson and the Democratic Party. Jackson's opponents called him King Andrew for his expanded view of presidential power and chose the Whig name with a nod to the American Whigs of 1776 and the early English Whigs who opposed the power of the British Crown.

Early Whig leaders were Henry Clay of Kentucky and Daniel Webster of Massachusetts. Whigs generally favored an active federal role in economic development, believing it crucial to build such infrastructure as roads, canals and railroads to boost the nation's economy. They also favored a national bank and high tariffs to protect American manufacturers and drew support from manufacturers, merchants and maritime entrepreneurs.

50

Maine's Whig Party revolved around the same issues. It became more anti-slavery than the Democratic Party and became the political base for the Maine Law, the nation's first attempt at prohibition. The Maine Law effort was led by the fiery, controversial and powerful prohibitionist Neal Dow of Portland.[18] The Democratic Party largely opposed the Maine Law and was dubbed "The Rum Party" by some Whig newspapers. Prohibition remained a powerful issue for nearly a century in Maine.

The Whig Party achieved some success, including twice electing Bangor's Edward Kent as governor of Maine, but it generally remained the nation's minority party. In the 1850s, the Whig party fractured and crumbled. Most former Whigs helped to create the Republican Party, a third party coalition of antislavery Democrats, free-soilers and other political splinter groups.

Elijah Hamlin came of age in this era of dramatic political upheaval and shifts. While living in Bangor, he was named land agent in 1838 and 1841 — two years when the Whigs held power and could give jobs to political allies and leaders — and played a role in the tense border standoff that nearly led to another war with Great Britain (see page 53). Elijah also served two terms as a state representative in the 1840s and two terms as a state senator in the 1850s.

Between his two stints in the legislature, forty-eight-year-old Elijah became the party standard bearer, carrying the Whig flag for governor in the summer of 1848. Despite growing fissures within the party, he was nominated at the Whig State Convention in Augusta on May 24, 1848, by a large majority, receiving 64 percent of the votes.

The party's fractures were caused largely by concerns over the party's national standard bearer, Zachary Taylor, known as "Old Rough and Ready." Maine Democrats pushed Lewis Cass for president and, as usual, attacked Elijah's Whig Party as successors to the now-dead Federalist Party. The Democratic organ, *Eastern Argus,* offered this vivid description, saying that after the party died "and its putrid corpse opened, then was its corruption fully displayed. It had spread ruin far and wide. It had beggared widows and orphans, and robbed the laborer of his hard-earned pittance."[19]

Elijah and such party stalwarts as Edward Kent were Taylorites and worked hard to unify the Whigs. The *Whig and Courier* implored Whigs to present a unified effort to defeat the Democrats and Democratic incumbent John W. Dana. Moderate and respected, Elijah was considered the Whig's best hope to unify the party.

The *Kennebec Journal* said, "Mr. H is a gentlemen every way qualified. His integrity we never heard questioned: his business talents are generally acknowledged even by opponents. H is a Whig of the old school, and yet not behind the progressive spirit of the age."[20]

The *Portland Umpire* wrote, "Among all the men in the state who have been in public life, scarce any one can be named, if in fact there is one at all, who has through life acted so uniformly under the guidance of his own unbiased judgment, without prejudice, or selfish purpose. No one has ever doubted for a moment the integrity of his profession, or the fairness of his conclusions. He never lost popularity in any position, for no one has ever thought him capable of being swayed by a selfish regard to his own interests or his own advancement."[21]

In the increasingly splintered state, Dana received the most votes, but not a majority. Ultimately, the race was decided by the Democratic-controlled legislature. In the general election, Dana received about 48 percent of the vote, to Hamlin's 37 percent and Free-Soil candidate Samuel Fessenden's 15 percent. (The Free-Soil party opposed the extension of slavery into federal territories or new states and succeeded the Liberty Party.)

Governors of the era served only one-year terms and the following year, Hamlin ran and lost again, this time to John Hubbard by a 51 percent to 38 percent vote. Once again a third party candidate, George F. Talbot, siphoned off thousands of votes. A cholera epidemic in Bangor also depressed turnout.

Hubbard was supported in the primary and general election by Elijah's brother Hannibal for his own political reasons. Hannibal believed Hubbard's election would ensure his reelection to U.S. Senate in 1850 by bringing in pro-Hamlin Democrats to the Maine legislature. In the 1850s, senators were chosen by state legislators, not popular vote. Thus, the party controlling the state legislature had the upper hand in choosing the senator.

Party loyalty and self-interest trumped brotherly love. But only briefly, for Elijah. As the senatorial election of 1850 drew near, Elijah worked behind the scenes to secure votes for his brother in a bruising fight as pro-Hamlin and anti-Hamlin forces waged war within the

The Aroostook War

In the mid-1800s, a dispute over control of a sparsely settled wilderness nearly brought the United States into its third war with Great Britain.

The northern border between British-ruled New Brunswick and Maine was vague. Established by the Treaty of Paris in 1783, it was defined loosely by rivers and highlands in a territory that had never been surveyed. This ambiguity caused increasing tension between the two neighbors by the late 1830s. At stake was control of the North Woods and its most valuable asset — white pine.

Lumber was fast becoming the lifeblood of Northern Maine's economy, and no tree was so prized as the majestic white pine. As mature trees became scarce, surveyors and scouts for timber companies pushed farther north and suddenly a land that did not seem worth haggling over in 1783 assumed great importance.

Maine's claim extended north nearly to the St. Lawrence, and included the headwaters and all of the tributaries of the St. John River to the already established eastern border at Grand Falls. The British also claimed the whole St. John watershed, a boundary that would have put the northern border of Maine at roughly the latitude of current-day Houlton. Rivers and watersheds mattered because no other way existed to transport lumber over large distances.

Several incidents occurred during the 1830s, and by 1839 the *Bangor Daily Whig and Courier* proclaimed that Maine had "had enough of diplomacy."[32] Soon, nearly 2,000 Maine Militiamen were in the disputed territory, with two companies of provincial infantrymen and British regulars positioned across the St. John.

Neither the United States nor Britain were eager for bloodshed. The United States sent Mexican War hero Winfield Scott to defuse the situation. He helped calm tempers and established the St. John as the de facto border until a formal agreement could be reached.

The dispute was finally settled without a shot being fired with the signing of the Webster-Ashburton treaty on August 4, 1842.

For Maine, the treaty opened what became Aroostook County to increased lumbering and agriculture. For Bangor, the treaty increased the size of its periphery and the amount of lumber that eventually made its way to its mills. And importantly for Bangor's businessmen and promoters, the agreement meant an increasing security for their investments in land and resources.

— Hoving

Democratic Party. Most Whig and Free-Soil legislators gleefully joined the melee.

In a letter dated April 5, 1850, Elijah wrote to Hannibal and told him he was out surveying the state's political scene. "I will do for you what I can and will attend upon the organization of the legislature if you think it advisable. I am quite intimate with Mems. Reed and Hagon, two of the Lincoln Senators, and as I shall not be a candidate for any office this year, I think I can have some influence with many persons."[22]

Meanwhile, despite two statewide defeats, Elijah's influence in Bangor remained strong. He served as Bangor mayor from 1851 to 1853, swept into power his final year by a landslide of 1,780 to 37 votes. In his mayoral address in the spring of 1852, Elijah discussed his political agenda and beliefs, including the need for infrastructure improvements, long a staple issue of the Whig Party. He highlighted a drop in crime and arrests, which he attributed to stricter enforcement of the prohibition on alcohol, and outlined attempts to alleviate traffic congestion in East Market and West Market Squares, "so choked with teams and wagons from the country, that the Marshall is often called upon to open a passage for travelers passing through Main Street."[23]

The former teacher also discussed public education, which he felt should not only address the mind, but physical and moral well-being as well. At the time, Bangor operated fifty-two schools for 5,130 pupils, with an average school population of just under one hundred. The city's attendance rate was 52 percent.

"The common idea seems to be that the physical powers will take care of themselves, and that the moral training belongs solely to the parents. All that is considered necessary to give a first rate education to any one, is to fill up the mind with a certain quantity of Latin, Greek, Algebra & c., and prepare it for the mastery of purely literary and scientific, rather than practical matters. This system is wrong. A young man arriving at the age of twenty-one, with his physical powers fully developed and hardened from habits of labor, and his moral powers well disciplined, will be more likely to become a valuable citizen and a happier man, than if he had acquired all the learning of the schools, and possessed a feeble body, and unsubdued passions."[24]

Furthermore, Elijah urged parental involvement, which he said undeniably improves student and school performance, and criticized the severe "intellectual" training of some younger pupils, spurred, he believed, by excessive competition between schools. "The real progress of a scholar is not measured, so much by the extent of studies passed over, as from the fixed habits of mental discipline acquired. Thoroughness, and not progress, should be the principal aim of the teacher."[25]

Elijah did not seek a third term. However, he did not step off the political stage. Three years later, he co-starred in a political event that affected politics in Maine for the next century. He shook hands with his brother.

The Grand Old Party

With the Maine Whig Party virtually disintegrated by 1856 and the Democratic Party wracked by dissension and defection, political upheaval swept through Maine and the nation.

In the nineteenth century, national politics drove state elections. It was an age of great men, great causes, great movements and seismic shifts in party loyalties. The Maine Law, abolition and slavery extension played out as issues on both the national and state stages.

A key national issue was the Kansas-Nebraska Act of 1854. The Kansas-Nebraska Act officially repealed an earlier compromise that excluded slavery from Western U.S. Territories and nullified most of the Missouri Compromise, the agreement that allowed Maine's admission to the union as a free state to balance the admission of Missouri as a slave state.

The Kansas-Nebraska Act unified abolitionists and spurred protest meetings across the nation. At two meetings in Wisconsin in early 1854, an antislavery coalition selected the name *Republican*, professing to be the true descendants of Thomas Jefferson's Democratic-Republican Party. They could also trace roots to Alexander Hamilton's Federalist Party of 1791 and the Whigs.

The birth of the Republican Party in Maine also emerged from the fusionist movement of the mid-1850s. It took place in Strong during the summer of 1854, when the Free-Soil Party, the Whig Party and the so-called Morrill (named after Anson P. Morrill) Democrats each held separate conventions on the same day and then held a unified convention.*

---

*The Maine Democrats were also sometimes divided into the Woolheads (anti-slavery) and Wildcats (pro-South).

Like the Wisconsinites, the coalition chose the name Republican
and adopted as their major platform an opposition to the extension of slavery.

Watching all this unfold was
an increasingly disaffected
Hannibal Hamlin, who observed
his beloved Democratic Party
become increasingly controlled by
Southern power sentiment. At one
point, in a letter to his wife Ellen,
Hamlin called his party "a putrid
mass of moral leprosy."[26]

Finally, in 1856, after the
Democrats at the Cincinnati
Convention moved to divest the
federal government of any power
over slavery, Hannibal Hamlin
denounced his party and abandoned it in a speech on the floor of
the U.S. Senate on June 12, 1856.

At the same time, the fledgling Republican Party was also

Maine Historic Preservation Commission
Hannibal Hamlin (1809–1891), Elijah
Hamlin's brother, was a powerful Maine
politician and served as Abraham Lincoln's
first vice president. He died on July 4, 1891
while playing cards at the Tarratine Club in
Bangor.

developing through a coalition of old Whigs, Free-Soilers, antislavery
Democrats and other splinter groups (such as the largely anti-immigrant
Know-Nothing Party). Some of Hannibal's Republican friends in Maine
courted him to join the "new party of Freedom."

Of course, practical matters were also in play. Republican leaders,
drawn from diverse elements, believed public conversion by Hamlin
would bring a slew of converts and add strength to the Republican
cause. And Hamlin, the master politician, realized that a conversion to
the Republican Party, given his recent positions, might be the only way
to ensure his reelection.

Hannibal's switch did not come without vitriolic attack from
Democrats. The *Eastern Argus* of Portland proclaimed, "He has left a

glorious, and renowned party, whose principles are ever young, and has united himself with a deformed monster whose embrace is destruction."[27]

The *Machias Union* also chastised him: "He has enrolled his name in the black catalogue of ingrates and traitors to the democratic party, — among those men whose resentments and ambition have overpowered their gratitude and devotion to principle."[28]

However, in other circles in Maine, Hannibal's decision generated tremendous excitement. On a June night in 1856, old Norombega Hall in downtown Bangor nearly burst with excitement as people gathered from about the countryside. There on stage stood Hannibal Hamlin, popular U.S. senator who only days earlier had bolted from the Democratic Party. Also on the stage was Elijah Livermore Hamlin, former Whig and chairman of the Republican Convention in Bangor. Since their days at Paris Hill, Elijah and Hannibal had long opposed each other's politics, even though they remained close and discussed many issues. But there on Bangor's greatest stage, Hannibal turned to his brother and said, "You and I, sir, for the first time in our lives stand upon the same political platform and battle for the same great cause. And let me tell you, sir, that that cause involves the destiny of your country and mine. When you were the candidate of the great Whig party for governor of our native State, in which we both feel so much pride, you did not receive my suffrage, and when I was the humble candidate of the late Democratic party for its national representative, I did not receive your vote. Now, thank God, we stand firmly together upon a platform broad as the Union, and with the Declaration of Independence and the Constitution for our principles. Those words, dear to every American, *liberty* and *union*, are emblazoned on it in letters of living light. Brother, I give you the right hand of political fellowship, and God grant, may we always remain side by side in the cause of our country and human liberty."[29]

The two brothers shook hands and embraced to thunderous applause, which prompted Hannibal Hamlin to remember later in life, "Didn't they howl, though."[30]

The meshing of the two political forces, symbolized by the handshake, formed a powerful Republican Party that would dominate Maine politics into the 1950s and gave Maine its most powerful politicians,

Courtesy of Bangor Public Library

Norombega Hall, built in 1854–1855, served as Bangor's primary hall for its major events. Shown here in about 1890, the great hall burned in the fire of 1911.

perhaps ever, in Hannibal Hamlin, Sen. William Pitt Fessenden, Gen. Joshua Lawrence Chamberlain, James G. Blaine, Israel Washburn and Thomas Brackett "Czar" Reed. Most commanded a national stage, while Chamberlain, although not a national political figure, was revered for his Civil War heroism.

That night at Norombega Hall also set the stage for Hannibal's election as governor of Maine, his subsequent quick resignation and return to the U.S. Senate. And it eventually paved the way for him to become vice president of the United States four years later.

Elijah enjoyed the ride, already understanding his role. Now in his mid-fifties, he felt his opportunity had passed for higher elected office and that a new generation stood at the forefront. Later in 1856, he attended a political gathering in Stoneham, Maine, with his brother. He told the crowd that for political success, he was born nine years too soon. As a result, it was now his fate to beat the bushes, while Hannibal, his younger brother by nine years, caught the bird.

Still, he was overjoyed with his brother's success. On the night of Hannibal Hamlin's nomination for vice president, Elijah wrote of the excitement that enveloped Bangor: "About twelve o'clock I was awakened by a crowd about my house [on Court Street] shouting your nomination for Vice-President. Augustus and I had to get up, and upon opening the door, the outsiders rushed into the house with loud cheers. After partaking of some refreshments, Augustus found a swivel and some powder, and a salute was fired in honor of the nomination. ... Two drums were obtained, and the crowd then went to the mayor's, Hollis Bowman, then to Wingate's, the street commissioner, and so on to other places until near sunrise. The nomination was everywhere enthusiastically received, and in some cases, persons came out just as they came out of bed. The Democrats complain that they had no sleep the last part of the night, there was such an infernal uproar in the streets."[31]

Building an Economy

Politics was but one passion for Elijah; he also felt strong businesses and economic development were crucial to Maine and Bangor. Despite the Globe Bank fiasco, he frequently stepped into the business world, often with political compatriots or friends at his side. His businesses included: Bank of the State of Maine, which he helped found with Samuel F. Hersey, Leonard March and Samuel H. Dale; Penobscot Mutual Fire Insurance Company, which he served as president; the Bangor Bridge Co., which he served as director and president; and the Oldtown and Lincoln Railroad, which he helped establish.

He lived in the south tenement of a four-tenement brick block on Court Street until his death. Although not a rich man, he lived an upper-middle-class life by Bangor standards. In 1861, he lived with his wife, two children and a domestic servant. His house included a piano and small library. He also owned a horse and chaise and his local investments included twenty-two shares of the Bangor Bridge Company, valued at $3,740; eighteen shares of Bangor Gas Co., worth $4,100 and twenty shares of Market Bank, worth $1,960.

Also, illustrating Bangor's nearly-forgotten maritime heritage, he held interests in local schooners, often with business partners. He owned a one-eighth share of the schooner *Adeline Hamlin*, named after his daughter and valued at $125; and a one-eighth share of the schooner *Westward*, valued at $450. Typically, owners received a share of trade profits as well.

West Market Square, shown here in the late 1850s, was the city's prime business district. It was formed by the intersection of Main, Hammond and Broad Streets.

In pursuing his varied interests throughout his life, Elijah also established a group of friends, political allies and business partners that formed the core of Bangor power. When working together as a force, these men could accomplish at any level almost anything they desired.

At perhaps the top of his game in the early 1850s, Elijah sought out twenty-three men for a venture that would combine private enterprise skill, business acumen and public service to benefit the emerging laboring class and the city's poorer residents — Bangor Savings Bank. He didn't have to look far for help: Bangor's best and brightest were close at hand, already helping build Bangor, and most just a short walk from his office in bustling West Market Square.

Chapter Four

The Founders

There was perhaps no better place to be in Maine, perhaps no better place to be in New England, than Bangor during the 1830s. The city was alive. It danced forward with an almost outsized sense of destiny and dreamed of not simply standing as a rival to Portland, but as a rival to Boston and New York. Queen City of the East was not a marketing slogan; it was a quest. People talked of building an eastern San Francisco on the Penobscot.

Driven by this dream and emboldened by what seemed like vast untapped riches to the north, businessmen adopted a freewheeling, often unregulated capitalism, creating a sense that anything was possible — both good and bad. The era produced rapid changes as hundreds of new buildings sprouted on riverbanks and an unprecedented gathering of talent and energy descended on Eastern Maine. So did quick buck artists. Land speculation bordered on the obscene. Outsiders sniped that in no other place in Maine were visitors more likely to have their pockets picked. Entrepreneurs headed into the woods to cut canals and build dams as they battled each other over the tall timber. They divined ways to reach ever more distant stands of white pine, the juice of the Bangor boom, and drive it down the Penobscot to sawmills. Unavoidably, the speculation boom came crashing down in the financial panic of 1837, pummeling the economy. Some fortunes withered. But by this time, financial turmoil could only delay, not derail, the city's momentum. Following the panic, wealth came from the actual timber, not the speculation on land. Even a prolonged recession that began in 1839 served as a

Courtesy of Bangor Historical Society

Map of downtown Bangor, 1853. Court Street intersects with Hammond Street (top left) and Harlow Street runs beside Kenduskeag Stream (top). What is called Wall St. Place is in the area of what became better known as Pickering Square.

mere speed bump. It seemed that more than two hundred years after Champlain declared that it did not exist, some adventurers traveling up the Penobscot had finally found Norumbega.

Like Elijah Livermore Hamlin, other entrepreneurs now woven into the fabric of Bangor history staked their claims, opened storefronts in West Market Square, hung shingles outside new law offices, and bought land in the great Maine forest. Some of their names are still recognizable in Bangor, even if only on street signs, buildings or other landmarks.

This generation of innovators included nearly all of those who came to found Bangor Savings Bank in 1852 — a breathtakingly active and entwined group of twenty-four men who started corporations, acquired land, oversaw nonprofit organizations, ran cultural institutions and rose to power in both state and national politics. Some became fabulously wealthy in the process.

Bank founders included men like George W. Pickering, for whom Pickering Square was named; Joseph S. Wheelwright, who built the Wheelwright & Clark Block; Samuel F. Hersey, one of the nation's leading lumbermen and major city benefactor; Franklin Muzzy, who ushered in the city's industrial age; and Isaiah Stetson who, as mayor of Bangor, helped rally troops to the Union cause during the Civil War.

In the 1840s and 1850s, most of these men moved about town in the same general circles, often co-owning schooners, starting businesses together, joining the same social organizations and making other joint investments. Most shared other similarities as well. They were self-made and sprung from humble origins. They were politically engaged in an era of tumult and reform, they belonged to the Whig Party and later the Republican Party after it was created in 1854, and they were steeped in religion, most attending either the city's powerful Congregational, Unitarian or Universalist Churches.

In some regards, Bangor proved a fascinating dichotomy: its notorious bars and brothels operated along the riverfront in the very shadows cast by the city's majestic church steeples that dotted the hillside. Its shanties and tenements stood only a stone's throw from Greek Revival mansions. While a list of Bangor Savings Bank's twenty-four founders reads mostly like a roll call of the city's nineteenth-century movers and shakers, some founders also stood at the edge of greatness and blinked, their reputations crumbling through personal weakness or simple misfortune: Mayor Samuel H. Dale allegedly committed suicide; George R. Smith participated in one of the state's most infamous embezzlement schemes; John Winn and Samuel Farrar skulked from the city in financial ruin; and Capt. Nathan Pendleton died in the state mental hospital.

But, then, that was the inherent excitement of a vibrant city filled with dreamers, of a city literally being drawn from a nearly blank slate. It was the possibility of building great fortunes and the real risk of losing it all.

Welcome to the entrepreneurial hotbed.[1] Welcome to Bangor 1852.

The Lumberman ~ Samuel F. Hersey

Samuel Freeman Hersey rose from a lowly paid Bangor store clerk to become one of the nation's greatest lumbermen, owning tracks of forest-land in Maine and the old Northwest Territory of Michigan, Minnesota and Wisconsin. He reigned as Bangor's wealthiest citizen after transforming one hundred dollars in savings into a million dollar fortune. General Hersey, as he was known, also became one of the city's greatest benefactors, and close friend and political confidant of Maine's leading politician, Hannibal Hamlin.

Courtesy of Bangor Public Library

Samuel Freeman Hersey (1812–1875)

Hersey was born in April 1812 on a farm in the Oxford County town of Sumner, the son of James Hersey and Olive Freeman and the grandson of two Revolutionary War soldiers. He attended school in Sumner and nearby Buckfield during both summer and winter, alternating his studies with farm work until he was fifteen. He began teaching school at sixteen and graduated from Hebron Academy in 1831, ending his formal education. He was an avid reader of nonfiction books and his favorite was Alexander Pope's *Essay on Man*, an eighteenth-century work that discusses man's role in the universe, man's ability to think and reason, and God and Christianity. Hersey said this book served as an important influence on his life. As an adult, he formed strong ties to the city's Universalist Church.

In the early 1830s, he left Oxford County for Bangor to work as a store clerk, laboring initially for board. His meager pay soon increased enough that he saved one hundred dollars. In 1833, he used that sum to launch a general merchandise business in Lincoln with his cousin W.R. Hersey, who also invested one hundred dollars.

Hersey's store grew slowly but steadily but was then nearly wiped out by the financial panic of 1837. Although the panic hit nationwide, in the Bangor area it was caused in part by a restricted money supply that followed years of rampant land speculation, easy bank credit and generous loan terms. The economy was a house of cards that could not stand.

Following the financial setback, W.R. Hersey sold his share of the business to his cousin. Unfortunately, Sam faced other difficulties as well. In 1836, his young wife, Eliza Stowell of South Paris, died. The two had been married but one year.*

Following his cousin's departure, Sam sought a new partner. He found one in Jesse Fogg and the two started Fogg & Hersey with general merchandise stores in both Milford and Bangor. Hersey tended the store in Milford, the town where he lived and served one term as state representative, but worked his way back toward Bangor by 1844. He lived on Harlow Street and later built a mansion on High Street.

Hersey's partnership with Fogg dissolved in 1850, but it had established Hersey as a Bangor businessman. While in business together Hersey & Fogg added an important product to their enterprise: lumber, the undisputed juice of the Bangor economy. More importantly for his personal fortunes, Hersey also invested in timberlands. The panic that pricked the speculation bubble in 1837 also provided a good buying opportunity for those with the money and the guts to invest. Hersey had no shortage of guts.

Operating from 2 Stetson's Block in the mid-1850s, Hersey also invested in western timberlands. He reasoned correctly that the nation was heading west and no doubt realized the supply of great white pine in Maine was dwindling. Hersey bought timberlands in Minnesota, Iowa and other parts of the Old Northwest, where some towns were subsequently named after him.

During the Civil War, Hersey was active in the state militia, helping organize and equip troops from Maine; he achieved the rank of major general. He helped raise the Second Maine Regiment and the First Maine Heavy Artillery. His son, Roscoe, served in the First Maine Heavy Artillery and was wounded at Spotsylvania Court House.

As Hersey's financial wealth grew, so did his political influence. He was

*Hersey later married Jane Ann Davis in 1839 and Emily M. Sanborn in 1871.

elected state representative from Bangor in 1857 and 1865, twice served as state senator in the 1860s and served on the executive council from 1853 to 1854. Originally a Hamlin Democrat, he, like Hannibal Hamlin, bolted to the Republican Party in the mid-1850s, helping build that party's century-long dominance in Maine. According to the *Whig and Courier*, Sam "was one of the sturdy band of pioneers who unfurled the standard of the Republican Party in Maine, and from the hour of its birth to the present has been an outspoken and unswerving advocate of its principles."[2]

Hersey served as a delegate in 1860 to the Republican National Convention that nominated Abraham Lincoln and Hannibal Hamlin, served as a delegate again in 1864, and served as a member of the Republican National Committee from 1864 to 1868. Furthermore, he worked as a key political organizer to secure Hamlin's nomination as vice president, even against Hamlin's wishes.

On his way to the 1860 convention in Chicago, Hersey stopped to visit Hamlin in Washington. Hamlin, a hardcore politician, gave Hersey instructions to canvass delegations from key states to decide whom to support for the presidential nomination. At the convention, Lincoln was chosen over William H. Seward of New York on the third ballot. Meanwhile, Hamlin had told Hersey not to place Hamlin's name on the ticket for either president or vice president. However, after Lincoln's victory stunned Seward supporters, Hersey ignored Hamlin's instructions and engaged in a "lightening campaign to nominate Hamlin."[3]

He rounded up support from other delegations and key party leaders by pointing out the benefits and practicality of a Lincoln-Hamlin ticket. Hamlin was nominated on the second ballot. Said Hamlin's biographer, H. Draper Hunt, "The 'naturalness' of Hamlin's nomination should not obscure the impressive politicking of Sam Hersey and the Maine delegates, who saw a golden opportunity and seized it."[4]

Hersey also stood at the center of two of Hamlin's more disappointing moments.

Hamlin was a famous practitioner of political patronage intended to reward friends and build loyalty. Lincoln allowed Hamlin to name the secretary of the navy and Hamlin chose a New Englander, Gideon Welles of Connecticut. During the Civil War, the Navy wanted new wooden gunboats. Hamlin received a promise from Welles that the contract would go

Baptist Church (left) built in 1820s, and the Universalist Church (right) built in 1860s.
Looking up from East Market Square in the 1870s.

to William McGilvery, a leading shipbuilder in Searsport, and his old friend Hersey. Both were strong Union men and submitted a low bid.

However, the contract went to an alleged Confederate sympathizer instead of the two men. Hamlin was livid. After confronting Welles, who told Hamlin he could no longer honor his promise, Hamlin learned that someone else had authorized the agreement. Regardless, Hamlin never again spoke to Secretary Welles, saying, "This terminates our relations. I will not have anything to do with a man who breaks his plighted word to me."[5]

Hamlin's second disappointment involving Hersey came nearly a decade later. Hamlin frequently urged Hersey to run for governor of Maine and in the spring of 1870, Hersey agreed to stand as a candidate, backed by the Hamlin machine. To Hamlin's amazement, Hersey was defeated in the Republican primary by Sidney Perham of Woodstock, a radical prohibitionist.

Hamlin was shattered. Only a short time earlier he had assured Hersey he was confident of victory, but finally wrote to his friend after the defeat, "To tell you the sober truth, I have not had courage to write you, I have

67

William A. Blake

William A. Blake was born in Hartford in Oxford County and probably came to Bangor in the late 1820s or early 1830s. He was a founder of Merchants Bank in 1850, serving as its president throughout the decade. He served as an aldermen and city councilor in the 1840s and 1850s and lived on Summer Street. In 1860, he lived with his wife, two children and two servants.

William's brother Samuel was a prominent Democrat and served as president of the Senate in 1842. Samuel joined the Republican Party during the Civil War.

Historian James Mundy offered this description of the Blake brothers:

"Following the death of his brother, William A. Blake, he [Samuel] assumed the presidency of the Merchants National Bank of Bangor, spending most of his time managing a rather substantial fortune that he and his brother had built up in a lifetime of shrewd investments.

"Both Samuel and William were powerful, calculating, conservative and secretive men, traits not uncommon among those who survived and prospered in the nineteenth century Bangor."[39]

While on his way to work on a Friday in December, William was "attacked by a hemorrhage of the lungs" and died five days later.[40]

He died December 11, 1861. He was fifty-one.

Albert W. Holton

Local merchant Albert W. Holton served as the first treasurer of Bangor Savings Bank and was instrumental in its founding. Born in Lancaster, New Hampshire, in 1807, he came to Bangor in 1835 and lived a modest middle-class life with his wife on Summer Street. He first worked as a clerk for Major Jesse Wentworth and later became his partner. He remained a merchant until 1851 and then became treasurer of Bangor Savings Bank when it opened in 1852. He served as a bank trustee for more than twenty-five years. He twice served as a city councilor and was president of Bangor Gas Light Company.

Holton was progressively ill for several years and died of "paralytic shock" in February 1888.

Waldo T. Peirce

Waldo Treat Peirce was born September 16, 1804, one of the thirteen children of Waldo Peirce and Catharine Treat of Frankfort.

Peirce started as a merchant in Bangor in the 1820s and eventually operated Peirce & Hayward Company, a lumber business at Peirce Block on Exchange Street.

Like many Bangor Savings Bank founders he had ties to various banks, insurance companies and railroads. Peirce was a corporator, with George W. Pickering, of Bangor Savings Institution in 1833, organized Kenduskeag Bank in 1832, and was a director of Mercantile Bank in 1834. He was also corporator of the European and North American Railway Company in 1850.

He acquired a considerable amount of property for a pittance in the aftermath of the 1837 financial panic. In one transaction, he and his brother Hayward bought shares in a land and lumber company for one dollar each. The shares were originally valued at a thousand dollars each.[41] Waldo also owned a lot of property with Pickering.

He was a city councilor and a delegate to the state Whig Convention in 1848 that nominated Elijah L. Hamlin for governor. He lived on Harlow Street with his wife Hannah Hills and six children, one of whom donated to the city both the Peirce Memorial located near the Bangor Public Library and the Civil War Memorial at Mt. Hope. He died in 1858. He was fifty-four.

Thomas W. Baldwin

In the early 1850s, Thomas W. Baldwin operated a dry goods business at 56 Main Street and lived on Third Street. He later opened a coal business, Baldwin & Bacon, on Front Street and lived on Ohio Street. As a retired merchant in 1870, the census listed his holdings as ten thousand dollars in real estate and fifteen thousand dollars in personal estate. He lived with his wife, Margaret Hopkins, two children and one servant.

He also served as a director of the Penobscot and Kennebec Railroad, and was a Bangor assessor and an alderman.

Baldwin died in 1874 in Boston.

felt so sad at your defeat — I am sure I have felt it as keenly as you could — I tell you nothing but the truth when I say I had much rather have resigned my place in the Senate than you should have been defeated."[6]

Hersey had other interests beyond politics and timber. He served as a director of the European and North American Railway Company, president of Market Bank, director of the Merchants' Mutual Fire Insurance Company, and founding trustee of Merchants Mutual Insurance Company in 1851.

He was an early promoter of railroads both to Bangor and to the north, no doubt understanding the impact of rail not only on Eastern Maine, but also on the value of his own land and operations. In the 1870s, he acquired more property when lands originally granted to the European and North American Railway were sold off.

In 1860, he also owned shares in several schooners, including a one-eighth share of the self-named *General Hersey*, a stake valued at $225. He lived in a mansion on High Street with a housekeeper, the housekeeper's daughter and five other servants.

Hersey was elected a U.S. representative in 1873, by then in his early 60s, and died while in office in 1875.

Shortly before his death, he valued his real estate in Maine at three hundred thousand dollars and his personal estate at one hundred fifty thousand dollars. Those numbers clearly do not indicate his true worth, but even they illustrate his dramatic rise in fortunes. In 1850, he listed his real estate value at eight thousand dollars. This was a time when skilled workers in blue-collar jobs earned in the neighborhood of four hundred to five hundred dollars per year. Shortly after his death city taxes on his estate remained the highest in Bangor — greater than the second highest taxpayer by a stunning 30 percent.

Local judge and historian John E. Godfrey estimated Hersey's value at death at roughly $2 million and sniped in his own journals, "Gen. Hersey died leaving $2,000,000 and many friends among Universalists and Spiritualists and many severe critics among other people."[7]

There can be no doubt the General was probably a hard-nosed businessman. The lumber business was a rough and tumble and sometimes shady business in the nineteenth century. Regardless, he generated strong loyalty. When he died, flags at public buildings were lowered to half-mast. His will helped established two vital building blocks of twentieth century Bangor, the Bangor Public Library and the old City Hall.

Hersey left a bequest to the city of Bangor that was to be payable in 1900 and equal to 30 percent of his "eastern" estate at the time. However, by 1882, the city grew concerned about the future value of timberlands in Maine and alarmed by the spending of Hersey's heirs. To protect its interests, the city negotiated with estate trustees and agreed to relinquish its 1900 claim in exchange for one hundred thousand dollars, immediately. Later the city combined that bequest with books and trust money received from the Bangor Mechanic Association to fund and establish the Bangor Public Library. In the 1890s, the city also financed construction of City Hall using money in the Hersey Fund.

Following his death, the Sunday School at his beloved Universalist Church wrote: "No more in the future, as in the past, shall we see, with every recurring Sunday, his noble and manly form cheering old and young with his hearty greeting and the genial radiance of his smiling face. No more shall we hear the clear, ringing tones of his voice, giving us words of encouragement, and stimulating all to the cheerful performance of our whole duty."[8]

The Mechanic ~ Franklin Muzzy

Franklin Muzzy, left fatherless as a young boy and forced to work to help support his mother, labored to learn skills and develop a business mind. His talents helped usher in Bangor's industrial age. He became a skilled mechanic and capitalized on the lumber boom by providing equipment to the industry. He served as a community leader in both the antislavery and temperance movements, stood as the last Whig Senate president and tirelessly dedicated himself to literacy efforts and the improvement of fellow artisans and mechanics.

Historian James B. Vickery said that Muzzy, along with two of his contemporaries, Daniel Hinckley and Thomas Egery, were "energetic and innovative, [and] they transformed a small river community into an important early manufacturing area."[9]

Franklin Muzzy was born December 8, 1806, in Spencer, Massachusetts, the youngest of ten children. His father died when Franklin was twelve years old, forcing the young boy to work away from home in spring, summer and fall. He returned home to attend school each winter. The first year away he lived with his brother and earned about $18 before returning home in October. Then at sixteen, Muzzy was left solely in charge of the family farm, but farm life was not what Muzzy desired.

At seventeen, he headed north to Gardiner, Maine, to live with his sister and work as an apprentice in a local machine shop. He wanted to become a machinist. Unfortunately, the shop closed shortly after he arrived, forcing Muzzy to take a series of jobs to survive, including one stint at a local cotton factory earning $6.50 per month, a job he hated: "I was therefore compelled to work at a business I did not like under the nod of a surly tyrant who regarded neither honor nor justice."[10]

He left after four months to pursue a career as a machinist, a decision that eventually took him to a New Hampshire shop where he again labored for low pay. He was not discouraged, but remained resolute, even though he took to heart one prospective employer who considered him "not worthy of employ under his lordship, so he very coldly told me that he did not want any such help."[11]

He soon realized he lacked the education necessary to reach his goals, so Muzzy saved enough money to attend a technical school back in Gardiner. He took classes to learn drafting, but his money ran out and he returned to New Hampshire. There he followed the advice of a man he met in a local tavern, who told him that instead of asking for only five or six dollars, ask for fifteen or sixteen dollars per month. Claim you are that good, the man told him, but then offer to work on trial for one month to prove it. The advice worked and Muzzy started as an apprentice, initially doing little but sweeping and cleaning castings, in a large, intimidating factory. He became nervous when he first looked across the crowded factory floor at the men and machines: "These, together with the searching look of the workmen, made me tremble for my fate among them."[12]

His boarding situation provided no relief. He shared space with other factory men and slept in a bed only inches from the roof, in a top floor room that became so hot he could barely sleep at night.

He eventually returned to Gardiner to form a partnership with A.A. Wing. The firm moved to Bucksport in the spring of 1830 and made its way to Bangor about two years later as the machinist company Muzzy and Wing. Muzzy operated somewhat successfully until a fire in 1841 wiped him out. The fire exacerbated problems for a business already struggling through the economic troubles of the late 1830s.

After the fire, Muzzy scouted Maine and other states for a place to rebuild. He finally settled on a Franklin Street site along the Kenduskeag Stream. There he built a four-story foundry and took on new partners. His Franklin Muzzy & Company was later incorporated as Muzzy Iron Works in 1868 and later became part of Union Iron Works.

In 1860, Muzzy employed thirty-five men whom he paid about $37 per month or roughly $444 per year. They produced steam engines, boilers and other goods valued at fifteen thousand dollars per year and produced lumber machinery valued at twenty-five thousand dollars per year. His company grew larger than most of his contemporary competitors. For example, in 1850 most Bangor shops employed about eight people, while Muzzy employed thirty-seven.[13]

Indeed, Muzzy was a man with vision and a tireless work ethic that abetted his rise in wealth and station. He seemed to easily make the transition from machinist to businessman, something many others could not do, yet he "continued to espouse traditional artisan values stressing the dignity of skilled labor, self-reliance and the commonality of masters' and journeymans' interests."[14]

Beyond his foundry, Muzzy became active in the life of Bangor and its businesses. He served as a director of both the Penobscot & Kennebec and Bangor & Piscataquis Railroads, as founder and president of Bangor Mutual Fire Insurance Co., director of Bangor Union Fire Insurance Co., and founder of Bangor Boot and Shoe Manufacturing Company.

He also promoted education and tried to elevate both skilled laborers and their professions. The *Whig and Courier* said, "He had a high appreciation of the dignity of the profession of a mechanic and had an intense desire to have its members educated intellectually and morally up to his high standard of excellence."[15]

As a school committee member for three years, he helped reorganize the early school system and establish an apprentice school similar to a vocational school. When the apprentice school closed, he used his influence to ensure similar classes were available at a night school.

At the heart of many efforts was the Bangor Mechanic Association, an organization specifically dedicated to the intellectual improvement of mechanics, or artisans. The association kept an expanding book collection for its members and arranged for speakers on business and social issues. A great believer in the power of books, Muzzy gave one thousand dollars to establish a trust fund to buy titles each year. Those books and the trust fund he created eventually became the initial book collection and a second critical source of funding for the Bangor Public Library. Muzzy also established a library at the city poor farm. He believed that anyone who could read should have access to books.

In politics, he was a strong temperance man, serving as president of the 1854 State Temperance Convention, and an antislavery activist. He wrote his wife Caroline in 1855 that his political activities were aimed at preventing the country "from becoming overwhelmed with slavery or sunk in intemperance."[16]

In 1848, he served as president of the state's Free-Soil Convention, a third political party with the slogan "Free Soil, Free Speech, Free Labor and Free Men." In Maine, the party largely focused on slavery and, nationally, supported the conveyance of cheap federal land to settlers, not speculators. He also served on the executive committee of the East Maine Kansas Aid Society, an organization formed to aid Kansas during the dark days of "Bleeding Kansas."*

Muzzy's outlook evolved from seeking the self-improvement of artisans to the improvement of society in general. In a letter dated September 14, 1845, he wrote his wife, referring to his varied interests: "We know dear Caroline that our happiness does not depend on wealth, but on other and higher and holier object."[17]

Furthermore, Muzzy was a devoted husband and father. During his absences in Augusta or while away on business, he wrote Caroline faithfully, discussing everything from politics to religion to family with an unfailing tone of affection, confidence and good humor. In a letter dated January 23, 1853, Caroline Muzzy wrote to Franklin in Augusta: "I feel utterly lost without you, like some wandering star loosed from its natural orbit and straying through chaos ... but I fear you will think me growing romantic in my *old age* [emphasis hers]."[18]

---

*Bleeding Kansas was the name used to describe the violence that occurred as proslavery and antislavery advocates fought for control of the new Kansas territory under the doctrine of popular sovereignty.

As a politician, the *Whig and Courier* said Muzzy took his time to make judgments and form opinions, but once made, he remained resolute. "While in the legislature he was not a frequent speaker. His speeches were concise, clear and forcible, and commanded the attention of its members. He was there as in other positions, a working man, and had great influence in shaping the course of legislation."[19]

Muzzy died in November 1873 at the age of sixty-six.

It was also said of Muzzy, in a grand Yankee tradition, that "His habits of expenditures, were economical, and his idea was that whatever was worth money, was worth saving."[20]

The Merchant ~ Joseph S. Wheelwright

Courtesy of Bangor Public Library
Joseph S. Wheelwright (1821–1895)

Teenager Joseph S. Wheelwright came to Bangor simply looking for work but would emerge as a dominating nineteenth-century figure, operating a store and large manufacturing center in the heart of downtown Bangor.

Wheelwright, born April 18, 1821, in Kennebunkport to George Wheelwright and Mary Carter, came to Bangor in 1834, the same year the town became a city. He clerked at the clothing store of Thomas Furber for three years. He then joined his father, who operated a cloth and carpet business on Main Street, to buy out Furber and run the clothing store as George Wheelwright & Son until his father died in 1845.

In 1849, Wheelwright joined J.G. Clark and ran a store in a wooden building at Taylor's Corner, located between West Market Square and the Kenduskeag Bridge. In 1859, their success prompted them to erect a large brick block — the Wheelwright & Clark Block — upon the same site as their old wooden store.

By 1860, Wheelwright was a force in Bangor with a beautiful new block bearing his name and a thriving store and clothing manufacturing business. He employed roughly 520 people, including 500 women, and his company produced $150,000 worth of clothing annually and stocked about $60,000 worth of inventory.

In 1861, Wheelwright & Clark helped clothe Maine's Union soldiers. The company and a group of volunteer women produced thirty-two hundred clothing items for the Second Maine.

Like many of the men who founded Bangor Savings Bank, Wheelwright dabbled in politics. He served as mayor of Bangor in 1872 following the death of Samuel H. Dale and in 1873. He served as a state representative in 1874 and a state senator in 1875 and 1876, including one term as senate president.

He was also a deacon at the Hammond Street Congregational Church and, later, at the Central Congregational Church, a trustee of the Bangor Theological Seminary, and a corporate member of the American Board of Foreign Missions.

He helped create organizations including the Bangor Historical Society and the Bangor Association for the Prevention of Cruelty to Animals and served as president of the Mt. Hope Cemetery Corporation.

Not only was Wheelwright a founding trustee of Bangor Savings Bank, he also served as such for more than twenty-five years, during which he was named as the fourth president.

Wheelwright, who lived at the corner of Broadway and State, died in October of 1895 at the age of seventy-four.

"He was one of the most clear headed businessmen in the State and his ability and sagacity enabled him to accumulate a larger property," wrote the *Whig and Courier* upon his death. "His death removes from our midst one intimately associated with all the best interests of the city."[21]

The Native Son ~ George W. Pickering

Unlike many other early Bangor businessmen, George W. Pickering was born and raised in the city. He gave his name to Pickering Square and rose to become one of the city's wealthiest and most influential business leaders — boasting to people that he would "never fail." He lived through Bangor's occupation by British forces and survived epidemics, weather disasters and all the other hardships that buffeted Bangor as it grew from outpost to town to city. Upon his death, the *Whig and Courier* noted, "Thus ended the useful, noble and generous life of a man who has been most intimately connected with every important public or mercantile movement in the history of Bangor."[22] These strong words were not far off. Pickering allegedly was consulted on every financial move made by the city of Bangor.

Pickering was born September 2, 1799, barely thirty years after Bangor was settled by Jacob Buswell. As a teenager, he worked as a clerk for Taylor Brown in 1818 — reportedly the "only important merchants" in Bangor. In the fall of 1821, he opened a "new goods" store in a wood frame building in West Market Square. Obviously possessing no small amount of confidence even at an early age, he opened his fledgling store directly opposite a well-established and thriving rival. He married Lucy Clark of Boston in the 1820s.

Pickering was a force in starting Kenduskeag Bank in 1832, a time when Bangor had only one

Courtesy of Bangor Public Library
George W. Pickering (1799–1876)

bank and remained short of capital. He served as president of Kenduskeag Bank from 1846 until his death; thus for a period of time he simultaneously held the presidencies of Kenduskeag Bank and Bangor Savings Bank. He was a founder of the Hammond Street Congregational Church, owned the first packet line between Bangor and Boston and sent the first cargoes of lumber from Bangor to the West Indies. Clearly, he stood at the forefront of the city's early economic development. And in turn, he grew fabulously wealthy.

By 1852, he held $84,480 in Kenduskeag Bank stock and he owned chunks of downtown real estate including storefronts along Broad Street and West Market Square.

He saw early the value in the Bangor shipping industry. In 1832, he owned shares in the schooner *Sophronia*, the sloop *Merchant*, the schooner *Katahdin*, the brig *Banner* and others. Twenty years later, he still owned shares in at least six vessels, including a one-eighth interest in the *G.W. Pickering* valued at $450 and one-fourth share in the *Adeline Hamlin*, co-owned by Elijah Hamlin and Albert Holton, valued at $4,700. The worth of his holdings in Bangor between 1832 and 1842 soared by more than 160 percent, rising from $46,440 to $124,140 — remarkable gains over a decade of economic tumult. In 1842, he reigned as Bangor's highest taxpayer.

Pickering also recognized the value of railroads and their importance to Maine, especially remote Eastern Maine. He was incorporator of Penobscot and Kennebec Railroad and the European and North American Railway Company and is said to have lost a significant amount of money in connection with the Maine Central Railroad.

He succeeded in politics. Pickering followed Elijah Hamlin as Bangor mayor in 1853 and 1854, winning election to his final term by a vote of 1,353 to 14. He served on the first city council in 1834 and was a delegate to the 1848 Whig Convention that nominated Hamlin for governor.

He also followed Hamlin to serve as Bangor Savings Bank's second president, holding that position from 1863 to 1877.

Beyond politics and his personal businesses, he devoted time to other endeavors and the city. He was a founder of the Bangor Mercantile Association, a founder of Mt. Hope Cemetery, first president of the Bangor Fire and Marine Insurance Company in 1833, and a founder of the city's first savings bank, Bangor Savings Institution that failed in 1840. He was also one-time president of the Merchants' Marine Insurance Company.

John Burt Foster

John Burt Foster was "another of the old businessmen who were the bone and sinew of Bangor's business prosperity."[42]

Foster was born poor on June 5, 1819, one of eight children on a farm in Petersham, Massachusetts. His father died when he was ten. Foster was educated at district schools and the East Maine Conference Seminary at Bucksport. He came to Bangor in February 1837 as teenager, after working as a clerk and farmer.

He clerked for Howard & Jenkins, and later formed a partnership with Jenkins under the name James Jenkins & Company, a lumber dealership at the West End of the Kenduskeag Bridge.

In 1845, he married Catherine McGaw, daughter of Jacob McGaw, one of Penobscot County's leading lawyers. He lived at 47 Broadway.

His businesses included Foster & Upton, which specialized in general merchandise and lumber. He also maintained various timberlands and real estate interests.

Foster helped start the Bangor Mutual Merchants' Marine Insurance Company and served as its president for about twenty years. He also served as president of Exchange Bank in the early 1850s.

He served as city councilor and alderman as well as a state representative in 1865 and 1866 and state senator in 1872 and 1873. He served as senate president in 1873. Foster began his political career in 1840, according to the *Whig and Courier*, as a Whig supporting Old Tippecanoe. He then joined the Republican Party upon its formation and later joined an independent Republican movement. In 1878, he supported a so-called Fusion ticket, an alliance between the Democratic Party and the Greenback Party, which produced the election of Gov. Alonzo Garcelon of Lewiston, Maine's first Democratic governor in twenty-four years.

As a member of the state executive council, Foster was also involved in one of the state's most famous political events, the so-called Count Out of 1879, which left state elections in doubt because of disputed ballots and counting methods. The drama nearly ended in violence as both parties tried to seize control. [see page 134]

Foster was a Congregationalist at the Hammond Street and Central churches for many years. He died January 19, 1907, and is buried in Mt. Hope Cemetery.

Charles Hayward

Born in the town of Readfield, Charles Hayward came to Bangor as a nineteen-year-old in 1832, starting his career as a grocery store clerk for Stephen Goodhue. He survived several disasters to become one of Bangor's top businessmen and third president of Bangor Savings Bank.

In 1835, Hayward began work at the wholesale grocery firm of J. & J. True, co-founded by Jabez True, and became a partner in 1840. The firm eventually became Charles Hayward & Company. A representative from the Hayward company regularly sat on the Bangor Savings Bank board of trustees for decades.

Hayward's business at 50 West Market Square was flooded to the second story during the Great Freshet of 1846 [see page 85] and destroyed by fire in 1869 — only the safe, books and papers were saved. After the fire, Hayward rebuilt on Exchange Street.

Hayward served as a director of the Kenduskeag Bank, director of the Bangor and Piscataquis Railroad Company, and helped found the Board of Trade, the Bangor Mercantile Association and

Courtesy of Bangor Historical Society
Charles Hayward (1812–1889)

Merchants' Mutual Marine Insurance Company.

Politically, he was a Whig and Republican who served as an aldermen, city councilor and mayor in 1847. He was also a member of the Bangor Fire Department.

He lived on Summer Street with his wife Amanda Leslie, who he married in 1847, and attended Hammond Street Congregational Church.

He died December 24, 1889. He was seventy-seven.

Courtesy of Bangor Historical Society

Pickering Square, shown here in the 1890s, was an outdoor market named after George W. Pickering.

Upon his death in 1876 as one of the city's wealthiest and most influential citizens, Judge John Edwards Godfrey wrote, "My old friend George W. Pickering died on Thursday morning at the age of 77 last September. He was in business here in 1821 — a fine looking young man as I recollect him; he never failed; was a model of integrity, and leaves a great void in this community."[23]

The Mayor ~ Samuel H. Dale

Mayor Dale rose from local sailmaker to dine with the city's cultural elite, play host to a United States president, and dramatically order flags raised, bells rung and bonfires set in West Market Square as Union troops pressed toward Richmond in the waning days of the Civil War. Yet, also while serving as the city's mayor, he allegedly killed himself, a shocking end for a man who had risen to prominence.

Samuel H. Dale was born in Salem, Massachusetts in 1812 and came to Bangor in 1833, a twenty-one-year-old looking for work. He joined forces with Lemuel Bradford to start Dale & Bradford, a sailmaking firm on Broad Street. He soon invested in shipping and left his sailmaking

firm in 1846 to form Fiske &
Dale, a ship chandlery and provisions dealer. By 1842, he partially
owned three schooners and ten
years later had acquired part ownership in seven. He married
Matilda Wadleigh in 1836.
Although the couple had no children of their own, they adopted or
raised several in their home.

In 1861, he started his own
ship chandlery business, S.H. Dale
& Company, built warehouses in
the city, invested in land and
erected the Dale Block, a pink
granite building on Broad Street.
He also served as president of the

Courtesy Bangor Historical Society

Samuel H. Dale (1812–1871)

Merchants' Mutual Marine Insurance Company, was a member of the
Bangor Water Company, and helped start a number of concerns —
Merchants Bank in 1850, City Bank in 1852, and the Bangor Historical
Society.* He was a deacon in the Unitarian Church.

At some point in the 1860s, Dale resigned from the Bangor Savings
Bank board of trustees and helped start its rival, Penobscot Savings Bank
in 1869.

During his life, Dale's fortunes flourished. According to census
records his reported assets rose from $6,000 in 1850 to $120,000 in
1870, at which time he employed four servants at his house located on
the corner of Union and High Streets.

The old sailmaker also acquired timberlands. After his death in 1872,
heirs auctioned off 106,965.5 acres of Dale lands for $117,159.35.[24]

When war erupted in 1861, Dale helped raise volunteers and provided other assistance. He followed Isaiah Stetson as mayor in 1863 and
remained mayor until 1866. He was elected again in 1871. But during
the latter term, he suffered financial problems or perhaps an unexplain-
able lapse in judgment. His difficulties were compounded, according to

*In 2002, the Bangor Historical Society is located in Samuel Dale's former house.

Godfrey, by mental health issues. According to Godfrey, Dale collected about ten thousand dollars to aid victims of the Great Chicago Fire, but instead of sending the money, Dale kept it, allegedly to improve his house for Grant's visit. When word of this began to filter out, Dale grew "much depressed," Godfrey said.

On a Sunday morning in December of 1871, barely two months after hosting President Grant during Grant's visit to open the European and North American Railway, Dale said good-bye to his wife Matilda as she left for church and then, according to legend and oral history, killed himself.

According to the *Whig and Courier*, Matilda returned home and found him dying on the floor, but the *Whig and Courier* made no mention of possible suicide, instead attributing the "swift work of death" to apoplexy.[25]

Dale's suicide is supported partly by the journals of Judge John E. Godfrey, who gives a brief account. Godfrey said the task of ensuring the death was suicide fell to the insurance agent, apparently to determine the company's life insurance liability. Godfrey wrote, "The insurance agent, that there may be no doubt that it was a case of self-destruction, caused his stomach to be sent to Boston that its contents might be analyzed."[26] The results of the test are unknown.

The Democrat ~ Amos M. Roberts

Amos Main Roberts lived as a powerful lumber baron and stubborn banker in Bangor for many years.

In the 1860s, he defiantly kept his state-chartered Eastern Bank operating despite the federal government's attempts to shift all such banks to national charters by imposing financial penalties. Eastern Bank didn't surrender its state charter until 1878, the last bank to do so in Maine. Roberts served as president of Eastern Bank from its founding in 1835 until he closed it in 1878. At the time, he was seventy-six and less than a year from death.

Roberts was born in New Hampshire and started his career as a clerk in Boston. He came to Old Town in 1826 to work in the lumber business and moved to Bangor in 1831.

He was unusual among Bangor Savings Bank founders for his lasting ties to the Democratic Party, even after the great wave of Republicanism washed over Bangor in the 1850s. He likely served on the bank board because the presidents of all city banks in 1852 (save for the controversial Samuel Veazie) were named as trustees.

While many Bangorites reveled in Hannibal Hamlin's nomination as U.S. vice president in 1860, Roberts served as a delegate to the Democratic National Convention that year. Roberts left the Bangor Savings Bank board in the 1860s and helped start Penobscot Savings Bank in 1869, serving as its first president.

He served as a city alderman in the 1840s, but was defeated in a run for mayor during the 1830s.

Roberts made most of his fortune in lumber and timberlands, operating a lumber firm at City Point in the 1850s. He also owned tracts of timberlands to the north, and accumulated some of his wealth in a shady but not uncommon way, perhaps in conjunction with landholders such as Waldo T. Peirce.

Courtesy of Bangor Public Library
Amos M. Roberts (1801–1879)

According to John C. Arndt, it was not uncommon at the time for a group of landholders to quickly buy and sell land to each other until it finally ended up back in the hands of the original owner at an inflated price. "Apparently Roberts and others borrowed against their interest in the land (which was purposely overvalued) and then passed the land on to someone else who would do the same. Such deals not only kept one out of debt, but were successful, though dubious, methods of raising capital."[27]

Roberts also played a role in one of the most famous dam and canal projects in Maine. The project, known as the Telos Cut or the Telos Dam, diverted water from the Allagash watershed into the East Branch of the Penobscot, thus allowing Penobscot lumbermen to gain control of a new region of timber that might otherwise have gone to Aroostook County and Canadian firms along the St. John River.

The Great Freshet of 1846

In the winter of 1846, Bangor residents were anxious. A dry winter caused an unusual amount of ice to form in the river, raising concerns about potential disaster when the ice broke up come spring. In the waning days of March, those fears were realized.

First, ice began breaking away upriver. The free ice raced downriver until it lodged against solid ice below. As this repeatedly happened, the icy mass grew deeper, higher and longer. Some upriver towns flooded and sawmills below Old Town were washed away. Such ice jams caused two problems: the ice dam caused flood waters to rise behind it and then, when the dam gave away, rushing water filled with ice and debris battered the river banks.

In late March, a jam above Bangor broke. Rushing water and ice swept lumber and buildings off wharves. Rev. John West said, "It came rushing on with a power that a thousand locomotives in a body could not vie with."[43]

Then the ice jammed at High Head, where the river narrows and the waters grow shallow. Water quickly rose throughout downtown, rising as high as eleven feet on Broad Street, submerging streets, homes and businesses.

And then came Sunday, which West called "the saddest most serious Sunday, probably, that ever passed in Bangor."[44]

Throughout the day, floodwaters continued to rise. Residents worked feverishly trying to save what they could and moved through the city by boat. Then that evening the alarms rang again — the ice jam at High Head was giving way. The flood waters in Bangor were about to rush away and ice, nearly four miles long, would roar down the Penobscot.

"The whole river was like a roiling cauldron with masses of ice upheaved as by a volcano. But soon the darkness shrouded the scene in part. The ear, however, could hear the roaring of the waters and the crash of buildings, bridges and lumber and the eye could trace the mammoth ice jam of four miles long, which passed on majestically, but with lightening rapidity, bearing the contents of both rivers on its bosom. The noble covered bridge of the Penobscot, two bridges of the Kenduskeag and the two long ranges of saw-mills, besides other mills, houses, shops, logs and lumber enough to build up a considerable village."[45]

The city quickly rebuilt its waterfront, but the worst flood in Bangor history was remembered for decades to come.

The plan was this: build a dam to hold back the waters of Lake Telos at the base of Chamberlain Lake, then cut a sluiceway from Lake Telos to Webster Lake, which ties into the Penobscot River. The project succeeded and lumbermen suddenly had a connection to the Penobscot River, allowing them to drive logs from the Allagash to the Penobscot.

Roberts, who installed a toll at the dam to collect money from other lumbermen, later sold his rights to Rufus Dwinel, a man who inspired both loyalty and hatred in Bangor. At one point, Dwinel brought in seventy-five armed lumbermen to collect tolls in what was known as the Telos Cut War.

Roberts also helped start Kenduskeag Bank in 1832, the Penobscot and Kennebec Railroad in 1845, and the Merchants' Mutual Insurance Company in 1851. He was an original director of the Bangor Mercantile Association, founder of Merchants Bank in 1850 and founder of the Oldtown and Lincoln Railroad Company in 1852 with Elijah Hamlin.

Roberts was also rich. In Bangor alone, his real estate rose from $3,475 in 1832 to $32,285 in 1842, an increase of nearly tenfold despite a depression during the ten-year stretch. A decade later, his Bangor assets had increased to $71,290. Roberts lived on State Street. The census valued his property in 1870 at $100,000 and his personal estate at $50,000. He lived that year with his wife, two servants and his daughter and son-in-law.

His son, Charles Wentworth Roberts, was colonel of the Second Maine Infantry in the Civil War, and later married Waldo Peirce's daughter, June.

He was a member of the Unitarian Church and played host to Transcendentalist Ralph Waldo Emerson in 1834 when that congregation tried to hire Emerson as its pastor. He died in 1879 at the age of seventy-seven at Boston's Tremont House, his base when working in Massachusetts. When he died he was heading to South Carolina for health reasons.

The Lawyer ~ Albert Ware Paine

Albert Ware Paine came to Bangor to practice law in 1835 and rose to great legal heights, arguing cases before the U.S. Supreme Court, helping create the State Insurance Department, and passing legislation that regulated savings banks. He lived on Court Street, and when he died he was the oldest lawyer in continuous practice in New England, a member of the bar for seventy-two years.

Paine was born in 1812, the second of eight children born to Frederic Paine and Abiel Ware of Winslow. Frederic, a cooper, and Abiel founded a Congregational church in that town in 1818.

Paine graduated from Waterville (Colby) College in 1832 and studied law with Thomas Rice and Gov. Samuel Wells before coming to Bangor. From his office in West Market Square, he wrote important legislation and won cases that shaped the future of Bangor and Maine.

Among his most important acts was procuring the right of an accused to testify on his own behalf, a right that did not exist in the U.S. or England until Paine's successful efforts in 1864 before the Maine Legislature after five tries. He successfully introduced the same legislation in Massachusetts and eventually the law was adopted in all U.S. states and numerous foreign countries.

Between 1836 and 1885, he argued 525 cases before the Supreme Judicial Court in Maine, two before the U.S. Supreme Court, and others before supreme courts in four other states.

Furthermore, he organized state laws taxing railroads and insurance companies and is credited with saving from destruction the historic records of Maine, which were being discarded by the Commonwealth of Massachusetts. He served as president of Maine Telegraph Company.

In Bangor, he argued numerous court cases for the city including the Hersey Fund case, the case involving the rights of Bangor to the shores of the Kenduskeag, and numerous dam cases. He also framed state law exempting cemetery lots from attachment and making fire inquests mandatory.

Despite all that activity, local businessman Elnathan Duren painted this picture of the lawyer: "His was an example of the simple life, devoted to his home, fond of his work in his fine garden, familiar with local history and often consulted on different points."[28]

Reportedly, Paine was reluctant to part with a dime. Godfrey said Paine's "eye to economy" was legendary. On one trip to Boston, Godfrey claimed that Paine complained about the cost of lodging for the entire trip home as Bangor luminaries egged him on. "In the morning he was thunderstruck to find that his lodging cost him two dollars, and did not get over it during the day. Every now and then the subject was introduced, and never failed to produce great hilarity, especially when Brother Paine would start off in a denunciatory speech of the imposition practiced upon him."[29]

He was a founding member and chairman of the first executive committee of the Bangor Historical Society, secretary of Bangor Lyceum and treasurer of Mt. Hope Cemetery. He died in 1907 at the age of ninety-five.

The Disgraced ~ George R. Smith

Former bookseller and City Councilor George R. Smith became the most notorious of the bank's founders — certainly the only one arrested for embezzlement.

Born in Gardiner, Smith moved to Bangor in 1834 and opened a bookstore in West Market Square with Jere Fenno. The business lasted until 1849. He left the book and stationery business to work as a bank cashier, putting in stints at Maritime Bank and Norombega Bank. He served as a city councilor in 1852 and 1855 and lived most of his life on Ohio Street.

It was his days at the fledgling Norombega Bank that gained him infamy. Smith was implicated and arrested in January 1860 for his ties to Maine Treasurer Benjamin D. Peck in an embezzlement scheme that shook the state. Peck was accused of embezzling tens of thousands of dollars from the state treasury and using the money for personal gain. Peck passed questionable checks to obtain funds from banks and at times applied pressure using his status as state treasurer. He was also tied to a company called Canada Corporation, a land and lumbering operation that received some of the embezzled money.

Smith, arrested January 4, 1860, was charged with conspiring to help Peck embezzle thirty thousand dollars from Norombega Bank between August 23 and December 28, 1859. Smith was also a partner in Canada Corporation.

At state hearings on the matter, Smith repeatedly told investigators, "I don't recollect," in response to questions. The state committee investigating the Peck case offered this opinion of Smith: "In the spring of 1859, Mr. Peck commenced a series of transactions with the [Norombega] Bank, but more especially with its cashier George R. Smith, of the most disreputable character."[30]

Arad Thompson

Born in Livermore, January 24, 1811, the son of Ira and Sophia Thompson, a nearly penniless Arad Thompson reportedly moved to Guilford at the age of twenty to work in his brother-in-law's store. Apparently seeing greater opportunity in Bangor, he moved there in 1832. He worked as a clerk for Franklin S. Remick and other firms.

He started Reed, Thompson & Company in 1842. He sold his interest in the company in 1867.

He served as a director of the European and North American Railway Company, was charter member and president of the Union Insurance Company, a director of Colby College, and a director of several banks. He was active in the state militia.

He was deacon and treasurer of the First Baptist Church. He married Margaret L. Cole in 1844 and later married Louise M. Baldwin.

A Republican, he served as state

Courtesy of Bangor Public Library
Arad Thompson (1811–1905)

representative and state senator.

He was the last surviving member of the original Bangor Savings Bank founders, dying in 1905 at the age of ninety-four.

Leonard March

Leonard March came to Bangor as a young man and worked at various times as a merchant, bank officer, and lumber dealer on Broad Street. He served as president of the Bank of the State of Maine, which he helped found in the early 1850s with Sam Hersey, Elijah L. Hamlin and S.H. Dale. He was a founding trustee of the Merchants' Mutual Marine Insurance Company and a corporator of the European & North American Railway Company. At one point he went to Cuba in search of renewed health.

He died in 1857.

Capt. Nathan Pendleton

Captain Nathan Pendleton is believed to have died in September 1857 while a patient in the Maine State Insane Hospital in Augusta. He was forty-nine. He was committed to the institution by the city of Bangor that January, less than five years after helping found Bangor Savings Bank. Why he was committed is not indicated on state records.

He married Lydia Gilkey in Prospect in 1832.

Captain Pendleton also was an incorporator of Maritime Bank.

As a mariner in 1850, he owned real estate in Bangor valued at about $1,050 and lived on State Street with his wife and three children. In 1851, he operated a ship chandlery, Nathan & Ross, on Broad Street and by 1855, he operated a towboat business and lived on French Street.

In 1852, he owned his home, a cow and maintained modest investments in Penobscot Stream Navigation Company and several vessels, including a one-eighth share in the ship *Dunbarton*, a stake valued at $1,375.

Jabez True

A member of the influential and successful True family, Jabez True served as high sheriff of Penobscot County and helped start a town in western Maine.

True, an aldermen and city councilor, was an original vice president of Bangor Savings Bank as well as a director of Peoples Bank which opened in 1836. A Democrat turned Republican, True also served as a state senator. He was a founder of the Bangor Mercantile Association.

In 1829, True was one of two men who purchased land that became the township of Shirley, near Moosehead Lake. True laid out lots, cleared an opening for a sawmill and began to bring in settlers. By 1832, he had established a growing settlement and a post office at "True's Mills." In 1833, he sold his land and moved to Bangor. He lived on High Street.

In Bangor, he ran a wholesale grocery business, J.& J. True, located at 50 West Market Square with his brother, John. The firm eventually became Charles Hayward & Company. True had hired Hayward as an apprentice in the 1830s.

True died in 1869 in Portland, where he worked as a customs house officer.

Norombega Bank was organized in 1857 and was liquidated in 1860. In a letter to Hannibal Hamlin in January 1860, Elijah L. Hamlin discussed the embezzlement case. He wrote that Peck and Smith were both in jail, referred to runs upon local banks sparked by fear of more widespread problems, and reported a city in shock.

"The run upon the banks has about stopped, and we think they will all go through safely. The affairs of the Norombega Bank look worse and worse. In addition to the $30,000 which the cashier let Peck have upon his draft, there is a large amount of the securities of the Bank missing, it is thought about as much or more, and to which no clue has yet been obtained. There are several gentlemen in the city high in office who appear nervous and are believed by everybody to be involved in this rascally business.

"Had a thunderbolt fell upon the city and destroyed one half of it, the consternation could not have been greater, than when it was first made known that the State Treasury and the Norombega Bank had been robbed the way it has."[31]

As the affair unfolded, Smith went from living with his wife, four children and a servant in 1850 to living in William D. McLaughlin's hotel on Harlow Street in 1860.

Smith apparently recovered enough of his reputation that ten years later he worked as a clerk in a government pension office.

He died in Rochester, New York in 1903. He was ninety-two.

The Immigrant Soldier ~ Capt. Michael Boyce

Of the founders, Captain Michael Boyce came the greatest distance to reach Bangor, crossing the Atlantic to seek his lot in America. Both nationality and religion distinguished him from most other founders. Boyce arrived in Bangor during a wave of Irish immigration to Bangor and America in the first half of the nineteenth century as the Irish fled poverty and famine at home. This increasing number of Irish Catholics in Bangor caused an unrest that at times grew downright nasty. Many of the Irish who came to America were exceedingly poor and were suspected of bringing disease, only increasing fear among natives.

There were other factors also at work. Poor, unskilled natives felt many unskilled Irish were not only taking their jobs, but also driving down wages. Furthermore, the Irish were mostly Catholic at a time when some feared that the power or influence of the Pope would damage the American way of life and its freedoms.

Many of the city's new Irish lived in small tenements and shanties along the riverfront, some adjoining an area that became known as "Devil's Half-acre" or "Hell's Half-acre" because of its sinful mix of booze and brothels, favorites of sailors and lumbermen.

The first ethnic riot occurred in 1833 when seamen — incited by a sailor who claimed that he was beaten by an Irishman and fueled by an ample supply of liquor — poured by the hundreds off ships and into the streets of Bangor to frighten Irish families and set a local bar ablaze. The next night they returned, setting fire to tenements. A mob was preparing to march elsewhere when it was confronted by armed residents. The town's inability to respond quickly to the riot was one reason why the town of Bangor incorporated as a city the following year. It became obvious Bangor needed a new organizational structure to handle its growing size and complexity.

The concurrent religious and ethnic tensions were exacerbated by other political events of the times. Among the issues were temperance and nativism. The temperance movement resulted in the prohibitionary Maine Law of 1851. Irish bars were a popular target. Nativism helped produce "The Know-Nothing Party" which began nationally in the 1840s. It enjoyed a short burst of popularity in Bangor in the 1850s. In 1855, the Party seized power in Bangor after running on a platform calling for strict enforcement of the Maine Law and an end to foreign influence. The Know-Nothing Party largely collapsed in Bangor when a key leader was found profiting from confiscated liquor.

Tension also arose from pressure to conform to political ideology within the Irish community. The Irish in Bangor were largely Democrats. In 1860, Elijah Hamlin wrote to Hannibal Hamlin asking him to bring or send a gift for a man named John O'Riley, who Elijah described as a likeable man with a likeable wife and a likeable family. According to Elijah, "It seems that two years ago he voted for you for governor and for this he was assaulted and badly beaten by some other Irishmen. I should like you to send me a book to present him."[32]

Politics were tricky during this era. Voters were required to ask for a party ticket before voting, so it was easily known at the polls for whom a resident was voting, sometimes leading to severe intimidation.

Ethnic and religious tensions involving the Irish in Bangor are considered to have subsided before the Civil War when both sides found a common cause. Also by this time, Irish made up a quarter of Bangor's population and some of the city's Irish immigrants had long ago become rich and powerful.

Michael Boyce came to America as a young boy and worked in a variety of trades. At one time or another he lived on Ohio Street and Court Street. In 1851, as a man in his forties, he ran a tailor and clothing business called Boyce and McKinnon at 15 West Market Square. Boyce owned a home and real estate worth fifteen hundred dollars and lived with his wife, who was a teacher, three children and three others at the corner of Ohio and Hudson Streets. By 1859, he formed Boyce and Casey, also a tailor shop, at the Kenduskeag Bridge. He was a former commander of the Grattan Guards, an elite Irish militia group in Bangor and the pride of the Irish middle class.[33]

His business career was soon overtaken by much larger events.

The strife engulfing the nation finally erupted into warfare when the South Carolina militia shelled Fort Sumter, igniting the Civil War in 1861. Boyce opened a recruiting office in the city. That fall, Boyce joined the Fifteenth Maine, Company I, raised primarily from Aroostook County. He mustered at Augusta and headed south from Portland on March 6, 1862. The company took part in operations in Louisiana, a region notorious for swamps and diseases that often killed more people than combat.

By that first fall, the regiment "was in a very bad state, from disease contracted amid the swamps of the Mississippi. The health of the men was very much broken down."[34]

In September of 1862, Boyce's regiment moved on to west Florida to recover. The rest was necessary. During a year in which it had not been in an actual battle, the regiment that numbered 962 when it left Portland had lost 329 men to desertion, death and disease.

In 1863, Boyce's regiment returned to New Orleans and later moved on to Texas, Virginia and Maryland. In January of 1865, four months before General Lee's surrender at Appomattox Court House, Virginia, Boyce mustered out.

After the war, Boyce was named captain in Company K of the Fifteenth Maine and his unit shipped to South Carolina as a peacekeeping force in an area rife with intimidation against newly freed slaves. He remained with his regiment until mustering out July 6, 1866.

Returning to Bangor, Boyce again ran his own small businesses, opening a meat market and a saloon at 2 East Market Square.

Captain Boyce, confined to his house for the final two to three years of his life, died at ninety-two. The *Whig and Courier* called him, "a man of the strictest integrity, warm and generous, a kind husband and father and a highly esteemed friend."[35]

The Debtors ~ Samuel Farrar and John Winn

Samuel Farrar, a member of the Farrar family that owned mills in Dexter, rose to prominence as a businessman in Bangor. He became one of its wealthiest and most influential citizens before leaving in shame.

During the 1850s, one of his primary business concerns was the Mercantile Bank, which he joined in the 1830s as treasurer and then served as its president into the 1850s. In the mid-1850s, he also served as city alderman.

In 1852, he owned a large house on Court Street valued by the city at eleven thousand dollars. In 1857, his businesses failed when a financial crisis hit the city.

Courtesy of Bangor Public Library

Samuel Farrar, died in 1862 at the age of 57.

As a result, he suffered "pecuniary embarrassments" and according to the *Whig and Courier*, "paid to the utmost of his ability, and then started life again in the great West, as a clerk."[36]

He started over again in Geneva Lake, Wisconsin working as a clerk for a company that manufactured flour. He died in December of 1862.

Meanwhile, John Winn at one time served as the state land agent (the government agent in charge of the state's public lands) and worked out of an office at Mercantile Square. He later worked as a lumber merchant at 38 Mercantile Square and owned a home on Broadway.

But somewhere along the line he overreached and left the city in utter financial ruin, trailed by debt and a string of lawsuits. According to court records, he amassed debts in the mid-1850s that he could not pay. By 1858, total judgments against Winn in cases handed down by the Supreme Judicial Court of Maine totaled more than $180,000, a staggering sum for the era. In comparison, the total assets of Bangor Savings Bank in 1858 were only $34,380.

Among those who sued John Winn were two of his fellow Bangor Savings Bank co-founders, Samuel H. Dale and Samuel F. Hersey. They were awarded $5,777 and $5,743, respectively.

Winn died in Salem, Massachusetts in 1858.

The Stovemaker ~ Henry A. Wood

Henry A. Wood, born January 27, 1817, in New Bedford, Massachusetts, was raised both in that town and on the island of Nantucket. He and his brother came to Bangor in the spring of 1839, opening a tin and iron manufacturing business under the name Henry A. Wood & Company.

In 1851 Wood's foreman, William A. Bishop, joined the brothers as a partner and the business became Wood, Bishop & Company. At about that time, the company employed just four men, paying them about $33 per month, for a monthly payroll of about $132. The company produced roughly eight thousand dollars worth of tin plates per year.

Business increased rapidly as the company's reputation spread throughout New England. By 1860, they held a tin and sheet iron inventory worth about twenty thousand dollars and produced about sixteen thousand dollars worth of goods annually. Employment doubled to eight. Wood eventually employed upwards of sixty workers and operated both a foundry and an impressive retail store at West Market Square.

Wood's personal situation improved as his business matured. In 1842, his assets in Bangor were $1,300, including his income and inventory, but by 1861 his personal assets reached $13,972, including a home on

Hammond Street. While not as dramatic a rise as realized by the city's lumber barons, this income does indicate escalating blue-collar success. By 1870, the census listed Wood's personal assets at forty thousand dollars and stated that he employed two domestic servants.

Like many in Bangor, Wood capitalized on the city's ties to lumber by developing associated goods or services to supply those in the industry. His Clarion brand stoves became famous throughout northern New England.

Wood, according to the *Whig and Courier*, paid strict attention to his business, but was also a "zealous advocate of the building

Courtesy of Bangor Public Library
Henry A. Wood (1817–1890)

up of the city."[37] He served as a director of several companies, including the Bangor Loan and Building Association, encouraging local mechanics to become shareholders in that company. He also served as director of the Second National Bank and the Farmers' National Bank. Wood was a prominent member of the Unitarian Church and served one term in the state legislature. He died January 8, 1890 at the age of seventy-three.

The War Mayor – Isaiah Stetson

Isaiah Stetson served as Bangor mayor from 1859 to 1863 and won election his final year by a stunning 1,307 to 2 vote. As mayor, he introduced military drill into the school system for physical training, military knowledge and good moral influences.

In 1861, he became part of Bangor history when he declined a request by Marcellus Emery, editor of the *Bangor Democrat*, for special armed protection. The *Bangor Democrat* was an anti-war, anti-Lincoln newspaper and was considered traitorous in Bangor. Following the battle of Bull Run, it called the Union mission one of "subjugation and death." Emery wrote:

Wood & Bishop store at the Flat Iron Block in West Market Square. Located on the second floor was Eastern Bank run by Amos M. Roberts. The building was built around 1835.

"Onward the shouting myriads will pour, until again met by the unequalled and invincible genius of Davis, Beauregard, Johnston and Lee, and the iron nerves of these noble men, who are defending their firesides and their homes, from the ruthless assaults of fanaticism and fury."[38]

As such stories continued throughout the summer, tempers built in patriotic Bangor, a place where businesses advertised products under the headline "Victory or Death" and "Stand by the Flag." So by the heat of August 1861, a gang of men that included prominent businessmen formed and upon a prearranged signal — the ringing of church bells — moved to attack the newspaper, which was located on the third floor of the Wheelwright & Clark Building. The mob smashed equipment, broke furniture and tossed it into West Market Square where they ignited a bonfire.

In an article looking back at the events, The *Bangor Daily News* claimed the mob intended to lynch Emery at Wood's Corner or tar and feather him. To avoid capture he hid in the attic of the Franklin House until tempers cooled. Several Bangor men were tried for the attack, but fourteen of the sixteen were found not guilty. In their remarks, the jury also said it felt the *Democrat* was a nuisance and should be stopped or destroyed. A few years later Emery started what became the *Bangor Daily Commercial*.

Founder Isaiah Stetson was born in Hampden, the son of Simeon Stetson, in 1812. He was educated at Hampden Academy and moved to Bangor in 1833. He started in business with Cyrus Emery in provisions and the West Indies trade. His brother Charles Stetson joined the company in 1835 and it became Emery, Stetson & Company until Emery's death in 1850, when it became Stetson & Company. Stetson eventually abandoned the mercantile business to concentrate on real estate and timberlands.

He served as state representative in 1865 and 1866, was the first president of Bangor & Piscataquis Railroad Company and was treasurer of Maine State College. He was an original officer of the Bangor Mercantile Association and first treasurer of the Bangor Historical Society.

By 1870, the federal census valued his real estate holdings at one hundred thousand dollars and his personal estate at fifty thousand dollars. He lived with his wife Sarah, his child, and four servants. He attended the Unitarian Church for many years and later attended the Third Congregational Church.

He died June 30, 1880.

Courtesy of Maine Historic Preservation Commission

Main Street, 1800s

At mid-century, these twenty-three men were among the most successful and forward thinking men the city had to offer. They had helped build the city of Bangor and stood among the city's most prominent and involved citizens, working with or near each other and traveling in the same general circles. Even with their extraordinary personal and sometimes far-flung success, they were also men committed to the city of Bangor and its people.

So, it was in this spirit and this environment that in the waning days of December 1851, fifty-two-year-old Elijah Livermore Hamlin, mayor of Bangor and also an active social, cultural and business leader, gathered a group of these men together to write a petition asking the legislature for permission to open an entity that would prove their lasting legacy and provide the people just what they felt was needed: Bangor Savings Bank.

Chapter Five

Widows, Orphans and the Daily Laborer

With the first blush of spring in 1852, the city of Bangor was entering its glory days, a two-decade run of growth, improvements and increased sophistication. To be sure, signs of problems existed for those who looked closely. Bangor remained stubbornly and dangerously tied to a single economic engine — lumber. The value of the famed white pine shipped from city ports was on the decline as stocks dwindled, giving way to less valuable spruce. The nation was moving westward, further from Bangor as a lumber source, making the city and the state ever more isolated. Shipping would soon begin its decline and with it Bangor's importance as a shipping port. But for most, these were problems probably hidden deeply in the recesses of the mind or defiantly ignored. Bangor, after all, was a city built on optimism and dreams.

So, instead, entrepreneurs discussed a rail link to connect Bangor with ports in Canada to shorten shipping routes to Europe and open up Eastern Maine to potential new riches. Soon, the great Norombega Hall would rise on the Kenduskeag and host political rallies and great speakers. Bangor was designated a port of entry, and a customs house would shortly be under construction. Bangor men, lumber and machines were going to aid in the California Gold Rush.

The economic troubles of the early 1840s were long past and banks and businessmen were fully recovered. Many of the men who arrived in Bangor during the 1830s to make their fortunes were now older men and richer

— some surely beyond their wildest dreams. They now turned their attention more often to city improvements and the trappings of fine society.

Yet, at the same time, not far from the mansions that sprouted on hillsides like dandelions and not far from the society balls, tea parties and carriage races, there was a Bangor struggling with change. There were shanties along the riverside, overcrowded tenement houses along unpaved roads, unsanitary housing conditions that bred disease, and poor farmers struggling against inhospitable northeastern climes. Increasing numbers of journeymen toiled in the expanding industrial economy, mill workers sweated in sprawling lumber mills and domestic servants worked and lived in the Bangor mansions. As in all cities during an industrial age, there was a developing wage-earning or laboring class, a developing middle class and, of course, the poor. With these developments came an increase in the social needs of the poor, a growing issue in Bangor. The number of residents at the city's almshouse doubled to more than three hundred between 1845 and 1853. Then from 1853 to 1858, a period which encompassed an economic depression, the number of people receiving assistance more than tripled, from 309 to 1,027.

One philosophy still in place in some circles held fast to the old Yankee standbys: industry and thrift. It was believed that hard work and the discipline to regularly save money, no matter how small the amount, was the only way to build wealth and the best way to help lift people from poverty or raise the poor and "middling classes" to higher stations. Thrift and industry would also lead to a temperate life, a major concern in nineteenth-century Maine, especially in a town as steeped in religion as Bangor.

Clearly, many people, even if they had a place to do so, could not save much at a time. Although, the *Whig and Courier* pointed out that a regular "pittance" could grow into a significant amount over time not only through accumulated savings but with the added value of interest. Given the incomes of some during the era, time was definitely needed.

In Bangor, women making clothes at Boyce and Casey tailors in 1860 earned twelve dollars per month; the women working for tailor Patrick Wall made eight dollars per month. Working for a clothing manufacturer was one of the few job options for Bangor women in the mid-1800s. Women could also help on family farms or could work as a domestic servant, a notoriously low paying job but one that did offer room and

The Ten-Hour Day

"We have been too long subjected to the odious, cruel, unjust, and tyrannical system which compels the operative Mechanic to exhaust his physical and mental powers by excessive toil, until he has no desire but to eat and sleep, and in many cases he has no power to do either from extreme debility. ... We cannot, we will not, longer be mere slaves to inhuman, insatiable and unpitying avarice. We have taken a firm and decided stand, to obtain the acknowledgment of those rights to enable us to perform those duties to God, our Country and ourselves."

With these words, distributed in an 1835 circular, the mechanics of Boston were among the first laborers to demand a regulated working day limited to a set number of hours. In many places, the campaign to obtain a ten-hour day met violent resistance from factory owners, resulting in strikes and general unrest. But when the movement came to Bangor in 1847, the ten-hour day for mechanics and artisans was achieved with no violence and relatively little discord.

Part of the ease likely was due to the small size of Bangor's manufacturing plants. There were no huge factories in the city like those in Lowell or Boston, or even Lewiston, and as a result, a closer relationship existed between master craftsmen and their employees. Many of these masters, including Franklin Muzzy, who ran a machinist shop, supported the idea of a limited workday as a means of improving their workers' lives.

Muzzy and four others from Bangor, including at least one other master, served on a committee that helped shepherd a state law that soon provided for the implementation of the ten-hour day for Maine artisans.

It was a less peaceful story some forty years later, however, when mill hands in Bangor tried to achieve the same ten-hour day. In June of 1889, workers at Morse and Company's lumber mills went on strike after management refused to negotiate a reduction from the current twelve-hour workday. There is little record of this strike, due to the interference of mill owners who used their influence to suppress publicity and became "very angry" at newspaper accounts of the worker demands.[46] While there does not appear to have been any violence, the Morse mill hands stayed out for almost two weeks before agreeing to a half-hour reduction in their daily schedule, to eleven and a half hours.

— Hoving

board. Most female workers were single and in their twenties or younger because women typically focused exclusively on raising the family and running the household after they married. After marriage, they might take in boarders or wash laundry as a way to earn money.

Meanwhile, men toiling for Benjamin Adams and Son making carriages earned twenty-six dollars per month. House builders at Wiggins and Fogg had slightly better paying jobs making thirty-five dollars per month, while sailmakers at Currier and Jones made thirty dollars per month per month and candy makers at Brown and Day earned about twenty-five dollars per month or $300 per year. (An annual salary of $300 in 1850 is roughly equal, adjusted for inflation, to $6,360 in 2001.)

These higher-paying, skilled jobs still required workdays of ten to fourteen hours, six days per week. Conditions slightly improved for some mechanics and artisans after they organized to seek a ten-hour workday in 1847. Others continued to work their long days. Sawmill workers did not strike for a ten-hour work day until 1889 (See page 103).

The worst conditions were reserved for day laborers, who were unskilled, often illiterate, and called upon only when necessary at usually less than one dollar per day. Historian James H. Mundy described their situation: "When Thomas Hobbes referred to life in a state of nature as 'nasty, brutish and short,' he could easily have been speaking of the Nineteenth-Century day laborer. The fourteen-hour days at intense physical labor until you were injured or your body wore out did not make for gentility or sweetness of spirit. If you were unlucky enough to be injured, there were no government or company payments, only public charity and begging."[1]

Into the 1850s, any accumulated savings were typically kept at home, perhaps hidden in jars, or given for safekeeping to a trusted merchant or tavern keeper. Savings were also important for old age or for injury — not uncommon for laborers during an era when Mainers drove logs down the Penobscot or made stoves in the local foundry. In the mid-1800s, no federal or state safety net existed, leaving only family or the poor farm for help. Likewise, there was no social security, no pensions, and no 401(k) plan.

To some public-spirited leaders, it only made sense to create a means of saving, and it was with that aim — not as a potentially lucrative investment — that savings banks came into existence. If successful, the *Whig and Courier* later wrote, "there will come a feeling of security, and of independence which will serve to give sunshine to many hours which might otherwise be overcast; the toil of labor will be lightened, the motive to labor quickened and the experience of life very much sweetened."[2]

Bangor Savings Bank

It was in this environment in 1851, in the cold December days that usually follow Christmas, that Bangor Mayor Elijah Hamlin fired off a petition to the state legislature seeking permission to open Bangor Savings Bank.

The petition, signed by eleven men, was officially received in Augusta in January and the charter was approved on February 14, 1852. The bank, not officially organized until March 27, opened for business on May 5.

At the time in Maine, only three savings banks existed, although by year's end the number reached seven. A special charter outlining general operating procedures was required to open any new bank, but Maine had no general savings bank law. As a result, regulations and conditions were not uniformly imposed on banks.

Bangor Savings Bank bylaws required a president, three vice presidents, twenty trustees and a treasurer/secre-

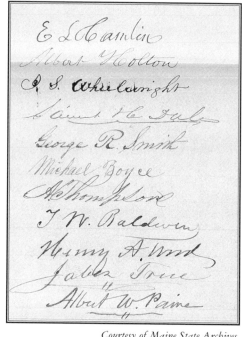

Courtesy of Maine State Archives

Signatures of the original eleven men who filed a petition with the state legislature in December of 1851 seeking permission to start Bangor Savings Bank. Eventually, twenty-four men would serve as the original trustees and officers of the bank.

tary. Officers, who were not to be compensated, were to be selected at the annual meeting and the trustees were to meet at least twice in every year, on the first Monday in April and October, to declare a dividend. The smallest deposit allowed was one dollar* and the maximum account balance was one thousand dollars.

The bylaws left all investment decisions up to a committee and imposed no restrictions. The bank would not pay interest on deposits withdrawn at any time since the last dividend. The bank would pay an extra dividend every five years based on accumulated profits. To calculate the extra dividend, the bank paid interest starting from the first Monday in April after a deposit was made. The bank had ten days to respond to any withdrawal request.

Elijah L. Hamlin was chosen as the first president and served for a decade. The original three vice presidents were businessman Jabez True, clothing merchant and manufacturer Joseph S. Wheelwright and sailmaker and merchant Samuel H. Dale. Albert Holton was named treasurer and secretary. The treasurer was the paid employee in charge of the bank's daily affairs.

The bank also needed an office. The logical place, of course, was West Market Square, the bustling heart of the business district.

Many bank founders were also founders of Merchants' Mutual Marine Insurance Company located at 28 West Market Place in the co-called Circular Building. Sure enough, the bank took office space upstairs from the Merchants' Mutual office at West Market Square in the section known as Mercantile Square. It paid twenty-five dollars for the first year's rent.

By April of 1852, the bank begin to trumpet its opening, leaving some leeway by stating only that the bank would open around the first of May. It ran announcements in the *Whig and Courier* amongst typical ads for fire proof paints, Shaker remedies for coughs and colds (Compound Cod Liver Oil and Fir Balsam Candies), information on securing passage to California, daily steam boat schedules and "ready-made clothing" ("Best Styles and Qualities — Cheap as the Cheapest").

On opening day, May 5, the hours of operation were 10 A.M. to noon and the bank offered depositors an interest rate of 4 percent.

The *Whig and Courier* heralded the new bank:

"One of the most difficult things for the poor and for young men and women, is the saving of their small surplus gains. In seasons of health

---

*Some people were concerned that a minimum deposit of one dollar was still too rich and that gave rise to the Five-Cent Savings Bank, which accepted deposits as low as five cents.

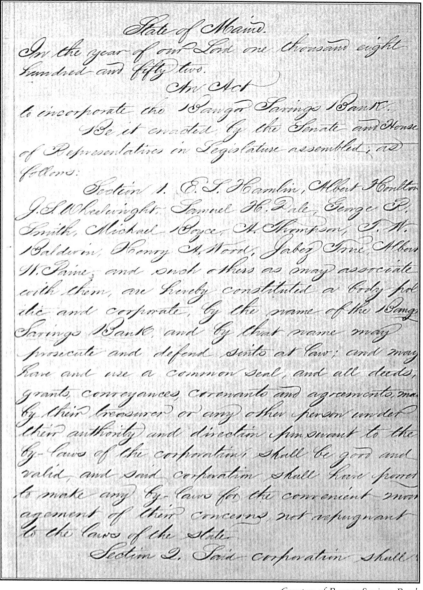

The first page of the original incorporation papers for Bangor Savings Bank.

and when they can earn good wages, the novelty of having on hand a few dollars of surplus funds too often tempts to the indulgence of, to them, small extravagances in living, in clothing, or something of the kind until their little treasure is exhausted; whereas, if they had safely laid away

Courtesy of Maine Historic Preservation Commission

Looking from Taylor's Corner (left) down Broad Street between 1864 and 1878. The Circular Building, site of the first Bangor Savings Bank office, can been seen near right, while the Flat Iron Block, home to the Wood & Bishop store, can be seen far right. Three Bangor banks are visible in this picture: Second National Bank (left), Kenduskeag Bank (center) and Eastern Bank (located in the Flat Iron Block).

these little sums, and had them increasing by the accumulation of interest, they would, in the course of a few years, have had an aggregate sum which would be then a little fortune, and render them independent.

"To enable those who are earning money by their labor, and who are able, occasionally to lay by a few dollars, there has been established in this city a Savings Bank, where money may be deposited, and draw interest at four per cent. This Bank is perfectly safe; its officers are men of integrity and of property, and every dollar will be safe, will earn its interest and will be ready whenever called for.

"We cannot do better than commend this Bank to the confidence of the public, and to advise all who are accumulating money by their labor to make their monthly or quarterly deposits at its counter, so that when they wish to get into business, or to build them a house, or whatever else may require the permanent investment or expenditure of their money, they will be able to lay their hands upon it readily, and to receive what it has earned."[3]

The doors were open, now the bank just needed customers.

The first depositor was not the targeted daily laborer, but Edmond Abbot, a Frankfort doctor. He did not appear at the bank in person; rather, a friend or associate deposited $440 for him.

Not until five days later when young Caleb C. Cushing came in with his grandfather to deposit $5 and Winthrop E. Hilton deposited $100 did the bank see a second and third customer. It would be another nine days before a fourth customer arrived.

In the coming days others would trickle into the new institution. City residents perhaps remained wary of banks in general or some might have recalled that a savings bank in Bangor went out of business a decade or so earlier. Perhaps the bank was just something new and it took people some time to consider it a worthy place for money. Slowly they wandered in.

In mid-June, Rebecca Graves, an immigrant from Nova Scotia who probably worked as a domestic servant for local merchant Jacob Thompkins, deposited $50.

Lumberman James M. Littlefield, who eight years later listed his combined real estate and personal assets at $1,000, deposited $117.

Eben Pool, a local merchant looking to save money for his young children, deposited $10 in separate accounts for Jane, Eben C., Samuel and Lillian.

By year's end, less than sixty people had opened accounts, a rate of fewer than eight people per month.

Over the coming years, though, the list would grow.

Mill worker William Pond of Orrington, married with four children, opened an account, as did local butcher Albert L. Spencer, farmer William H. Fisher of Newburg, Rev. Moses H. Tarbox and Postmaster Otis Gilmore of Brewer. Merchant C.S. Bragg opened accounts for his children, Augusta, George and Eva.

Fan Jones: Bangor Madam

Enterprising businesswoman Fan Jones came to Bangor in the mid-1800s and became madam of the most famous downtown brothel in Bangor history.

Fannie Jones owned and operated what was known as the "Blue House," on Harlow Street near where the Bangor Public Library now sits.

Raised on a West Brooksville farm, Jones launched her business sometime before 1858, the year she first appeared in court charged with running a house of ill fame. She may have continued in business until near her death in 1917.

The legend of "Fancy" Fan Jones holds that she painted her tall chimney sky blue and "its heavenly color served as a landmark for women-hungry loggers coming downriver from the woods, and a promise of snug harbor to the sailors coming upriver."[9]

Jones and her brothel were well known in Bangor. She was believed to run a relatively respectable establishment and reportedly didn't hire women who were too young. But she was still a local celebrity and the *Whig and Courier* frequently tweaked Jones in its columns.

Meanwhile, the federal census sometimes listed her as a seamstress and noted that she rented out rooms to as many as eight young ladies at a time.

Richard R. Shaw and Wayne E. Reilly, who have conducted the most extensive research into her life, describe her as "a woman who lied about her age and carried a wad of money rolled up in her garter; that she jousted frequently with the law during her nearly sixty-year career; that she dressed up and rode about town in a horse-drawn carriage with her 'girls.'"[10]

She was a product of her times, rising to fame during the wild times of the Queen City when "Ladies of the night were as common as fistfights. Maine was a 'dry' state, yet rum, also know as 'white eye,' could be had at a dozen groggeries on Peppermint Row near the corner of Harlow and Franklin streets (not far from Fan's establishment) or in Devil's Half Acre down by the waterfront."[11]

Over time her legend grew, no doubt because many customers spent months in the woods or at sea waiting to return. She even became the subject of folk songs.

"Fan Jones she runs a cat house/ Way down on Harlow Street/ And if you are a woodsman/ Your friends all there you'll meet."[11]

As each of the customers opened an account and received their bank book, they were required to acknowledge they understood and agreed with the bylaws. Those who could write signed their name in a bound book with lined blue pages, while the many who couldn't write simply signed with an X — known as his or her "mark."

At the end of the first year, Bangor Savings Bank had total assets of $7,461.53. The bank paid its first dividend in October 1852 — a total of $33.00. Its profit, in excess of its dividend, was $42.37.

Loans developed slowly and were rather small, mostly because the bank had little money to lend. The first interest payment received on a loan was $20 from Albert Smith in 1854. C.A. Babcock, a local merchant and later a coal dealer, borrowed $444 in 1856, probably for his business, and finally paid it all back twenty years later. Meat market owner H.A. Crocker borrowed $650 in 1866 and did not pay it off until October of 1877. Lumberman Samuel B. Gilman borrowed $2,500 in 1870.

The bank's entire investment portfolio in 1852 consisted of deposits in three local banks, Kenduskeag, Exchange and Mercantile, run by trustees George W. Pickering, John B. Foster and Samuel Farrar, respectively. Not until the second part of 1853 did the bank receive any income from an investment outside a local bank and that was interest on a city note.

The bank later expanded its investment portfolio to include railroads, war bonds and other increasingly risky investments. Many other savings banks pursued riskier investments as well, and began offering interest of up to 7.5 percent to attract depositors.

For the six months ended April 6, 1856, the bank generated a gross interest income of $1,011.99 on investments that included city notes and notes to merchants. Many founders took notes from the bank including Pickering and Roberts, and the bank also took notes and invested in the bonds of businesses tied to founders including Bangor Gas Company, Marine Merchants' Mutual Insurance Company and Fiske & Dale.

The bank was not an expensive operation to run. Expenses for the first full calendar year of 1853 totaled roughly $285.50. The two largest costs were a $200.00 salary to Albert Holton as treasurer and secretary and $33.33 to trustee George W. Pickering for rent. By 1854, Holton's salary was $400.00 per year, and he received a paycheck every six

West Market Square, the heart of the city's nineteenth century business district. Bangor Savings Bank opened its first office at 28 West Market Place, not far from this intersection. The bank, although it moved to 1 Main Street, remained in this general area until 1889 when it moved across Kenduskeag Stream to the Kenduskeag Block, now 3 State Street. The Wheelwright & Clark Block (right) was built in 1859–1860. The Smith Block (center) was built around 1835 and is the building where Elijah Hamlin practiced law in the 1850s.

months. Also in 1853, the bank paid Wood & Bishop $5.33 to either buy or rent a stove and $1.92 for a man to deliver and cut wood.

Clearly, the savings bank concept took root very slowly in Bangor and Maine, despite a relatively flush economy. Statewide, only eleven savings banks existed in 1855. Assets trickled in so slowly that in 1858, after more than six years, Bangor Savings Bank still had only about $33,515.00 in deposits and only 242 customers, an average of roughly forty new deposit customers per year. The average account balance remained small, at $138.49.

A severe economic panic in 1857 and subsequent depression took a toll on Bangor Savings Bank and its savings bank contemporaries. For Bangor Savings Bank, total deposits in 1858 decreased 2.3 percent from the previous year while the average account balance slipped 3.9 percent.

Bangor in the Civil War

Maine contributed more soldiers, as a proportion of its population, to the Union cause than any other state and was second only to Vermont in the proportion of casualties it suffered as a result of the Civil War, 1861–1865.

Many soldiers came from the Penobscot Valley and Eastern Maine. Four major regiments were raised in Bangor, enlisting several thousand men. Additional soldiers from the region served in other Maine regiments, as officers in the units of other states, or as sailors in the Navy. All told, nearly 73,000 Mainers fought in the Union Army (another 6,750 joined the Navy and Marines) and more than 7,300 died. Another 18,000 or so were seriously wounded.

Despite its name, the Second Maine was the first unit to ship out after President Abraham Lincoln's call for troops in 1861. The Second Maine saw action in major battles from Bull Run to Antietam to Chancellorville, before being mustered out June 9, 1863.

Even after much of the regiment went home, 125 men were forced to serve a third year in Joshua Lawrence Chamberlain's Twentieth Maine.

Meanwhile, the First Regiment Heavy Artillery organized at Bangor as the Eighteenth Infantry and mustered in on August 21, 1862. It fought from Fredericksburg to Appomattox and was present when Confederate General Robert E. Lee surrendered his troops on April 9, 1865. The First Maine had the heartbreaking distinction of sustaining the greatest loss in battle of any regiment in the Union Army. During the siege of Petersburg the regiment suffered 632 casualties (of 900 men engaged) in about ten minutes of fighting. During the war, 23 officers and 400 enlisted men were killed of some 2,200 enlisted. An additional 260 died of disease.

The Twenty-second and Twenty-sixth Infantry Regiments were also largely raised from Bangor and mustered into service in October 1862. Both regiments were stationed in Louisiana and Florida and fought in several battles in the Gulf district. Both were harder hit by disease than combat; in the Twenty-second, only nine of 170 dead fell in battle. Likewise, in the Twenty-sixth, of the 154 who died, all but 23 succumbed to disease.

The women of the Penobscot Valley also contributed to the war effort. Dorothea Dix of Hampden, well-known for her work with the mentally ill, served as superintendent of women nurses for the Union Army. Other women quietly followed their sons, brothers and husbands to battle, working as nurses in field hospitals.

— Hoving

Yet, also in 1858, the bank distributed its first extra dividend as required by the bylaws. That dividend, which included all profits made during five years, excluding interest paid, capital and so forth, totaled $522.15.

The turmoil of 1857 proved a low point for savings banks, but set the stage for a period of remarkable growth. The growth was no doubt tied to the improving economy, progressive industrialization and the Civil War.* In addition, banks increasingly sought to entice customers with higher interest rates.

Perhaps an even bigger factor was the growing acceptance of savings banks. While several commercial banks failed or liquidated during the mid- to late-1850s, including Mercantile, City and Maritime in Bangor, no savings banks failed.

From 1859 through 1864, annual deposit growth at Bangor Savings Bank was never less than 23.7 percent. In 1863, deposits rose a stunning 80.1 percent, and the number of depositors reached 1,564 in 1864, a six-fold increase during the previous six years. The average account balance stood at $229.88, a 66 percent increase during that same stretch.

Clearly savings banks had emerged as a factor in the lives of Bangor citizens and those of surrounding towns. They were also becoming a force in the economy. The state bank examiner noted in 1861: "That these institutions have been constantly growing into favor and acquiring more and more of the public confidence, may be inferred from the steady increase of deposits, and from the fact that they are springing up in various parts of the State."[4]

Statewide, the number of savings banks increased from three at the beginning of 1852 to fifteen in 1864, with total deposits of $3.67 million. Furthermore, the state was finally paying attention to the power and importance of savings banks and, as a result, to the potential devastation to small depositors should the banks pursue risky investments and fail. Not until 1855 did the state require that bank examiners even look at savings banks and report on their condition, although there was still no effective oversight.

---

*Paychecks were given to soldiers and money was raised to help their families who remained at home with no provider. It is likely that some of this money was deposited in savings banks and then withdrawn when they returned home.

In 1856, the bank examiner made this recommendation. "They constitute a safety fund for the benefit of the daily laborer, the widow and the orphan, and wisely managed, are the means of promoting the general good, and the welfare of the many who embrace the advantages they hold out. ... It will be perceived, that as moneyed institutions, they are becoming of much importance, and have, in fact, attained a position which in our opinion, requires that the Legislature should pass a *general law for their management and regulation*. They are now all subject to the terms of their respective charters, and without any statute defining their powers. These charters, we noticed, in almost every instance, vary from each other; and we know of no reason why corporations of this character should not all be established and governed by fixed and uniform laws."[5]

The state examiner consistently emphasized that caution and extreme safety should be paramount in all investment decisions made by savings banks. He especially cautioned against investments in unfinished railroads and other potentially risky schemes, but again, these were cautions, not restrictions, against such investments.

Not until the late 1860s did the state finally address the situation. In 1868, the state revamped its departments and created the office of Examiner of Banks and Insurance Companies and in 1869 passed the first substantial general savings banks laws. By this time, thirty-seven savings banks operated in Maine, with more than $10.8 million in assets and more than 39,500 customers.

The General Savings Bank Law of 1869 was weak, but it did establish investing guidelines by formally charging banks to make investments in whatever manner "the trustees regard as perfectly safe." The law forbade banks from making loans on names alone or making loans to trustees or companies of which a trustee was a member. The state required savings banks to establish a reserve fund, initially a mere 0.5 percent of assets, but eventually rising to 5 percent. As the savings banks grew in size, the state would also tap them as a source of revenue through taxation, another controversial issue.

Unfortunately, the laws remained somewhat toothless and a few banks openly disregarded them. Still, they were a start and the state would steadily increase its regulatory powers throughout the 1870s and 1880s.

The End of State Commercial Banks

The remarkable growth of savings banks during the 1860s coincided with the dramatic end of the often-maligned state-banking, or "Wildcat" era. In the early 1860s, the federal government moved to shut down state-chartered banks through the National Banking Act of 1863. The act was largely created to find a market for government bonds needed to fight the Civil War and to create a uniform and stable currency for the nation. Creating a uniform currency meant driving from the system all state bank notes. State banks did not convert as quickly as expected, so in 1865 the government ratcheted up the pressure by imposing a 10 percent tax on the notes of state banks. The effect was dramatic and banks converted to national charters in droves. In Maine, forty new national banks came online in 1865, with the first opening in Bath and the second in Bangor. Most of the new national banks were state banks that converted their charters.

To illustrate the effect, in 1857, there were seventy state-chartered commercial banks in Maine. By 1866, only nine remained. Of the seventy that had been operating in 1857, two had failed, eight had liquidated and fifty-four had converted to national banks.

Meanwhile, Bangor still had nine state-chartered banks in 1857. During the previous nine years three other banks had not renewed their charter and two others, Exchange Bank and Grocers Bank, failed. That meant that during the early to mid-1850s, fourteen different state-chartered commercial banks operated in Bangor. They would all convert, fail or go out of business. Yet more than any other city, Bangor remained stubbornly attached to its state-chartered banks — or maybe the community just had the most stubborn bank presidents. Of the last nine such banks still operating in Maine in 1866, four of them were in Bangor. Eventually, two of those four converted to national banks: Veazie to Veazie National Bank in 1873 and Farmers Bank to Farmers National Bank in 1868. However, even though he agreed to convert in 1873, the irrepressible Samuel Veazie did not do so without a fight. He challenged the 10 percent tax, claiming it was unconstitutional, and argued his case all the way to the U.S. Supreme Court (Veazie Bank v. Fenno). Ultimately, he lost.

Arts & Entertainment

"Two hundred singers were present and for four days they had a jubilee. Norembega {Hall} was crowded all the time — afternoon and evening — to the astonishment of Miss Houston {a singer from Boston}, who ... inquired beforehand if there was a room in Bangor capable of containing two hundred people, and if two hundred people would probably attend the concert!"

– John Edward Godfrey, April 30, 1865

Judge Godfrey had reason for feeling indignant over the snobbery of the Boston singer. After all, Bangor's first theater, seating around one thousand, had been built nearly thirty years before, in 1836. That theater burned in the 1850s, but its replacement was even grander. Norombega Hall, an imposing Georgian structure built on the Kenduskeag Stream in 1856, impressed even big city performers. Many celebrities crossed its stage, including Oliver Wendell Holmes, Frederick Douglass, Harriet Beecher Stowe, Ralph Waldo Emerson, Henry Ward Beecher, Benjamin Harrison, Ulysses S. Grant, Edwin Booth and Laura Keene.

Courtesy of Maine State Archives
Playing croquet on a Bangor lawn.

A second great hall, the Bangor Opera House, was built in 1882, and seated two thousand. The old Bangor Auditorium, designed to accommodate the audience and participants in the Maine Music Festival, was built in 1897.

From minstrel shows to Shakespeare, there was no shortage of public entertainment in nineteenth-century Bangor. Operas, concerts, balls and costume parties, magic shows, circuses and gymnastic exhibitions were held in the public halls and city parks. People enjoyed sleighing trips, card parties, picnics at Pushaw Lake and the Dedham hills, croquet, ninepin bowling and billiards. Athletically-inclined Bangor residents could enjoy baseball, sailing, ice skating, bicycling, swimming, horse racing, fencing and golf.

Indeed, for more than half a century, the glitter of social life was one of the brightest gems in the Queen City's crown.

— Hoving

117

*Bickford's market, owned by Thomas Bickford, was located at the future site of Bangor
Savings Bank on State Street. S.B. Fifield, a clothier, also occupied part of the building.
Bangor Savings moved to this location in 1889.*

The last two state-charted banks still operating in Maine were also
located in Bangor. They were Mercantile Bank and Eastern Bank, the latter run by Amos Roberts and his son Charles. Mercantile quit the fight
in 1876 while Eastern finally gave up in 1878, its assets having dwindled to a miniscule $27,307.38.

Bank historian Walter W. Chadbourne estimates that during the state
banking era, a full 20 percent of the banks that had opened eventually
failed. He attributed seven failures to the manipulation of speculators
from outside the state. Many other banks voluntarily liquidated for various reasons, especially following the financial panics of 1837 and 1857.
Many of those that liquidated also lost a considerable amount of money
for investors and those holding bills.

Some critics are very harsh on the Wildcat era as a whole for its corruption and failure, even while they acknowledge the crucial role banks
played in raising capital, funding businesses and issuing currency and
also note that many banks operated honestly and effectively. Chadbourne

admits there were some problems: "The notable defects, from which few states were exempt, were unsound methods in paying in of capital, unsatisfactory limitation of note issue, lack of uniformity, unsound loans and inadequate supervision."[6]

Perhaps the greatest problem, he said, was the lack of consideration given during boom times to whether yet another new bank was necessary. Too often they were not.

Regardless of its pros and cons, the age of wildcat banking was officially over.

Savings Banks Continue to Roll

Savings banks, having overcome the negative image of banks and initial customer resistance, continued their runaway success into the 1870s. The old state-chartered banks had been replaced by national banks, but they, like their state bank predecessors, were prohibited from accepting savings deposits.

During the entire decade of the 1860s, only in 1865, as thousands of soldiers returned from the war, did assets and deposits drop at savings banks. At Bangor Savings Bank, the drop was dramatic — 16.4 percent in deposits and 114 fewer customers — but temporary.

By 1871, forty-nine savings banks operated in Maine, including Bangor's second one, Penobscot Savings Bank. Penobscot Savings Bank was started by former Bangor Savings Bank trustee Amos Roberts and former Bangor Savings Bank Vice President Samuel H. Dale. The bank, although growing, was only a fraction of Bangor Savings Bank's size.

Indeed, by 1871, Bangor Savings Bank had accumulated 5,112 depositors (in a city of 18,289 people) and had built its total assets to $1.86 million. The average account balance was up to $363.14 and the bank had moved its headquarters to Main Street. Undivided profits soared to $85,081, an increase of 70 percent from the previous year despite the high 7 percent interest rate it was paying depositors.

To pay the high interest rates, the bank's investment portfolio had become increasingly aggressive as trustees shifted more money into railroad stocks and bonds, which now made up 33.5 percent of the bank's investment portfolio, excluding loans on real estate.

Times were good and only looked to get better for the banks and

Courtesy of Maine Historic Preservation Commission

A busy Kenduskeag Stream, seen here in the 1860s or 1870s, as well as the forest of masts looming above the Penobscot River illustrate the still bustling nature of the Bangor riverfront as the nineteenth century entered its final decades.

Bangor. On the horizon was the long awaited opening of the European and North American Railway, connecting Bangor with Europe through ports in Canada. In terms of lumber — still the undisputed lifeblood of the Bangor economy — shipments were about to hit an all-time high.

With all this going on, Oliver Frost showed as much optimism about Bangor's future in 1869 as had others before him. "The time may soon arrive when the three great cities of North America – Bangor, New York and San Francisco — shall be representatives of the wealth, population, intelligence, and enterprise of the eastern, central and western divisions of our country."[7]

Yes, these were good times indeed.

Chapter Six

A Financial Crisis

O n October 18, 1871, the people of Bangor were giddy with excitement and the city itself was never more resplendent. President Ulysses S. Grant was in town, the first president ever to visit Bangor.

On a cool, overcast fall morning, red, white and blue streamers and festoons hung from nearly every building in downtown Bangor, as did the American flag and the flag of England. Bunting hung from the grand old Bangor House and Norombega Hall. Pictures and mottos were posted everywhere.

The *Whig and Courier* said the downtown was "transformed into fairy vistas of enchantment, reproducing under the mellow sunbeams all the splendor of the autumn woods,"¹ while a Boston newspaper proclaimed, "The smartest little city in Maine has fairly outdone itself."

Visitors poured into the city. More than a thousand came up the Penobscot on steamships such as the *City of Richmond* and hundreds arrived in twenty-two rail cars with President Grant. As many as fifty thousand people jammed the streets and city squares to watch a seemingly endless parade that wound under ornamental arches and through streets such as State, French, Broadway and Union. More than a thousand soldiers, firemen and police walked the parade route, as did more than four hundred lumbermen wearing black felt hats, bright red shirts and black pantaloons. School children clad in red, white and blue snaked along the route. Four young women representing America, England,

Courtesy of Maine Historic Preservation Commission
Archway over Main Street welcoming President Ulysses S. Grant to the city for the grand opening of the European and North American Railway in October 1871.

Justice and Liberty stood high on one riser with Justice holding a drawn sword. Nearby, stood thirty-seven high school girls dressed in blue silk, representing each of the United States.

President Grant, architect of Union victory in 1865 and the man who tapped Maine's Joshua Lawrence Chamberlain to accept the sword of surrender at Appomattox Court House, walked the streets of Bangor and then stood on the balcony of the Bangor House to deliver a short speech. The cheers were thunderous.

It was a day of optimism and pride and a display of state, national and international power never previously witnessed in Bangor and never equaled since. Along with Grant came the governor-general of Canada, the Canadian premier, Canadian provincial leaders, the U.S. secretary of war, the U.S. secretary of the navy, various military generals, the postmaster general, Senator Hannibal Hamlin and many other dignitaries.

They came to celebrate the official opening of the European and North

American Railway, the brainchild of a railroad legend and from-Bangor lawyer, John A. Poor. The railway, as dreamed for two decades, was to unite the economies of two countries, open access to Europe and energize Eastern Maine. With this rail, the principal route from London to Canada, New York, and the sprawling American West would run through the Queen City.

Twenty-one years earlier, an original leader of this rail effort was Elijah L. Hamlin. On this day, Hamlin, seventy-one, and less than a year from death, finally saw the fruition of a dream he shared such a long time and so many delays ago. Since those days, he

Courtesy of University of Maine, Orono
A ticket issued to Elijah Hamlin in 1853 for ceremonies related to the European and North American Railway. The railway would not be completed for another eighteen years.

had watched continued growth in Bangor, helped run numerous companies, and guided the blossoming of Bangor Savings Bank into an important city institution. He surely must have been gratified by the railway's completion and no doubt believed it meant great things for the city.

Hamlin had no way of knowing on that grand day that the mighty European and North American Railway would help nearly ruin Bangor Savings Bank.

The European and North American Railway Company

Some people had recognized for years that Maine's general isolation and its position at the extreme northeastern corner of the United States would eventually serve to its detriment. As a nation moved west, that sense grew ever more pronounced. Since the first explorers arrived, Eastern Maine leaders believed the region was teeming with untapped potential. How to tap it remained a mystery.

Joshua Lawrence Chamberlain, Maine governor in 1870, highlighted some of his concerns in a speech to the legislature. "What this State needs is capital — money in motion, whether gold or currency. Our material is stagnant, our industry is crippled, our enterprise staggered for want of money, which is power. ... Maine strikes me as quite different in

123

her circumstances from the other New England States, with their denser population, developed arts and industries, their centralization of forces and accumulation of capital. She reminds me more of the western states in her condition and needs, — a virgin soil, undeveloped powers, vast forests, and vigorous men, but no money."[2]

Transportation (even as it remains in the twenty-first century) was seen as a key to opening up Maine. The era's most important transportation system was rail, already displacing the sea as the nation's main transportation thoroughfare. Even Bangor, despite its lumber riches, saw problems. In the 1870s, Maine and Bangor trailed the rest of New England in railroad building.

The greatest and most dynamic railroad proponent in Maine history was Bangor's own John Alfred Poor. Poor possessed a vision, a religious zeal and wild dreams — some of which actually came true. He viewed the railroad "as the great achievement of man, the most extraordinary instrument for good the world has yet reached."[3] And as a champion of Maine, the Bangor lawyer viewed rail as a way of "redeeming his native state from economic stagnation and for staying the emigration to Massachusetts and to the American West."[4]

Rail, he felt, would bolster the state's agricultural markets, convince farmers to stay in Maine and temper the lure of the American Heartland. Given improved access to markets and improved overland transportation, he was convinced the state, with its superior proximity to Europe, would benefit and the seaboard would thrive.

In the 1840s, Poor relentlessly pitched Portland as a rival, not a satellite, of Boston and, if necessary, stirred the cauldron of city bitterness to his advantage. Poor's first grand idea was to build a rail line from Portland to Montreal. He said it would dramatically shorten the distance from England, the world's great economic power, by bringing ships to a United States port and then sending goods and people over rail to Canada.

Portland was a half-day closer to Europe by boat than Boston, and more than one hundred miles closer to Montreal by rail. It was two days closer to Europe than New York. Thus by sheer geography, Portland would emerge a thriving port, especially when the St. Lawrence was frozen, and Maine would benefit.

Railroad historian Edward Chase Kirkland said, "Though not yet a resident of Portland, John A. Poor of Bangor became the flaming evangel of her railroad greatness."[5]

Poor pitched his bold ideas with a religious fervor and lobbied for legislative and financial support. By the winter of 1845, he drew ever so close to his dream. But Poor, who now lived in Portland, got wind that a long-standing and well-financed rival group in Boston was close to reaching a deal to build its own rail line to Montreal. Canadian officials were already considering a proposal and seemed close to making a decision that would tie that city to Boston, thus pushing Portland aside. Not to be denied so late in the game, Poor, despite a severe February storm, gathered himself and shortly after midnight, started toward Canada by horse and sleigh to rescue his dream, reaching the city in the wee hours of February 10.

"The weather was bad when Poor left Portland. The stableman from whom he'd rented the team refused to accompany him, so he prevailed upon a friend named Cheney to come along. Bundled in fur coats and fur caps and under fur lap robes, they rode through a raging blizzard. As Poor graphically described it 'Our only protection was the covering of ice which hung in masses from our eyebrows.' ... Poor and his friend sped over snow so deep that it covered stone walls and woodpiles. They were lost five times. The temperature was 18 below zero when they crossed the frozen St. Lawrence and entered Montreal."[6]

It took him roughly five days and he was just in time. Poor successfully convinced officials in Montreal to delay approving the Boston proposal. The following week a Maine delegation arrived with a copy of a new charter for the Atlantic and St. Lawrence Railroad and offered a proposal. The Maine plan was chosen. Still, the project remained a struggle and Poor overcame numerous obstacles, including topography, political conflicts, financing and repeated attempts by Boston — which dismissed Portland as a "ninth-rate city"— to quash it by any means necessary.

The railroad opened in 1853 and a revitalized Portland — previously known as "the deserted village"[7] — became a key port with rail connections to the West via Canada.

As an additional backhand to Boston, the line was built using a broad gauge measure, as opposed to Boston's standard rail measure. This meant that lines to Boston could not easily connect and thus future business could not easily be diverted to Boston. Later, the state legislature passed

The Steamboats

The first steamboat to journey up the Penobscot River to Bangor was the Maine, which arrived in port Sunday, May 23, 1824. To generate interest in the new form of transportation, the *Maine* took 120 people on a pleasure cruise to Bucksport. On July 8, the vessel began weekly trips from Bangor to Portland. The service lasted one year before the boat was shifted to another route.

In 1834, the Boston and Bangor Steamship began passenger service between the two cities with the *Bangor*. That line soon faced competition from Sanford Steamers and its famous ships, including the *Penobscot* and *Katahdin*. The original fare was about five dollars, but competition reduced prices to one dollar by 1848.

The *City of Bangor* began service at the height of the steamboat era, in 1894, and made three trips to Boston each week.

Compared to slow, bumpy and uncomfortable stagecoaches, which might take a day or so from Boston, steamships were elegant, comfortable, and fast. They were the preferred form of long distance travel until the passenger railroad, and later the automobile, rendered them obsolete. In 1935, the last steamer left port in Bangor for its final voyage down the Penobscot, marking the end of an era.

— Hoving

Courtesy of Bangor Public Library

The steamer *City of Bangor.*

a statute forbidding any other rail lines from tying into the track from the west.

By the time it was completed, however, the railroad was financially strapped and was almost immediately leased to the now-famous Grand Trunk Railway Company of Canada for 999 years.

Even before the Atlantic and St. Lawrence opened, Poor unveiled an even grander vision: the European and North American Railway Company. The idea was to build a wilderness railroad from Bangor through New Brunswick and Nova Scotia, to Cape Breton island and, if possible, to the old French port of Louisburg in Canada. From there steamers would cross the Atlantic to Galway and from there goods and people could speed on to London. The combined rail and "Atlantic Ferry" would cut three to four days off a trip from London to New York. The rail would become the principal route from Europe to the United States for freight, mails and passengers; it would open up Eastern Maine to development and stem the outflow of men and capital.

Poor offered this dramatic vision: "With a more extended line of sea-coast than any other state in the Union, and more good harbors than all the states together, Maine will present at some future day, along her bays and rivers, a line of cities surpassing those which are now found upon the shores of the English Channel, or Baltic Sea."[8]

Poor's lobbying campaign for the European and North American Railway opened with a Portland convention in July of 1850 attended by dignitaries and powerful men from Maine and Canada. Among those attending was Elijah Hamlin, who was named a vice president of the convention and one of three Maine-members of the executive committee. Elijah, an original incorporator of the railway, had officially signed on with the railroad rabble-rouser. Also on board from the beginning were George W. Pickering and Waldo T. Peirce.

Throughout the early 1850s, Poor pressed on, upping his rhetoric with a dramatic new vision of a united Canadian and Maine region: "Let village, and city, and country share each other's pleasures, without labor and without fatigue, while the dreaded inconveniences of our climate are dispelled or subdued, and the arm of labor is here made strong, bringing at will its richest rewards. When this shall come to pass this region of the continent, this great peninsula between the river and the sea, so long

Courtesy of Maine Historic Photograph Collection, University of Maine, Orono
The European and North American Railway wharf on the Bangor riverfront at the end of
Exchange Street in the late 1800s. Rail bridge in center was a draw bridge that allowed
vessels to enter Kenduskeag Stream.

overlooked, and so sparsely populated, shall become, from its commercial
advantages, its healthful climate, and its geographical position, the finest
portion of the earth."[9]

The project faced resistance and obstacles, including political infighting, the interference of world events such as war, and tentative financing.
Bangor leaders who were either reluctant or "jealous" of the railway
caused further delays. Promised financing by British capitalists soon vanished. In 1853, the project went on hiatus, though Poor continued to
believe in its importance and was determined to overcome obstacles and
opposition. "Had Mr. Poor been merely a businessman, he would at once
have left Maine, gone where there were new railways to be built, and
allowed Bangor to take the consequences of her inconceivable folly."[10]

A decade later, the project suddenly reappeared, this time because
"the hitherto hostile Bangorians summoned him [Poor] to harmonize
and promote their railroad interest."[11] Despite new interest from Bangor,
success remained contingent on numerous difficult issues. But by the
late 1860s, Maine finally contracted a case of railroad fever. Even the city
of Bangor stepped up and lent Poor's operation $1 million.

Through what was at times a tenuous coalition and through a complicated combination of public assistance, land grants and land claim settlements, the railroad project came together, though in a somewhat less
grandiose fashion than planned and, unfortunately, with some shortcuts

taken for expediency. Before the project was completed, John Poor was forced out of the corporation amidst internal squabbling. The Canadian destination shifted to Halifax and the rail was now promoted as a way to "weld the trade of the Maritime Provinces to Maine, stop the drain of commerce eastward from Aroostook into the alien land of New Brunswick, enhance the value of the wild lands in northern Maine and serve as a means of military defense."[12]

The line was completed from Bangor to Vanceboro, Maine, in 1871, six weeks after John Poor died. Finished too late for Poor to witness, it was also probably finished a decade too late for it to succeed.

The railroad was fraught with problems including shoddy construction, continued political infighting, miscalculations, opposition from Portland and Aroostook County and inadequate financing. Furthermore, since its original conception, transportation had changed. Sea travel became faster, lessening one key advantage. Even more devastating, the long-delayed opening meant the railway was launched on the eve of perhaps the nineteenth century's greatest economic depression, caused in no small part by speculation in western railroads.

The European and North American Railway Company developed financial problems almost immediately. It soon plunged into insolvency, suspended its credit payments and defaulted on loans. It finally sold off its lands and leased its lines to other companies, including the great Maine Central Railroad. Some of the lines did emerge as important pieces of the Maine economy. One feature of the European and North American not developed at the time was a proposed spur into Aroostook County. A separate line was finally built in the 1890s and the Bangor and Aroostook Railroad became a force in Northern Maine for years.

Still, Poor's original grand vision of a thriving intercontinental railroad system died an ugly death. His hometown and Bangor Savings Bank, a major holder of the railway company's bonds, suffered the consequences.

A Developing Crisis

With the nation in a full-blown depression by the mid-1870s, the European and North American Railway defaulted on its loans and suspended interest payments on its coupons. Times were tough as another speculation bubble burst.

However, savings banks, despite troubled investments and the general turmoil of the 1870s, seemed to hold their own. The state bank examiner maintained a relatively rosy outlook for them, even as railroads and towns in the western United States defaulted on their bonds because of the nation's deepening financial woes.

In 1874, a year after the panic began, he was quite heartened as savings banks reported an increase in total deposits. "The fact that they came through the recent panic responding to all the calls made upon them gives them a record — draws around them the full confidence of more people than ever before. They are stronger now than before the panic."[13]

Like its contemporaries, Bangor Savings Bank saw increased deposits during the years leading into 1874; perhaps because trustees, concluding the bank remained in good shape, continued to offer a relatively high interest rate of 6 percent. Yet, its asset quality was eroding. During the 1860s and 1870s, Bangor Savings Bank had pushed its investment portfolio beyond bank deposits and local notes as it competed to offer high interest rates. Perhaps trustees got caught up in the boom times. Certainly, President George W. Pickering, a powerful man in Bangor and at the bank, was an avid promoter of railroads.

On the eve of the crisis in 1872, Bangor Savings Bank had 5,554 depositors, total assets of $2.19 million, and $371,761 invested in railroad stocks and bonds, the majority in bonds of the European and North American Railway Company. This stake was not surprising, given the role founders and trustees played in the railway for the previous two decades and the railway's perceived importance to Bangor. The railway's bonds made up 37.2 percent of the bank's investments, not including loans on real estate.

It started to unravel in 1875, when Bangor Savings Bank reported a decrease of 1.7 percent in deposits and a net loss of seven depositors.

More alarming, the European and North American Railway suspended interest payments that June and soon after defaulted. Over half of the railway's bonds held by savings banks were held by Bangor Savings Bank — nearly $240,000. Other bank investments also suffered. Still, the bank examiner said he believed Bangor Savings Bank had sufficient assets to cover its liabilities.

In 1876, the banking landscape worsened. Four savings banks in

Maine failed and were placed into the hands of receivers: Winthrop
Savings Bank, Solon Savings Bank, Bucksport Savings Bank and the
Lewiston Institution for Savings.

Bangor Savings Bank remained afloat, but hemorrhaged both money
and customers. In 1876, total deposits plunged 32.2 percent to $1.52 mil-
lion while 24.4 percent or about fourteen hundred of its customers closed
their accounts. During the same year, the savings bank industry as a whole
lost 13 percent of its deposits and about 11 percent of its depositors.
Clearly, all banks suffered, but Bangor Savings Bank's large stake in the
European and North American Railway only exacerbated its problems.

In 1877, the situation continued to deteriorate and the bank made
some internal moves. Charles Hayward became president, following
George W. Pickering's death at the age of seventy-seven. The previous
year, the bank had replaced its treasurer with Samuel D. Thurston and
for the first time hired an assistant treasurer, Levi Murch.

As the year dragged on, Bangor Savings Bank lost another 12.4 percent of its deposits and another three hundred customers. There was no
end in sight as its problems gained momentum. In the latter half of
1877, four more Maine savings banks declared insolvency.

On the streets of Bangor, even those steadfast in their belief in
Bangor Savings Bank's safety grew anxious. Rumors circulated throughout West Market Square and beyond about the bank's stricken condition
and its possible failure. By late fall 1877, roughly 1,830 depositors had
closed their accounts during the year, and depositors had withdrawn
nearly $1 million from the bank.

Those concerns intensified in December. A long winter was looming
and the continued depressed economy in Bangor meant insufficient work
and income for residents. In late December, depositors began to show the
unmistakable signs of a potentially deadly run on the bank. A significant
or sustained run would kill the bank by forcing it to sell assets at a
greatly reduced value in order to pay off its depositors.

Trustees grew increasingly worried. For years, the bank's operating
policy was to meet any depositor's demand for money within ten days,
even though the banks could legally take thirty and sixty days, depending on the amount of the withdrawal. Given the city's current state of
agitation, the previous course seemed no longer prudent so the bank

announced it would take the allowed thirty to sixty days. That
announcement only caused more panic.

At the same time, bank trustees moved to assure the public of the
bank's safety by asking the state bank examiner, William W. Bolster, to
examine its operations and issue a report. He complied and his state-
ments appeared in the *Whig and Courier* on January 3, 1878. He proclaimed the bank solvent, said it could cover all liabilities if given time,
and urged restraint on the part of its customers. "Depositors must be
aware to force a sale of the assets, especially real estate, at this time when
depression rests so heavily upon this class of property, would result inju-
riously to their interest and induce additional and needless loss."[14]

It was not an imagined threat. The bank had already sold most of its
investment in the European and North American Railway at a loss of
nearly $140,000. Its two largest real estate holdings were the Bangor
House, a property that cost the bank (through the original loan)
$76,437, but had a current market value optimistically pegged at
$40,000, and 74,500 acres of land for which the bank had originally
loaned $88,000, but now had a current value of $50,000.

The city's newspapers tried to calm people, urging them to follow
Bolster's advice. On January 3, the *Bangor Daily Commercial* said, "Should
the depositors generally or to a large extent, within the next 30 to 60
days, give notice of their intention to withdraw their deposits, there will
be no other course open but to place the bank in the hands of receivers."[15]

The next day the *Commercial* explained how banks operate and again
urged patience. "So many savings banks, having been obliged to stop
paying out, have caused some distrust with our Bangor Savings Bank;
and while there has been no run upon it, there has been a disposition
among the depositors to steadily withdraw their funds."[16]

On January 5, "A.W.P." — possibly Albert Ware Paine — wrote the
Whig and Courier, declaring the bank in good health and also urging
restraint. He explained the bank's reasons for adopting the thirty- and
sixty-day waiting periods as an enforced cooling down period to allow people to ask questions that should alleviate any panic. "If this be true, it may
be asked, why does the Bank interrupt its former and well understood
practice of paying depositors on ten days' notice. The answer is ready and
plain: For some reason, no matter what as long as it is imaginary, a distrust

Courtesy of Maine Historic Preservation Commission
Looking down Exchange Street toward Penobscot River in the 1860s or 1870s.

of the Bank has become quite general in the community, leading to large calls under the ten days' rule. The call had well nigh amounted to a panic, which the discreet and highly competent trustees saw foreboded an injury to the bank by compelling an untimely sale of their assets at great loss."

The people would not be calmed. The bank closed its doors to save itself.

On January 10, the bank appealed to the Supreme Judicial Court for permission to "scale" its deposits — reduce the value of deposits across the board to balance its assets and liabilities. If approved by the court, every depositor would see their account balance slashed by the same percentage, thus spreading losses equally. Total deposits would be scaled to meet the reappraised value of the bank's assets. The petition dated January 10 was signed by four officers of the bank, including three of its founders: Charles Hayward, Albert Holton and Joseph S. Wheelwright.

"The undersigned, trustees of Bangor Savings Bank, of Bangor respectfully represent that by reason of loss on certain of its assets, and by

Joshua Lawrence Chamberlain Stares Down a Mob

After years of Republican dominance of state politics, the rise of the Greenback Party and its alliance with the Democrats (known as "fusion") wreaked political havoc in the late 1870s and temporarily interrupted Republican rule. In 1878, no candidate for governor received a majority of the popular vote, forcing the election into the legislature for resolution. There, the Democrats and Greenbackers combined to eliminate front runner Seldon Connor, the Republican candidate. Forced to choose between their two rivals, the senate majority's Republicans chose Democrat Alonzo Garcelon, who had finished third in the race, over the stronger Greenback candidate.

A year did nothing to relieve the divisions, and the election of 1879 proved even more messy and divisive. Again, no candidate for governor received a majority vote, though the Republicans claimed majorities in both the House and Senate sufficient to see their candidate elected. But before the issue could come to a vote, Governor Garcelon (once again the Democratic candidate) and his council declared their intention to investigate Democratic and Greenbacker claims that Republicans used fraud and graft to win their elections. The investigation and subsequent recounts,

which involved some dubious recounting techniques, realigned the balance of power, putting the Republicans into a minority.

Outraged Republicans, led by powerful U. S. Senator James G. Blaine, claimed that it was the Democrats and Garcelon who had committed fraud and that the council acted illegally. Blaine set up an armed camp of disgruntled Republicans at his Augusta home, conveniently located next to the capitol. Responding with equal anger, Garcelon hired one hundred armed men to guard the capitol building, which Republicans derisively dubbed "Fort Garcelon." At this point, the Greenbackers stepped in, siding with the Democrats to raise their own force, headquartered at a nearby hotel.

With tempers at hair-trigger stage and Augusta an armed camp, Garcelon called in the state militia on January 5, 1880. This action brought to the center of the fray General Joshua Lawrence Chamberlain, Civil War hero, former governor, and major general of the state militia. Though he ordered the militia to be ready to mobilize on his command, Chamberlain came to Augusta alone and unarmed, determined that violence be avoided. Ignoring all requests, even from his own Republican party, to simply settle the matter by naming a winner, Chamberlain insisted that the legislature must choose the governor, and that only the state Supreme Court could decide which legislators to seat.

Using the city police force and his own calm presence to keep the peace, Chamberlain braved death threats and angry mobs. On January 12, Republicans took possession of the two legislative chambers and refused to leave. Fusionists demanded Chamberlain eject them and when he refused, replying that was not his duty, an armed mob formed outside the capitol. It was then that he famously stood on the capitol steps, unbuttoned his coat and faced down the armed mob, declaring:

Courtesy Maine Historic Preservation Commission
Joshua Lawrence Chamberlain (1828–1914)

"Men, you wish to kill me, I hear. Killing is no new thing to me. I have offered myself to be killed many times, when I no more deserved it than I do now. Some of you, I think, have been with me in those days. You understand what you want, do you? I am here to preserve the peace and honor of this state, until the rightful government is seated — whichever it may be, it is not for me to say. But it is for me to see that the laws of this state are put into effect, without fraud, without force, but with calm thought and purpose. I am here for that, and I shall do it. If anyone wants to kill me for it, here I am. Let him kill!"[22]

Overcome by emotion at the speech, a veteran who had served under Chamberlain was heard to yell, "By God, old General, the first man that dares to lay a hand on you, I'll kill him on the spot!"

Chamberlain survived unharmed, despite last minute maneuverings by all the parties, including an attempt by Greenback candidate Joseph Smith to have him arrested.

Eventually, the Supreme Court ruled that the Republicans should retain their majorities in both houses of the legislature; duly seated, they chose their candidate Daniel Davis, who assumed office without further incident. The twelve-day crisis was over.

— Hoving

depreciation of the value thereof, without the fault of Trustees, the said Bank is unable within the time allowed by law after demand or notice to pay all its debts and liabilities and is therefore insolvent."[17] Accounts were frozen. No depositor had access to his or her money and a Supreme Judicial Court hearing on the bank's fate would not occur for nearly two months.

It was the dead of winter. Times were tough, indeed.

A *Bangor Winter of Discontent*

In Bangor, at least some merchants took seeming delight at the bank's woes, or at least tried to capitalize. Advertisements in the *Whig and Courier* offered deals to bank depositors. One advertisement read: "Bangor Savings Bank! Orders taken on the Bangor Savings Bank payable in Clothing, in sums of FIVE dollars and upwards. James Tobin. Peoples Clothing House."

Another advertisement, an obvious shot at the bank, read:
SAVINGS BANKS, AHOY!

"The subscriber, being unable to work at his vocation, will accept a situation as President of one of the above institutions (one that will pay 50 cts on the dollar preferred.) Until I get such a situation I shall derive

Courtesy of Bangor Public Library

Hugh and Cornelius Gallagher ran this market, shown here in the 1890s, at 139 State Street.

my scanty subsistence from the small profits that accrue at 36 Hammond Street, opposite Court House, where you can still get any article of jewelry made or repaired you wish."

But in most places, the lighthearted were tough to find.

As they had for decades, calls continued to beckon from the Midwest encouraging Maine farmers to come out for better farmlands. In many cases they worked. The 1870s represented the first decade in Bangor history that the city saw a population decline, from 18,289 in 1870 to 16,856 in 1880. Advertisements in the *Whig and Courier* in February of 1878 sought "Men Looking for Farming Lands in the West." John Peirce, a railroad agent in Sioux City, Iowa, advertised choice lands along rail lines and said he had eleven hundred non-resident property owners looking to sell.

John C. Flint offered a dairy and stock farm in the Floyd Valley of Iowa and in another advertisement announced he would be available in Bangor for most of February to sell lands in northwestern Iowa. He promised secure, special rates of transportation beyond Chicago.

Certainly, some people could have used such a break, but most probably didn't have the money to move.

Mayor Augustus C. Hamlin (Elijah Hamlin's son) in 1877 reported that great expenditures by the city and other relief organizations "appears to represent a vast amount of destitution,"[18] while the Overseers of the Poor commented, "The continued depressed state of business, the large number of men and women out of employment, owing to the scarcity of labor in the winter season, taken in connection with the unusual severity of the past winter, have caused large demands on the department."[19]

The *Whig and Courier* reported, "We are informed by the Overseers of the Poor that there are one hundred and fifteen persons at the Alms House; [five hundred ninety-four] outside and some twenty more in other towns being supported in whole or in part at the expense of the city, making a total of seven hundred and twenty-nine, and this number will be largely increased before the winter is gone."[20]

The total people receiving aid at the almshouse in 1878 was 1,385, up sharply from the last existing records in 1870 when the number was 445. Two hundred and thirteen people lived at the almshouse during the year, up 87 percent from the last pre-depression year of 1872 and up 28 percent from 1877.

State clerks, who typically received an entire month's pay at a time, instead received checks for about ten days from the cash-strapped government in 1876. Also in 1876, postal carriers and clerks in Portland had their paychecks slashed ten percent. In January 1878, Bangor Mayor Augustus C. Hamlin tried to explain to residents why city taxes had risen so disastrously high. He blamed it in part on the city's troubled investments. And because of declining tax revenues, the city slashed its appropriations for the 1878–1879 fiscal year by 30 percent, from $344,557 to $240,262. It was easy to see why such actions were necessary: taxes paid to the state by Bangor, indicative of a drop in the taxes collected by Bangor, dropped from $57,142 in 1872 to $20,142 in 1877, a stunning 47 percent plunge.

Meanwhile, the courts kept busy with bankruptcy cases.

In March, Charles D. McDonald and John D. Hopkins declared bankruptcy individually and for their firms J.D. Hopkins & Company and Hopkins, McDonald & Company; Joseph Isaacson of Rockland declared bankruptcy; Caleb, George and Prince Estes of Bangor declared their Caleb Estes & Son was bankrupt; James A. Monroe of Abbot and Jesse and Charles A. Dorman of Corinna declared themselves and their businesses bankrupt. The list went on.

Not everyone suffering business setbacks during the mid-seventies depression declared bankruptcy. Some couldn't handle the pressure or perhaps the shame. In August of 1876, forty-seven-year-old Thomas B. Holt of O.D. Holt & Son in Pickering Square simply walked into his office as usual at about 9 A.M. But on this morning, he took out his large revolver, descended into the cellar, placed the barrel above his right eye and killed himself.

The *Whig and Courier* declared: "A Well Known Merchant Shoots Himself Mental Derangement and Business Difficulties the Causes."[21]

Resuscitation

Finally, on Friday, March 8, 1878, at 10 A.M. the Bangor Savings Bank trustees and a throng of depositors gathered in the court house for a hearing before Justice Appleton to determine the bank's future. Albert Ware Paine, a Bangor Savings Bank founder, served as bank counsel. Bank Examiner Bolster agreed with a trustees' request to scale deposits and recommended reducing all deposit accounts by 30 percent. He also said he believed that in time, depositors should recover all their lost principal.

138

After arguments and deliberation, Judge Appleton determined that the bank was insolvent by $403,696.60 and agreed to the 30 percent reduction. Appleton's decision forestalled the immediate chance of closing, but was at least a temporary blow to strapped depositors, many of whom remained unsure the bank would recover.

As a result of these actions, Martha Dunham saw her account balance fall from $83.86 to $58.82. John Marshall's account dropped from $257.56 to $180.29. John Fox's balance fell from $441.79 to $309.25. However, despite the scaling and the bank examiner's assurance of safety, not everyone was convinced. Or perhaps they just desperately needed the money. Some people withdrew their seventy cents on the dollar.

By the end of 1878, the year's damage to the bank was this: a 52.9 percent drop in deposits to $627,061 and the loss of another 933 customers, or 22.4 percent. The average account balance, only in part because of the 70 percent scaling, dropped 39.3 percent to $193.78. The losses only continued to mount in 1879.

The bloodletting finally abated in 1880, but the damage inflicted over the previous five years was staggering. The bank's deposits had fallen nearly 77 percent to $525,936 and it had lost 3,345 or 55.8 percent of its customers.

On the brighter side, the bank examiner's confidence of ultimate success expressed in the dark days of 1878 proved correct. With corrective measures taken and buoyed by an improving economy, Bangor Savings Bank was able to restore the entire 30 percent reduction to its customers in September 1881.

Customers at some other savings banks were not so lucky. During the same period, five savings banks in Maine failed and another fourteen scaled their deposits. Of those fourteen, only five, including Bangor Savings Bank, restored the full amount to depositors. The total lost by depositors from Maine institutions that scaled deposits was $238,449. Depositors in failed banks lost another $261,138.

Also lost during the crisis was the long-cultivated sense of trust and safety. It took some time to recover. Bangor Savings Bank did not reattain its pre-crisis deposit base until 1888, nearly a decade after the recovery commenced.

Aftermath: A Changed Banking World

The world in which Bangor Savings Bank found itself in the post-crisis 1880s was much different from the one that existed when economic problems began.

The European and North American Railway had leased the last of its track to Maine Central Railroad and sold its land holdings. In the 1880s, the city of Bangor introduced telephone service to residents, the famous Bon Ton ferry started between Bangor and Brewer, and track was laid for the Bangor Street Railway system. Meanwhile, the *Bangor Daily News* started publication, giving the city three daily newspapers*, and work began on the Bangor and Aroostook Railroad.

While it was an age of modernization, the era also witnessed a continued slow loss of political clout for Bangor and an ebbing of the great wealth it once enjoyed. The lumber boom, although not completely over, would soon give way to the pulp and paper industry. Shipping had slowed dramatically, and the famed, rowdy waterfront grew quiet. Furthermore, Bangor's growth lagged that of Portland as the lumber boom wound down. In 1860, Penobscot County and Cumberland County were nearly equal in population at 72,731 to 75,591, respectively. By 1900, Cumberland County had grown another 33 percent to 100,689 while Penobscot County had grown only 4.8 percent, to 76,246. That disparity would continue during the twentieth century.

Meanwhile, Bangor Savings Bank faced more stringent state regulations, which were passed in response to the banking crisis. Maine regulators restricted the states in which the savings banks could invest, restricted the size of investments in corporations, banned investments in unfinished railroads, mandated substantially greater reporting practices, banned gifts or other compensation to trustees based on any bank transaction they were associated with, toughened conflict of interest laws, established a 1 percent state tax on deposits, doubled reserve fund requirements to 10 percent, capped interest rates, and increased penalties. Other restrictions followed, but a few loopholes remained and not everyone learned the lessons of the 1870s. Many savings banks lost

*The *Bangor Daily News* bought the *Whig and Courier* in 1900 and published under a combined name for a short time before dropping the historic *Whig and Courier* banner altogether.

Bangor Savings Bank
Elegant Rooms in Kenduskeag Block

The Bangor Savings Bank officials began business yesterday at the new rooms in Kenduskeag Block, and while the new rooms have not been fully completed they show that the bank is finely equipped with handsome apartments and excellent facilities for handling business. A WHIG reporter called at the bank yesterday and was shown about the rooms by the Treasurer, Hon. S. D. Thurston.

The bank is divided into two rooms, the main business room in front and the Directors' room in the rear. Both are finely lighted by the large windows. The floors are of birch and the long, handsome counter in the main part is of polished cherry. The counter is surmounted by a gilded railing of iron, arranged in squares. The ceiling is paneled, and with the walls, is painted a buff and light yellow in color in the rough, grained style, which gives a handsome effect. The large vault, made by the Hall Safe and Lock Company,

is of steel, and is surrounded with twenty inches of brick work. It is fourteen feet long and ten feet wide upon the interior and eleven feet high. The foundation is of solid masonry, which rests upon the bed of the stream. In the vault are two large safes and several boxes. The vault is fire and burglar proof and has time and combination locks.

The Directors room is of good size and will be elegantly fitted up. Over the entrance is an arch, which will contain a large pane of stained glass. The new quarters make one of the handsomest and best fitted up banks in the State, and in them the prosperity that has always attended the business of the bank will undoubtedly be continued.

— Reprinted from the
Bangor Daily Whig and Courier
June 18, 1889

Courtesy of Amos Kimball
Schooner docked on the west side of Kenduskeag Stream between 1889 and 1911. Bangor Savings Bank and Bangor Public Library are located in the building at right.

money because of heavy investments in street railways — the great investment mania of the 1890s. Furthermore, after having the playing field pretty much to themselves for years, savings banks now faced a new and powerful banking competitor: trust companies.

Meanwhile, the city of Bangor, its people and its businesses faced even greater competitors at the turn of the century: out-of-state corporations, advancing technology and shifting national demographics. In short order, this would mean, quite literally, the end of Bangor as it was known so famously in the nineteenth century.

Chapter Seven

The Fall of King Lumber

C hastened by the memories of past financial crises and buffeted by increasingly stringent state regulations and new competition from trust companies, Bangor Savings Bank spent the two decades before 1910 enjoying steady, but slow, growth. The mostly low, single-digit annual gains were a relatively new experience for a bank that once produced a three-year run of 38.7 percent, 80.1 percent and 65.9 percent deposit gains. But they were the type of results that would define the bank for decades.

Collectively, the state's savings bank industry generated similar steady returns, not producing an annual gain of more than 5.3 percent for any of the twenty years prior to 1910 nor recording a year of double-digit growth in nearly three decades. There were several reasons for this development. After the crisis of the 1870s, banks began paying substantially lower interest rates to depositors — from an average of 5.91 percent in 1875 to 3.81 percent in 1910 — and shifted their portfolios into more conservative investments. The industry also matured. After hitting a high of sixty-three in 1875, few new savings banks opened in Maine and the number gradually declined. This decline was caused in part by competition from trust companies starting in the 1880s.

The bank and the city seemed on parallel courses. Bangor itself had also mellowed. Largely gone was the nineteenth century explosiveness and devil-may-care attitude. Bangor's goals and image at the dawn of a new century were more sedate and refined, more characteristic of a maturing city than a dream-fueled boomtown. Even Henry Lord, one of the most powerful men in Bangor's shipping industry and a respected businessmen, sensed the change when he addressed a meeting in 1914 to celebrate the fiftieth anniversary of the Bangor Historical Society. "Bangor appeared 'prosperous and happy,' according to the venerable Henry Lord, who addressed the gathering of fellow members. It was a larger and wealthier city than in 1864, but, he added with obvious sadness and nostalgia, Bangor was no longer famous or boldly enterprising."[1]

With the swirling reform movements that defined the mid-1800s — slavery, maverick political parties, and the Civil War — having largely played out, Maine settled into a more tranquil mood. Of the older passions, only prohibition continued to generate heat.

There, of course, remained dramatic events. In 1893, the state economy plummeted again in a by-now-familiar financial panic caused in part by a restricted money supply. However, while two savings banks in Maine failed and one scaled deposits to remain solvent, the duration and severity in Bangor were minor compared to the economic pounding that crippled the city from 1873 to 1878.

In 1898, war again came to the United States after the USS *Maine* exploded in Havana, Cuba, killing 266 men. The explosion served as a catalyst that propelled the United States into war with Spain, which contemporary opinion blamed for the *Maine*'s destruction. The war marked the nation's birth as a world power. The dramatic explosion and death toll ignited patriotic fever in Maine and across the country. "Remember the *Maine*" became one of America's most famous rally cries. A monument to the *Maine* stands in Bangor's Davenport Park.

In March 1902, the city suffered another great flood the likes of which had not been seen in Bangor since the devastating Great Freshet of 1846. The *Bangor Daily News* described the 1902 disaster as "The twin monsters, ice and flood, which had for 22 hours laid devastating and terrifying siege to Bangor."[2]

Flood water rose to several feet on parts of Exchange and Broad Streets, rising so high on Broad that businessmen used canoes to move about. Ice containing logs frozen in the river since the onset of winter took out the railroad bridge and the toll bridges between Bangor and Brewer. Hundreds of communication wires connecting Eastern Maine were severed. The ice and surging waters also swept away wharves and lumber sheds along the riverbanks.

Broad Street during the flood of 1902.

But, in general, turn-of-the-century Bangor ambled along on a remarkably steady course, one characterized by internal improvements and steady modernization. There were no European and North American Railway dreams, and Bangor men no longer drove into the forests and reshaped the land by sheer force of will to bring timber to market. No one on Bangor streets boasted anymore that the Queen City would soon rival New York or reign as the San Francisco of the East.

At the same time, there was a transformation taking place that was changing the fundamental character of Bangor. King Lumber was dying.

The Coming of the Pulp and Paper Mills

The decline of the lumber industry was no small development in a city born and bred by lumber. For decades, Bangor was lumber. It was not that the vast Maine forests were depleted in the early 1900s, but rather that the products created from her timber had changed and their main destination was no longer Bangor. No longer did Bangor Tigers (a famed group of rivermen) drive logs to the lumber mills of Old Town

145

and Bangor to be sawn and shipped around the world. Now the logs were sent by river and rail to the pulp and paper mills north of Bangor.

The mightiest mill of all was the Great Northern Paper Company, built on the West Branch of the Penobscot River. At the turn of the century, Great Northern was so powerful it literally took a patch of wilderness and built Millinocket — known for years as the "The Magic City" or "Magic Millinocket" because it rose from a single farm to a thriving town in what seemed a finger-snap. Within Maine, Millinocket (and later East Millinocket) became almost as synonymous with paper as Bangor had been with lumber.

But there was one key difference. Unlike old Bangor, Millinocket had no local lumber barons running full-speed into the woods with big dreams, hard work, and local pride. Millinocket was a paycheck-driven, punch-the-clock company town, and a corporation controlled building and development. The new forest economy would not be run by Bangor lumbermen and work crews from Exchange Street, but instead controlled by corporate executives and investors from Wall Street. Rather than Bangor sawdust and fresh cut wood on the Penobscot, the new economy smelled of New York money and sulfur dioxide.

The changes evolved over a couple of decades before accelerating in the early 1900s.

Into the late 1880s, Bangor proprietors still owned vast stretches of the Maine forest. In 1888, these men owned nearly half of the 8.5 million acres of wild land in Maine or roughly one-fifth of the state's total acreage.

In the 1890s, a group of Bangor men, led initially by future Bangor Mayor Charles W. Mullen, began plans to tap the power of the Penobscot for a power site near the confluence of the West and East Branches. Hydroelectric projects were all the rage. Through the Northern Development Company, these ambitious men secured rights to the water and began buying up land in the area. Their vision was based in part on the growth of Rumford Falls in Western Maine, a town that boomed after the Rumford Falls Power Company and Rumford Falls Paper Company were established and a community built around them. Historian Charles E. Clark said Rumford Falls "quickly took on an appearance reminiscent of Bangor in its boom days."[3]

Courtesy of Bangor Savings Bank
Bangor Savings Bank moved into this office in 1889. It burned in 1911.

Eventually, Rumford Falls Paper Company was absorbed by the new International Paper Company when it was founded in 1897 by combining more than twenty smaller mills in New York and New England, including several in Maine. International Paper soon controlled nearly 90 percent of the newsprint business in the East.

Meanwhile, a group of New Yorkers, including famed publisher Joseph Pulitzer, became increasingly disturbed by the monopoly that International Paper enjoyed in newsprint. These men, led by former International Paper executive Garrett Schenck, looked to build a competitor and subsequently hooked up with the Bangor-based group and became involved in Northern Development Company. From this group eventually evolved the Great Northern Paper Company, the ultimate entity created to carry out the plans.

While the Millinocket project moved ahead, its cost grew beyond original expectations. With more and more money required, other wealthy New Yorkers joined Pulitzer, effectively forcing out many of the Bangor men. Lumber historian David C. Smith said, "As the price of

Courtesy of Bangor Public Library

Wood stacked along Valley Avenue on Kenduskeag Stream for use in the S.A. Maxfield Tannery, sometime after 1898. The Standpipe is seen in the background.

Wall Street support, most of the Bangor men dropped out and their places were taken by New York money men."[4]

The Great Northern Paper Company incorporated in 1899, and began building Millinocket. By June 1900, Millinocket had one hundred homes and when the plant opened that fall, the town already had two thousand residents. Led by Schenck, Great Northern developed hydropower and built blocks for local businesses, schools, hotels, libraries and homes. And, true to its goal, it became the largest newsprint mill in the United States. It eventually controlled more land than any other company in Maine.

The growth of International Paper and Great Northern also meant that an increasing percentage of the Maine forest was controlled by forces located outside of Maine, a significant change in both ownership structure and raw power.

The lumbermen of Bangor — regardless of how people regarded their political and economic clout in the 1800s — lived in Maine. But with

148

Courtesy of Maine Historic Preservation Commission
Morse's Mills on Kenduskeag Stream, 1800s.

the coming of the mills, the paper and pulp industry took "ownership of the land, control of the rivers, and domination of the politics and economics of the state."[5]

The Battle of Bangor

Corporate control of the Maine woods didn't come without a fight or popular resentment.

In her classic 1904 book *Penobscot Man*, Brewer-native Fannie Hardy Eckstorm told of the old Maine woodsmen and wrote with contempt of the changes imposed by the "Great Company."

"The times had changed indeed. That year the great stranger company had taken the drive to show us how much better Millions of Money can manage those things. There was a railroad to its own doors; there were steamboats at its service on all the lakes; it had a telephone the length of the river; it had unlimited capital — and all these our own leaders lacked, fighting the wilderness bare-handed. Besides, the Great Company very nearly owned the state: it owned the water-power; it owned the forest land; it guided legislation; it had made enormous improvements and was contemplating others which will end god knows where, if they do not improve us all out of existence. It was supreme, the incarnation of the Money Power, the eidolon of the Juggernaut Capital which is pictured as ready to crush all who will not bow down — and some who do. Never before had we seen anything which quite so boldly flaunted the legend, Money is Power. It could do what it pleased. It could buy what it pleased. It could buy everything.

"Everything but men!

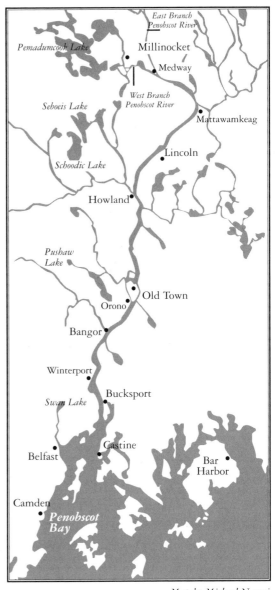

Map by Michael Nasuti

The Penobscot River valley showing the tributaries of the Penobscot from Millinocket to Penobscot Bay.

"So not a single man of the old West Branch guard had bowed down to it, not a single man who knew the river had bent to its magnificence, but every man of them had shouldered his cant-dog and marched off to work for one who was 'a lumberman from the peavey up.' It was superb. It was epically large."[6]

It was also the end.

Great Northern essentially gained control of the Penobscot River, particularly the West Branch, after a bitter feud with Bangor lumbermen and businessmen. Great Northern needed to control water levels to effectively run its power plant and mill. Thus, it needed to decide when the river would flow freely and, significantly for the local lumber drives, when it would not.

Bangor lumbermen, businessmen and sawmill owners — "downriver men" — balked at such an idea. Since 1846, the river and the log drives had been managed through a co-operative, the Penobscot Log Driving Company. Many felt the state's rivers belonged to the people or a collective, not to a single corporation. The first attempt at a legal change came in 1901 when the forces behind Great Northern filed a bill to create the West Branch Driving and Reservoir Dam Company to replace the old Penobscot Log Driving Company. The bill sought to give an entity controlled by Great Northern command of the West Branch. It caused an uproar in Bangor. *The New York Sun* called it "the long-expected struggle between the Penobscot River lumbermen and the corporation known as the Great Northern Paper Company, which is chiefly composed of New York men. It is a fight for control of the water of the Penobscot River, and upon its result depends, in the opinion of the lumbermen, the fate of the industry upon which the prosperity of the City of Bangor and many other towns hangs, the cutting and sawing of logs."[7]

Among the Bangor forces opposing the bill were Samuel Prentiss, John Ross, Edward Stetson and businesses such as the Bangor Boom Company and Eastern Trust Company. The Great Northern forces included local men such as Joseph P. Bass (owner of the *Bangor Daily Commercial*), Appleton and J. Fred Webster.

Prentiss was particularly vocal in opposing the bill. He and others voiced their concerns at a critical Board of Trade meeting that winter. At the meeting, the Bangor Board of Trade officially moved to lobby against a bill it said, "would mean the end of Bangor shipping and sawing."[8]

The fight led to compromise and what amounted to a postponement of

Driving Lumber

Bringing timber down from the vast Northern woods and turning it into the product — and profit — that made Bangor the Queen City of the East was a circular process, repeated year after year.

The journey often began in Bangor itself, where young men looking for work in the woods signed up for the lumber camps with recruiters. From there, many workers would travel overland on foot or by stagecoach to Greenville, where a steamer ferried them across Moosehead Lake to Mount Kineo and used the Northeast Carry, where boats and baggage were carried across by ox carts on rails, to reach the West Branch of the Penobscot River. By bateau, canoe and eventually on foot, the woodsmen then traveled to their camps, often fifty to one hundred miles from the nearest village.

During winter and into spring, trees were cut and then hauled by horse and sled (and later by the steam powered Lombard log hauler) to the edges of rivers and stream to await the spring thaw.

In late March and early April, the ice broke up and the men began rolling the logs into the water. To be a river driver required nimble feet, reckless courage, and the ability to endure cold and discomfort, as workers often toiled from daylight to dark in icy water, crossing rolling logs to free up jams that could suddenly burst and drag a man under, and sometimes using dynamite to clear stubborn blockages. Time was always a factor as the drivers raced against falling water levels that by late spring or early summer made certain drives impossible.

From the rivers, the logs went to mills, many of which were located a few miles above Bangor in towns like Old Town, Stillwater, and Veazie. Henry David Thoreau, a visitor to the area, noted in 1837 that there were 250 sawmills on the Penobscot and its tributaries near Bangor, sawing 200 million board feet a year.

Once processed, lumber was rafted to the port at Bangor, where in the 1830s, it was said, so many ships were anchored that one could almost walk to Brewer by stepping from deck to deck. Ships carried the lumber to the West Indies, England, and the growing cities of the East Coast.

Meanwhile, the lumbermen themselves returned to Bangor to collect their pay, "have a good time," and get ready for the next season's work in the woods.

— Hoving

Courtesy of Bangor Public Library

Logs were hauled out of Maine's forests during the winter months when the ice and snow allowed the heavy load to be carried out by horse drawn sleds or in later years the Lombard log hauler. This lumberjack is leaning on a pic-pole or peavy, manufactured by the Peavey Company of Stillwater in the later 1800s.

the legislation for two years. In the meantime, Great Northern was given control of drives in 1901 and 1902. Those drives proved disastrous in the eyes of Bangor lumbermen. The losses locals incurred, whether by mismanagement or unfortunate weather, prompted lawsuits against Great Northern.

In 1903, the battle finally played out in the legislature and courts. A compromise bill eventually passed that, while providing some measure of victory to the downriver men, for all intent and purposes gave Great Northern the control it sought. It was the death knell for West Branch drives to Bangor and hastened the decline of East Branch drives as well. Bangor would never be the same.

Perhaps most significantly, it heralded the arrival of the powerful, out-of-state corporation as a force in Eastern Maine.

Clark provides historical perspective to Eckstorm's contemporary account: "And at the same time new giants of the industry, International

Paper and the Great Northern, imposed the entrepreneurial spirit of the age, largely with outside capital, upon a waiting state. They overcame with financial and political power whatever resistance stood in the way of their gaining domination of Maine's northern forests and utter control of the big rivers that had been used primarily up to then by co-operative log-driving groups for the benefit of small native woodcutting companies. The transition could not have been more profound."[9]

The Decline of Bangor Lumber

In one sense, of course, the paper and pulp industry reinvigorated the forest industries in Maine, and Millinocket, for one, would thrive as a wage-earning company town. Bangor benefited in some ways by virtue of its location as the closest city to Millinocket — thus the primary source of goods and services — and as the jumping off point for visitors. But the shift cost Bangor important parts of its economy and heritage and all but killed its waterfront.

Great Northern and the pulp and paper mills delivered a stinging, perhaps fatal blow to an already ailing lumber and shipping industry. The volume of long lumber shipped from Bangor ports peaked in 1872, twenty-seven years before Great Northern was incorporated. Bangor's reign as "Lumber Capital of the World" ended in the late 1880s, and by 1890 the amount of long lumber shipped from Bangor had dropped 27 percent from its peak. Short lumber, such as shooks, staves, shingles, clapboards, lathes, fruit boxes and other wood products, also declined.

Despite this trend, leaders in 1888 remained optimistic about the industry, writing, "the lumber trade of Bangor is still in a flourishing condition, and the timber supply shows no sign of early exhaustion."[10]

Such public optimism was perhaps understandable in that Bangor had never known nor really tried to know any other economy. No doubt, great fear existed simply because no one in Bangor could know how the decline of lumber would damage the city. No one had ever seen a Bangor that didn't rely on lumber.

By 1900, the year Great Northern opened, lumber shipments from Bangor were 42 percent off the 1872 peak. By 1915, they had plunged a staggering 82.7 percent to 42.6 million board feet, a shipping volume not seen since 1834. Thirteen years later in 1928, the last long logs for

Shipping vessels on the Penobscot River, just off the railroad wharf.

downriver mills floated down the lower Penobscot River.

Clearly, by the early 1900s, the lumber industry was dying as a major force in the Bangor economy. Its character had already changed.

In 1914, an early end to winter work and a late spring start in the woods left lumberjacks broke. In Bangor, some twelve hundred men were out of work. On one April night alone, the city, operating its own version of a breadline, fed two hundred woodsmen on Exchange Street. "The police furnished bread, sausage and bologna sausages to the woodsmen, who were nearly famished," wrote the *Bangor Daily Commercial*.[11] Bangor patrolman Golden, whose beat included Exchange Street, where many woodsmen gathered, took $5 from his pocket to buy canned beans. After seeing these cans of food, the woodsmen, "fell upon them like wolves, calling down upon his head all the blessings in the calendar," according to the *Bangor Daily News*.[12] Others sought shelter in city buildings during cold spring nights, but available space was limited to thirty-five men. All this was a far cry from the old days when the lumber operations were run by local men. "Twenty-five years ago, it is pointed out by one familiar with lumbering operations, the operators would have staked their men in Bangor, not allowing them to go hungry. That was when operators were personally acquainted with their own men. It is different now, large corporations conducting most of the operations, the officers, of course, knowing nothing of the men."[13]

A Lonely Port

The lumber decline, combined with the increasing use of railroads for shipping and the nation's move west, produced a radical transformation in the Bangor waterfront, as well as many other ports along the Eastern seaboard. Gone were the glory days when hundreds of masts rose like a forest from Penobscot waters and when, legend claims, you could walk from Bangor to Brewer across the decks of vessels. In those days, the ships might come in by the hundreds and leave laden with goods on voyages around the world. They would head to the United Kingdom with spoolwood, take fruit boxes to Palermo and Naples, and carry deals (fir or pine wood) to South America and pine boards to the West Indies. Vessels like the brig *Harry Smith* were renowned for trips to the Mediterranean. For a short time, the great Maine clipper ships sailed from Bangor with equipment, men and dreams to California during the Gold Rush. Thoreau, referring to Bangor in the 1840s, said it was a city that sent to the West Indies for its groceries.

Gone were men like black-bearded Thomas J. Stewart, "kingpin of the shipping business" (and founder of the *Bangor Daily News*), who patrolled the docks, and Henry Lord, a powerful turn-of-the-century businessman who built his reputation on the waterfront. Exchange Street had been lined with the offices of lumber manufacturers, ship brokers, shipping agencies and chandleries. The wharves had crawled with stevedores.

But as the sawmills closed and shipping firms shut down, the *Bangor Daily News* in 1921 said, "A sailor would be a stranger there now and no longer is there any place where shipmasters might sit around a fireplace, whittle and smoke and swap amazing yarns, as in the olden days."[14]

Some in Bangor had foreseen such days. Although many years premature in issuing an outright obituary of Bangor shipping, Bangor Mayor Augustus C. Hamlin did see the lumber endgame more clearly than most. During the economic woes of 1877, he said, "Once she [Bangor]

Courtesy of Maine Historic Preservation Commission
Bangor waterfront, late 1800s.

was the first lumber mart of this continent, if not the world. Not many years ago the sails of her commerce might have been seen on almost every sea. It is no fault of hers that her forests have vanished and her ships have disappeared. These misfortunes do not arise from want of prudence or energy of her citizens. They are due to causes over which the mercantile communities have but little control."[15]

Numbers also tell the story. In the 1860s, up to 190 vessels per year were cleared for foreign ports; by 1890 that had dropped 80 percent to 39 vessels and by 1910 it had dropped to two. Likewise, in 1860 at least 3,376 vessels were cleared in port, that number shrank 33 percent to 2,250 by 1890, by 66 percent to 1,161 in 1910, and by 86 percent to 471 in 1918. In the 1880s, more than a thousand vessels were cleared to pass the drawbridge and unload in Kenduskeag Stream. By 1914, there were barely a hundred and the numbers were dropping like an anchor.

Coal became the biggest import instead of goods like flour and molasses. There was little romance to be found in a coal barge, often the depress-

Both Bangor and Brewer were significant shipbuilding towns during the age of sail. Here, a two-master and a three-master are under construction at McGilvery Shipyard in Brewer, around 1860. Note men in rigging.

ing hulks of old schooners fallen from their graceful, full-masted glory.

The Bangor shipbuilding industry also vanished. By 1888, shipbuilding in the Queen City had declined to a mere twenty-five thousand dollar per year industry. The age of the wooden schooner was fading fast, although Bangor leaders naively hoped it could be revived. In 1888, the

Board of Trade wrote, "This port possesses every possible advantage for building and repairing wooden vessels, and with the revival of the trade which is certain to come before long, must again become an important shipbuilding center."[16]

It would never happen. Steel-hulled steamships would rule the seas.

This decline produced dramatic cultural and social changes on the Bangor riverfront. When the Penobscot River served as the economic artery of Bangor, it was famous. Rowdy sailors in from sea, rowdy lumberjacks from the woods and stevedores and workers from local docks all converged at "Hell's Half-Acre," thirsting for liquor, prostitutes and a fight or two.

Exchange Street was a street of gilded dreams, the place where lumbermen ran their operations and planned their next moves and where shipping businesses of all sorts flourished.

The raucous riverfront and the dream of riches gave the city its romantic, Wild West image (and many of its problems) throughout the nineteenth century. Now parts of it were simply derelict and seedy or shifting to retail shops.

Finally, the harbormaster resigned in 1951, citing lack of business. A city committee concluded bluntly that year that the job of harbormaster was one that had "outlived its purpose."

Maine author Bill Caldwell perhaps captured the waterfront's decline best when, after coming up the Penobscot River in early 1983, he wrote, "the only half-safe place to tie a boat to was a decrepit piling beside a garbage-strewn, abandoned coal yard. To get a meal ashore we had to walk the railroad tracks into the Queen City. It was a hell of a way to arrive in Bangor. But that's what has happened to the head tide of the river. A sad, sleazy, deserted slum is what is left of the port of Bangor, which once boasted that here was the busiest lumber port in all the world."[17]

A New Direction

All was not lost, however. While lumber faded, the waterfront declined and major manufacturers stayed away, much of the city was not crumbling — it was just changing. Bangor's energy moved from the riverfront to downtown and the city continued to develop a reputation as the cultural, financial, commercial, retail and service center of Eastern Maine. Bangor was increasingly commercial, not industrial. This commercialization, underway at the turn of the century, picked up speed in succeeding decades.

Already, Bangor served as a hub for the rail lines — most importantly, the Maine Central Railroad and the Bangor and Aroostook Railroad — that brought people and business into the city in the early 1900s. Steamships still carried people up the Penobscot into the mid-1930s. Overall, transportation improved in all respects, increasing the mobility of Eastern Maine residents. As the automobile age took hold and road systems improved, Bangor's status as a commercial center only strengthened. Highlighting its superior garages and hotels, the city promoted itself to automobile travelers. The descendants of all those professionals who arrived in the 1830s to service the lumber economy could still find plenty of work in Bangor, which by 1900 had surpassed twenty thousand in population.

Bangor looked to improve through both public and private projects. In the 1890s, electricity brought electric lights and trolley cars to once-rutted but now newly-paved city streets. An increasing number of city people used the new telephone system. The Bangor Opera House opened in 1882 and would eventually feature such greats as Maude Adams and Ethel Barrymore. The Tarratine Club was founded by leading businessmen in 1884. A new city hall rose up in 1894. In 1892, five local physicians started Bangor General Hospital, later Eastern Maine Medical Center, and Eastern Maine Insane Hospital, later Bangor Mental Health Institute, opened in 1901. All brought an increasing number of professionals.

The Bangor Symphony Orchestra gave its first performance in 1896 and The Standpipe was built on Thomas Hill in 1898. The old Bangor Auditorium was built in the 1890s and with it came the popular Maine Music Festival. Soon the first silent movies would flicker across screens in downtown Bangor.

All the while, manufacturing was holding its own, remaining an important part of the economy. In 1900, there remained 760 small manufacturers in Penobscot County collectively employing 6,916 people. Manufacturing employees earned on average about $425 per year. By 1920, the number of manufacturers in Penobscot County had dropped 60 percent to 306, but manufacturing employment climbed 29 percent to 8,945, meaning certain firms were getting larger while fewer people owned and operated their own small businesses. Despite the drop in the number of manufacturing companies in the county, the value of the products produced per employee soared from $2,055 in 1900 to $5,790 by 1920. This development — increased worker productivity — was at the heart of the industrial age.

By 1930, the number of manufacturers in the county plunged to 193, with most located outside of Bangor, but at this time employment also dropped, falling to 6,560. Meanwhile, average pay rose to $1,262 and with continued productivity gains the value of products produced per employee climbed to $9,857 — a fivefold increase in individual productivity in just three decades.

Among the biggest manufacturers in Bangor in 1910 were Morse and Company's lumber mill on the Kenduskeag Stream, with more than 200 people; Bangor Shoe Company with about 150 employees; Wood & Bishop with more than 80 people; and Bangor Moccasin Company with about 40 people.

Perhaps the city was ultimately blessed by certain things that didn't develop. The lack of major industrial development certainly kept Bangor from becoming a booming "mill town," but it also prevented the inevitable decline that befell many of the great one-industry New England towns when their industry, whether it be shoes or textiles or paper or cotton, died.

In many ways, Bangor transitioned quite nicely from lumber.

As seen in the 1860s and throughout the industrial age, a weekly paycheck economy versus an agriculture-based economy typically meant more disposable income, simply because people began earning more steady wages. The change also required people to buy more staples, such as food and clothing, instead of producing them themselves. These items became more affordable because of industrialization and increased productivity.

And all this gave rise to the need for more retail stores and service businesses, including consumer banking services. The rise of savings banks and increased deposits throughout the decades clearly mirror the rise of disposable income and the ability of common workers to save and spend money.

Likewise, as transportation systems improved, people more easily came from greater distances to Bangor, the region's largest and most advanced city, to buy goods and services. This only fueled further retail and commercial growth.

Among the most notable Bangor developments in the late nineteenth century was the evolution of retail establishments serving more than basic needs, including the opening in 1892 of a small store by A. Langdon Freese. Freese, a retail entrepreneur and visionary, built Freese's department store, the self-described "Fifth Avenue in Maine" and a landmark in Bangor. At one time it stood as the largest department store in Maine.

Also in 1899, city residents caught a glimpse of a more distant retailing future when F.W. Woolworth opened downtown. One day, national chains would rule the city's retail world, but not yet. Instead, the next great era of Main Street was still around the corner.

Trust Companies

While economic shifts swirled around the city, Bangor Savings Bank conservatively chugged along, surpassing twelve thousand customers in 1904 and passing the $5 million deposit mark in 1905, fueled by the continued need of its services by the working people of Bangor.

Leadership also continued to change. When Joseph S. Wheelwright was replaced as president by Samuel F. Humphrey in 1895, it marked the end of the long era in which the bank was guided by founders. Wheelwright had been with Bangor Savings Bank for forty-three years when he was replaced by Humphrey. Humphrey remained president until succeeded by Charles Veazie Lord in 1903. Lord was the former president of Veazie Bank, founded by his grandfather, Samuel Veazie. Lord was involved with numerous companies, including serving as president and treasurer of Union Iron Works (the company which had absorbed the old Muzzy Iron Works), president of the Bodwell Water Power Company and the Union Land Company, and director of the Bangor Railway and Electric Company. Lord also served as a Republican state representative in 1880 and 1881. Upon Lord's death in 1905, Frederick H. Appleton, a one-time prosecutor and law partner of Samuel F. Humphrey, became president. Treasurers also changed. John L. Crosby took over in the early 1890s and Everett F. Rich took the post in 1909 after fifteen years as assistant treasurer.

In another reflection of the changing city, the trustees' professions had also changed. By 1911, four of the five trustees were lawyers, while in 1852, only two of twenty-four original trustees were lawyers.

In Bangor, banking competition was heated. Like Bangor Savings

Bank, in-town rival Penobscot Savings Bank also grew steadily. In 1880, it reached $539,531 in deposits with 1,320 customers. By 1910, it hit $2.4 million in deposits, although it remained less than one-half the size of Bangor Savings Bank.

In 1910, Bangor Savings Bank had total deposits of $5.7 million, total assets of $6.18 million and 13,808 depositors who maintained average account balances of $413.72. At no point during the preceding ten years had annual deposit growth exceeded 5.8 percent; in fact, only twice during the preceding 20 years had it topped that rate.

Meanwhile, the number of savings banks in Maine had dwindled from sixty in 1880 to fifty-one in 1900. New trust companies were partly responsible for that decline. In 1883, the state of Maine reentered the commercial banking business after effectively abandoning it twenty years earlier. That year the legislature chartered the Portland Trust Company and gave it the power to receive deposits, disburse interest, serve as an agent to register bonds and stock, execute trusts, and hold real estate for its own purposes. What the legislature actually did was set the stage for a banking revolution.

The state chartered a second trust company in 1885, the Peoples Trust Company of Farmington. In 1887, the number of trust companies began to increase dramatically. That year, Eastern Trust became the first trust company in Bangor and the third in Maine. The next trust company to open in Bangor was Merrill Trust Company in 1903.

In general, trust companies operated with broader powers than savings banks or national banks. They could offer the deposit functions of savings bank and the commercial functions of a national bank. They had fewer investment restrictions and, generally, fewer regulations. In the early years, each trust company operated with an individual charter, thus creating a hodgepodge of restrictions. This lasted until 1907 when the state passed a comprehensive banking law to create uniform regulations. Even with that, trust companies operated with broader powers than savings banks and became aggressive institutions.

As a result, only a handful of savings banks were organized after 1880 and the number steadily declined as savings banks were acquired by trust companies. Savings banks remained in the older towns, while the newer industrial and growth centers opted for trust companies.

Some trust companies, based on their individual charters, were also allowed to open bank branches, a revolutionary concept in Maine. Several early trust companies took advantage of this power, including Eastern Trust, which by 1900 operated branches in Machias and Old Town. It was the first Bangor-based bank to operate a branch. The legal power to operate branches allowed trust companies to open banking centers in smaller or more distant towns without having to maintain a more costly full-sized bank, a distinct advantage.

From 1887 to 1907, a stunning 164 trust companies were chartered, although only 42 actually organized and operated. By 1907, there were 39 trust companies and 17 trust company branches, bringing the total to 56 trust company locations with total savings deposits of $29.9 million.

In comparison, total savings deposits of savings banks remained a formidable $85.4 million — nearly three times that of trust companies — but the new type of bank was closing the gap.

National banks also remained a banking force in Maine, but they too would suffer from trust company competition. The number of national banks in Maine reached a high of eighty-six in 1902. By 1907, there were seventy-nine national banks with $32.4 million in deposits. Overall in 1907, Maine had 170 separate banks, not including branches or building and loan associations.

The industry was ripe for consolidation. This led to another concept introduced largely by trust companies: mergers or acquisition for the purpose of growth. This activity developed slowly during the first decade of the 1900s, but picked up steam in the second and third decades. By 1933, trust companies had acquired twenty-eight national banks and twelve savings banks.

The most active acquirer in Bangor was Merrill Trust. Merrill Trust first acquired Kenduskeag National Bank of Bangor in 1906 and then Veazie National Bank of Bangor in 1908. In the following years, it bought the Second National Bank of Bangor in 1917, Dexter Trust and Banking Company in 1919, Machias National Bank in 1921, Old Town Trust Company in 1927, First National Bank of Bangor in 1928, and Kineo Trust Company of Dover in 1929. Other acquisitions followed.

Meanwhile, like savings banks, Bangor itself remained in a somewhat tranquil early-twentieth-century state. Population from 1880 to 1910 had grown 47 percent to 24,803. President Theodore Roosevelt had vis-

Courtesy of Maine Historic Preservation Commission
Main Street between 1889 and 1900. The city began laying track for the Bangor Street Railway in 1888.

ited in 1902 and President Taft, in 1910. Adm. Robert E. Peary arrived in Bangor after his historic adventure to the North Pole. The first synagogue opened in 1897 and Union Station opened in 1907. By 1905, four auto dealerships operated in the city and more automobiles were seen about town. America was at peace. The Spanish-American War was over and World War I was still several years a way.

Then the city's calm was broken by a hellfire that swept through downtown on a spring morning in 1911, wiping out huge chunks of Bangor, including the Bangor Savings Bank building.

Chapter Eight

From the Ashes

By the fall of darkness on April 30, 1911, seemingly all of Bangor was in flames. The hellish glow from the raging fire on a dry, windswept Sunday could be seen as far away as Brunswick. And by the time the sun rose that Monday, huge chunks of Bangor and its glorious history were gone. Gone was old Norombega Hall where brothers Elijah and Hannibal Hamlin shook hands in 1856. Gone was the Customs House that symbolized Bangor's rise as a port. Gone was the Bangor Public Library. Gone was the Bangor Historical Society. Gone were seven churches. Gone were stretches of houses on elm-lined Harlow Street and on Center Street. Gone were elegant homes on French Street and Broadway. Gone was all of Franklin Street and most of Central and Park Streets. Gone was much of Exchange Street where so many lumbermen and shipping merchants had made their fortunes. Gone was the post office, Bangor High School and the Windsor Hotel.

And gone too was Bangor Savings Bank, its headquarters on the banks of the Kenduskeag leveled to a smoldering pile of rubble.

If there was any doubt during the first decade of the twentieth century that an era was ending in Bangor, such doubts were swept away in a spectacular ball of fire.

The Great Fire

By 1911, the population of Bangor was nearly twenty-five thousand and the city was developing as a manufacturing, retail, wholesale and commercial center. The downtown and the waterfront still had many

Courtesy of Maine Historic Preservation Commission
Looking up State Street before the 1911 fire, which destroyed many of the buildings shown.
Bangor Savings Bank is on the right side of State Street while the steeple of the old First
Parish Church (now the site of All Souls Church) can be seen in the center of photo.

wooden buildings, warehouses and industrial buildings, as well as sheds filled with hay and other materials. Most city streets remained narrow and pedestrian-friendly, not yet developed as traffic arteries. While the downtown was clearly evolving, in many ways it remained remarkably similar in architectural character and function as in its glory days as a lumber center. There had been no catalyst for dramatic change.

Spring that year arrived dry. Maine was a veritable tinderbox. Small fires were reported throughout Eastern Maine as April dragged toward May and the summer season seemed to arrive weeks early. In Bangor, sometime during the afternoon of April 30, a fire broke out in a shed owned by J. Frank Green on lower Broad Street. The shed, filled with hay, tarpaper and other flammable materials, burned fast and the fire quickly spread. A stiff spring breeze swept flaming embers from Pickering Square across Kenduskeag Stream, igniting small fires wherever they touched down.

The Universalist Church tower was soon ablaze. A wooden storehouse in the rear of the Kenduskeag building on State Street caught fire and quickly engulfed the entire Kenduskeag Block. Located in this block,

Bangor Savings Bank was among the first to incinerate. The nearby Stearns Building on Exchange Street was consumed, as was the Morse-Oliver Building at State and Exchange.

The inferno on State Street was just the beginning. The fire chewed through downtown Bangor, leaping down streets while firemen and citizens, some armed with garden hoses, battled to knock it down. Swarms of people hurriedly carried furniture, clothes and other belongings from threatened houses. Other people, many dressed in their Sunday-go-to-meeting best, gathered to watch the spectacle. Finally, stymied by a long brick firewall, the fire was stopped between Franklin and Central Streets late Sunday night and early Monday morning.

By the time the fire flickered out it had leveled fifty-five acres, destroyed more than $3.2 million in property, wrecked about one hundred business buildings and nearly three hundred houses, killed two people and injured others. Some estimates placed the number of families left destitute at seventy-five, with hundreds of people left homeless. Some households suffered the plunder of vandals. Businesses and jobs were lost.

But in the fire's aftermath, Bangor, harkening back to its cockier days, vowed to rebuild — without help if possible. Refusing help seemed to generate an important sense of community pride. Bangor exuded Maine's famous independent spirit and its skepticism of charity. Mayor Charles W. Mullen initially refused all outside financial assistance.

The city moved quickly on many fronts. A fifty thousand dollar relief fund was raised for victims. Merchants hastily built shacks in old Centre Park and along city streets to keep their businesses alive. The *Bangor Daily News* said that "Shacks sprung up like mushrooms until the upper East side section looked like a mining camp."[1]

Leading the rhetorical charge was the *Bangor Daily News*. On May 3, 1911, with embers barely cooled on city streets, the *News*, in fiery language reminiscent of the old *Bangor Daily Whig and Courier* and Biblical verse, defiantly wrote, "Many fires cannot consume, many waters cannot drown, many croakers cannot discourage, many cruel blows cannot kill Bangor, which remains the Queen City of the East, which will spread and prosper and make glad the Eastern world, when envious backbiters and pessimists and harbingers of woe shall have retreated to their mountain caves, and their memorials shall be leveled to the earth."[2]

Courtesy of Bangor Public Library
Bangor Savings Bank building at 3 State Street catching fire on April 30, 1911.
Buildings to the right were located along Kenduskeag Stream.

The Vault

The Bangor Savings Bank offices were located by Kenduskeag Stream at the foot of Kenduskeag Bridge on State Street. On the top floors of the bank building were the Bangor Public Library and the Bangor Historical Society, both established in large part by bank founders. Among the irreplaceable materials destroyed by the fire were a large collection of artifacts donated by Bangor Savings Bank's founding president, Elijah L. Hamlin, also the historical society's first president and its inspirational leader.

Bangor Savings Bank's nearly fourteen thousand depositors were more concerned about what might lie ruined beneath the rubble of 3 State Street, namely, more than $5 million in securities, cash and other valuables. Bank Treasurer Everett F. Rich ran a notice May 1 informing people that "The vault is apparently intact, but it will take several days for it to become sufficiently cool so that its doors can be opened with safety."[3] For days, bank officials and depositors held their breaths waiting to learn whether the contents of the bank's vault — representing life savings for many — remained intact.

Bangor Savings Bank, Bangor Public Library and Bangor Historical Society at 3 State Street fully engulfed in flames, April 30, 1911.

After a few days, the rubble had settled and cooled enough for "vault experts" Herring, Hall & Marvin Company of Boston to begin clearing debris and digging out the vault. They dug through the rubble of the bank and drilled through steel, practically destroying the vault's door to gain access. In the meantime, trustees had arranged for heavy security. A guard was posted on the sidewalk to keep "an eye out for desperadoes."[4] Four rifle-toting marshals sat on the pile of rubble, a Bangor police inspector surveyed the scene and a private detective roamed the perimeter. In all, perhaps eight armed men guarded the vault, which included two large safes inside.

After a couple of days, the Boston firm notified Rich and bank trustees that the vault was ready to examine. Rich, the treasurer, stepped into the pile. The crowd waited. Rich worked the combination and tried to open the vault, but failed. He stepped away while the Boston firm took shots at the door with a sledgehammer and removed a piece of warped floor that still blocked it. The crowd still waited. Rich stepped forward again. This time he succeeded in opening the vault doors and,

Courtesy of Bangor Historical Society
Aftermath of the Great Fire of 1911 looking from East Market Square across Kenduskeag Stream.

although their view was partly obscured by steel bars, the crowd on State Street could see the contents were safe. All burst into applause.

"The news that the securities and valuables of the bank are safe will be the best kind of news to hundreds of depositors who have been fearing that when the vault was opened its contents would be destroyed," wrote the *Bangor Daily Commercial*.[5]

However, with the vault opened, trustees certainly couldn't just leave five million dollars sitting there — no matter how many rifles stood guard. After all, $5 million represented more assets than that held by any other bank in the city.

The bank moved with signature caution. Arriving on the scene were horse-drawn American Express wagons accompanied by armed guards. Iron chests were unloaded from wagons and filled with the valuables. The chests were taken to Merrill Trust where the contents were stored in that bank's vaults. Bangor Savings Bank also stored valuables at Merchants' National Bank.

Meanwhile, trustees moved to find new quarters. To notify the public of the new location, officials stuck a painted wooden sign in the rubble that was once 3 State Street that simply read: "Bangor Savings Bank Located Over Kenduskeag Trust Co. Broad Street."

The task of rebuilding the bank, securing temporary quarters and calming the public fell to the bank's officers and trustees: President Frederick H. Appleton, Matthew Laughlin, Erastus C. Ryder, Walter L. Head and Charles H. Bartlett. All but Head, who was treasurer of Charles Hayward & Company, were lawyers. Appleton, who had been involved with Great Northern Paper Company when it was created, was also a founder of Merrill Trust in 1903.

For more than eight months the bank operated over Kenduskeag Trust in an office formerly occupied by rival Penobscot Savings Bank. The bank shared the tight space with the real estate firm of Pember & Carter. Such limited space made business difficult for customers, so the bank extended regular operating hours from the traditional "banker's hours" of 9 A.M. to 3 P.M. to 8 A.M. to 5 P.M.

That summer, the bank ran advertisements noting its temporary location and its $5.6 million in deposits, while looking to assure the public of the bank's inherent safety: Bangor Savings Bank "is not in any sense a commercial bank, but confines its efforts to investing safely the funds of its depositors to whom it has paid in dividends of $4,442,331.39."

The bank had also adopted Safety First as its motto and it aimed to keep its word in the way it invested money. By the time of the fire, nearly 50 percent of its resources were invested in municipal and county bonds. One newspaper claimed Bangor Savings Bank was one of the "most conservatively managed institutions of the kind in New England."

Still, as Penobscot Valley leaves began to turn in the fall of 1911, trustees were forced to quell nasty rumors about the bank's condition, an effort that kept them occupied even as they decided how to rebuild.

The Smoke Clears

By late August and early September financial concerns once again gripped the nation. The stock market gyrated wildly, fueled in part by rumors that U.S. Steel would be dissolved. In Bangor, financial stability was shaken by the failure of Bangor-based banking and insurance firm

Tyler, Fogg and Company, which had invested too heavily in shaky western railroads. The failure of such a well-known firm affected thousands of people and ignited a rumor mill that Bangor banks, particularly Bangor Savings Bank, were in financial trouble. No doubt the April fire also exacerbated the public's general feeling of uneasiness.

Throughout that fall, the bank continued to run small advertisements emphasizing its safety. One headline read "Prudent Men" and the smaller copy below read, "believe in saving and that they may have a place of safety for their funds, make regular deposits in the Bangor Savings Bank where they will earn a liberal rate of interest. Conservative investment of funds guarded by the restrictions of the State Banking Laws and the required Reserve Fund." And another one read, "Just What You Require ... to increase your surplus funds is an account with the Bangor Savings Bank. Every safeguard provided — Every courtesy extended."

However, by late September rumors about the bank's condition only intensified, forcing the bank to mount a more direct offensive. It ran more advertisements, larger than usual and in the form of an open letter to depositors: "The Trustees of the Bangor Savings Bank, having observed that reports are being circulated questioning its financial condition, deem it advisable to make the following statement in order to allay any anxiety which may exist among the depositors.

"The Bank was never in better condition than at present."[6]

The city's newspapers also came to the bank's aid. Under the headline "A False Alarm," the *Bangor Daily News* on Sept. 29, 1911, wrote, "Within the past few days Bangor has witnessed a remarkable demonstration of the mischief that idle rumor can accomplish — of what a great alarm may exist in the public mind without just cause. The failure of the private banking firm of Tyler, Fogg & Co., although having no effect whatever upon other banking institutions here, seems to have created something like panic in the minds of many depositors in the old and substantial Bangor Savings Bank, who have been hastily withdrawing their funds from that ark of financial safety," and the newspaper concluded by saying, "There is not the slightest ground for alarm concerning the big savings bank. Let the deposits remain!"

The campaign eventually allayed most fears and the bank ended 1911 on solid financial ground despite the rumors and devastating fire.

However, it was still forced that year to report its first decline in deposits and customers since 1894, a drop of 1.8 percent and 3.9 percent (536 customers), respectively.

As the crisis passed, trustees devoted themselves to the other issue at hand: building a new office. Apparently, like Bangor itself, trustees were not content to simply rebuild. They wanted to make a grand statement, a "decided ornament to the downtown section of the city."[7]

The plans became clearer in early January of 1912 when the bank announced it had commissioned Carrere & Hastings of New York, the firm that designed the New York Public Library and Portland City Hall. The firm planned to design and build an ornate, one-story granite bank office on the former bank site. The bank's design included an alleyway surrounding the bank to ensure its isolation

Meanwhile, the bank, co-owner of the Kenduskeag Block in which it was located, cut a deal with its fellow partner to acquire sole ownership of the bank site. The following day, trustees announced plans to move from its temporary office on Broad Street to a temporary office at 73 Central Street, between the post office and Kenduskeag Stream.

Seventeen months later, in June 1913, the bank opened its new head-quarters at 3 State Street. As promised, the headquarters were grand. *The Industrial Journal* of Bangor described it as "one of the handsomest bank buildings in New England.

"It is splendidly adapted to their large and expanding business. The building is built of white granite from the Hallowell Granite Works with partitions of terra-cotta and concrete floor. The interior is finished in hollow metal, steel and marble. The doors and roof are of copper and the building is absolutely fireproof. ... Internally as well as externally the building is a gem and a most welcome addition to the architectural adornment of the new Bangor."[8]

In the post-fire days, it seemed people often emphasized those last three words: the *new* Bangor.

Bangor Rises Again

As everyone promised so boisterously even as they watched flames destroy parts of their city, Bangor rebuilt. (In fact, Bangor even became boastful, proclaiming that Bangor had one of the largest fires in New

England history.) Businesses and residents raised tens of thousands of dollars to support those hurt by the fire. Some leaders claimed the fire was actually a boon to the city and rebuilding became a rally cry, although exactly how to rebuild at times ignited a bitter controversy. A grand plan, championed by the *Bangor Daily News*, called for sweeping changes including new public buildings, new parks, a walkway along both sides of the Kenduskeag, wider Centre, French and Central streets and better quality buildings, all to "make Bangor an example to the world." Meanwhile, the *Bangor Daily Commercial*, controlled by businessman Joseph Bass, denounced such plans as too costly and impractical.

Startlingly different headlines over stories about the same meeting illustrate the conflict. The *Bangor Daily News* headline read: "Civic Improvement Gets Grand Support. Splendid Gathering of Bangor's Progressive Men and Women Indorse [sic] and Applaud the Committee's Report and Ask Favorable Action by the City Council."[9]

The *Bangor Daily Commercial* headline read: "Impractical Plans Meet With United Opposition. Civic Improvement Scheme Would Entail a Cost of Millions and Increased Taxes Would Drive Commerce Away From Bangor, So Business Men Say."[10]

In the end, compromise won out, and substantial, although scaled down, rebuilding did occur.

Across State Street from Bangor Savings Bank, the Eastern Trust & Banking Company built a six-story building, the tallest in the city. John R. Graham, President of Bangor Railway & Electric Company (forerunner to Bangor Hydro-Electric Company), built the new Graham Building on Central Street. A new Windsor Hotel was built on Harlow Street. As a safety precaution, wooden structures were forbidden.

The city planned Norumbega Park at the former site of Norombega Hall with Charles H. Bartlett, president of Bangor Savings Bank, chairing the fundraising committee, and Everett Rich serving as treasurer. A new high school, public library and federal building, new theaters, five new churches and a synagogue were all built. New sidewalks were laid, city streets were paved and Central Street was widened.

The Chamber of Commerce boasted in 1915, that "block after block has been rebuilt, and in almost every case the new building is a very material improvement on the old in every way, more modern, more spacious and more attractive."[11]

The new Bangor settled into growth that would last for nearly two decades.

Bangor Savings Bank Soldiers On

Once in its new offices in June 1913, Bangor Savings Bank barely skipped a beat, continuing its own steady growth. One of its banking neighbors, Merrill Trust, acquired banks right and left, but Bangor Savings Bank continued along, almost desperate to assure the public that it was not a commercial bank and that it remained perfectly safe.

Indeed, it was a crowded banking scene in post-fire Bangor.

In 1912, nine Bangor-based banking companies operated in the city: two savings banks, two national banks, three trust companies and two loan and building associations. They were: Bangor Savings Bank and Penobscot Savings Bank; First National Bank and Second National Bank; Eastern Trust and Banking Company, Kenduskeag Trust Company and Merrill Trust Company and Bangor Loan and Building Association and Penobscot Loan and Building Association. The loan and building associations provided loans to build houses and were relatively small, $396,957 in assets for Bangor Loan & Building and $142,183 for Penobscot Loan & Building.

Bangor Savings Bank remained the biggest bank in Bangor in terms of total assets with $6.27 million in 1912. Merrill Trust, although growing, tallied $2.67 million in assets and Kenduskeag Trust Company $1.69 million. The strongest commercial bank was Eastern Trust. Eastern Trust had $5.56 million in assets, including more than $2.7 million in savings deposits. Furthermore, its real estate owned was $183,933, more than double that of any other trust company in the state.

Clearly, Bangor had no shortage of banking. The new trend of establishing branches also meant Bangor-based commercial banks were reaching out into Eastern and Northern Maine, further solidifying Bangor's position as a regional hub. The commercial banks didn't build new branches, but expanded by buying existing banks and renaming them as their branches.

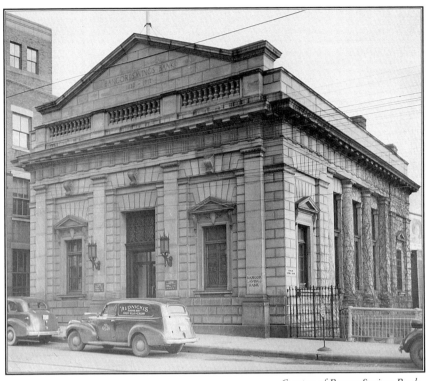

Courtesy of Bangor Savings Bank
The new Bangor Savings Bank offices at 3 State Street. The office opened for business in June of 1913.

The teens and twenties of the new century were years of steady growth for Bangor Savings Bank, largely mirroring the state of the Bangor economy as it recovered and rebuilt in the post-fire, post-lumber era. The Chamber of Commerce termed the city's growth "a growth that is stable, honest and gratifying — no mushroom boom, ephemeral and vanishing, but a progress that is bound to continue and to bring prosperity to the city and its people."[12]

From 1912 to 1929, Bangor Savings Bank recorded drops in deposits only in 1915 and 1918. By 1929, the bank had reached $8.8 million in total assets and $7.9 million in deposits, a cumulative growth of 43.9 percent and 41.0 percent, respectively, since the Great Fire.

While Bangor Savings Bank held steady, the trust companies continued to make inroads into savings banks' business. The number of savings banks in the state dropped from fifty-one in 1900 to forty-three in 1920 and to thirty-three by 1929. Many savings banks were either folded into trust companies or turned into trust company branches. National banks were also acquired by trust companies.

One other trend illustrated a slight shift in fortunes for Bangor in the post-lumber, post-fire Bangor economy. For the first time in decades, the average savings account balance at Bangor Savings Bank fell below the statewide average. Across Maine, accounts were growing at a faster pace. Perhaps, without the lumber economy, workingmen were not able to find jobs that could fully replace the income lost with the industry's decline.

The bank president during this era was Charles H. Bartlett[13] and the treasurer was Walter A. Danforth. Both made long-term commitments to Bangor Savings Bank. Bartlett served as president for twenty-two years and Danforth served as treasurer for thirty years. One or both of the men were in a position of power at the bank from shortly after the Great Fire through the Great Depression and into the post-World War II era. They didn't deviate from the tried and true formula; if anything, they cemented the bank's conservative image and practices by constantly pushing the bank toward safer investments.

Walter A. Danforth served as long-term treasurer of Bangor Savings Bank, meaning he ran the day-to-day operations and essentially performed the same role that a chief executive officer would in later years. After serving as treasurer of the Bangor & Aroostook Railroad Company, he joined the bank as treasurer in 1917 to replace the late Everett Rich. Danforth helped set the agenda for Bangor Savings Bank for decades through his own term and that of his understudy and successor, Harold L. Nason. When Nason started at the bank, there were five employees.

Danforth married Susie Herrick and after her death, married Anne Wyman. He was a staunch Baptist and a pillar of the Columbia Street Baptist Church. Through his association with the Columbia Street Baptist Church, he organized and taught the Danforth Bible Class for Men, an influential group. Hundreds of men attended the class during Danforth's years of teaching, not only learning the Bible but also studying "material welfare" and making key social and business connections. Danforth ran the class like his bank — with no arguments and in a highly dignified manner.

Danforth was a trustee of the Home for Aged Women, the YMCA and YWCA, the University of Maine and the Salvation Army. He was trustee and president of Higgins Classical Institute at Charleston and served as a city alderman. Active in the banking industry, he served as president of the Savings Bank Association of Maine and lobbied for banking legislation during his career.

Danforth, proper and ramrod straight, ran a tight ship at the bank from 1917 to 1947. But he was also good with customers. "People would go in with a complaint and they would come out smiling; he was very diplomatic," said Malcolm Jones, who started work at the bank in 1954 and became president in 1975. Above all, Danforth was a strong temperance man. He once told an employee seen coming out of a local saloon on Harlow Street that "People at Bangor Savings Bank don't drink. I don't want to see you coming out of that bar again." The employee later said, "He never did. I always went out the back door."

It was also said that in the days after prohibition when a person buying liquor at the state store had to sign a name on a receipt, many of the men who bought liquor on Exchange Street scrawled the name "Walter A. Danforth" on their slips.

Social Changes and Bangor's Next Era

In the teens and twenties, the city began to look ahead, first by commemorating its bygone era with statutes and tributes. The Peirce Memorial River Drivers sculpture was dedicated in 1926, just as log drives on the lower Penobscot officially ceased. (The Peirce Memorial and the Civil War Memorial at Mt. Hope were donated by the son of Bangor Savings Bank founder Waldo Peirce.) In 1927, the city finally unveiled a statue of its most famous resident, Hannibal Hamlin, where Norombega Hall once stood.

WABI radio began broadcasting in 1923, bringing yet another form of entertainment to greater Bangor and once again positioning Bangor as a hub. In the future, all three major television stations in Eastern Maine would emanate from Bangor. The Opera House on Main Street and the Bangor Aviation School opened in 1926.

Two of the big social and political issues of the day in Bangor were suffrage and Prohibition. In 1917, Bangor soundly defeated a ballot question

The Killer Flu

It is one of the ironies of history that just as the First World War was drawing to a close, an even more deadly threat took the global stage, the influenza pandemic of 1918–1919. The epidemic, known as "Spanish Flu," "La Grippe," or "the Grip," killed more people in a single year than the Great War. Somewhere between twenty million and forty million people died worldwide.

Because of the United States' late entry into World War I, relatively few American soldiers were killed in combat. Likewise, the oceans separating the United States from Europe protected civilians from the worst effects of war. But the flu respected no boundaries, and many American soldiers and civilians suffered from the disease. Twenty-eight percent of all Americans were infected and an estimated 675,000 died. Some 43,000 infected United States servicemen died; half of those who died in Europe fell to influenza, not in battle.

For Bangor residents, the first signs of alarm came from Boston, where the disease struck early and hard. At the beginning of September 1918, Boston public health officials announced that an epidemic had broken out at nearby Camp Devens and would likely spread to the city. Normal business and travel between Bangor and Boston guaranteed that the highly contagious influenza would spread north, and throughout the month, cases began to appear in Bangor. On October 1, city health officials took the extreme measure of closing all public gathering places, including churches, schools and theaters.

Bangor newspapers were full of recommendations for avoiding contagion. The *Bangor Daily News* recommended plenty of fresh air and exercise and counseled residents to "avoid the sneezers." They also attempted to debunk popular remedies, such as drinking rum, smoking or wearing bags of camphor around one's neck or sulfur in one's shoes.

By the time the ban on assembly was lifted on November 2, fifty-four people in Bangor were reported dead of the disease. The Report of the Bangor Board of Health for the year 1918 to 1919 listed sixteen hundred cases of influenza and 110 deaths in the city, a toll that might have been even heavier but for the judicious actions of city leaders.

— Hoving

to give women the right to vote. The city's women did not receive the vote until August 1920 when the Nineteenth Amendment to the Constitution was ratified. The Maine League of Women Voters then replaced the Maine Women Suffrage Association and became an important political group.

Also showing signs of cracking was Maine's staunch support of Prohibition. Maine stood at the forefront of the temperance movement in the mid-1800s, passing the first state law banning alcohol, and the issue remained at the center of Maine politics for decades. In the era before women could vote, Prohibition gave socially conscious women perhaps their strongest voice and most-enduring cause. The Women's Christian Temperance Union ranked as perhaps the most powerful women's organization in Maine.

An important event in the state's slow drift from Prohibition occurred in the summer of 1911 when Maine placed the repeal of Prohibition before voters. Voters chose to keep existing laws in place, but by a majority so slim that the outcome remained uncertain for days. The narrow victory probably signaled the end of dominant and popular opposition to alcohol although Prohibition remained the state law for two decades longer. Perhaps more interesting was the vote in Bangor, which favored repeal 77 percent to 23 percent. As the tide went against Prohibition in Bangor that day, some women wept at the polls. A young woman at Ward One became so upset that she was comforted even by men voting against Prohibition. Others gathered for prayer services at local chapels.

Still, it wasn't as if the issue went away in the Queen City. In May of 1916, Reverend W.S. Berry took to the pulpit and compared Bangor to a modern-day Babylon, a city filled with saloons, prostitution and gambling. He said an evening walk through the vice-filled streets of downtown horrified him. His words were hotly debated in the newspapers.

Drunkenness itself also remained an issue for the city. For example, in 1893–1894, 75 percent of all arrests were for drunkenness. In 1903–1904, nearly 82 percent of all arrests were for drunkenness and those rose still further to 85 percent in 1913–1914.

Charges were also periodically leveled at the city or police department for not properly enforcing anti-liquor laws. Those charges prompted occasional raids and other police activity to root out liquor. Such efforts occurred throughout the early 1900s.

The United States did not pass its Prohibition laws until 1919. Despite the close vote in 1911, Maine's Prohibition laws were not officially repealed until 1934 when an amendment to the Constitution gave states the local option of liquor laws. But in Bangor, it had never been difficult to find a drink. Even at the height of mid-1850s Maine Law, the *Bangor Democrat* quoted a Boston newspaper in 1857 as saying, "There had been enough rum sent hence to Bangor lately to give even river water a contraband tincture."[14]

Bangor: At Your Service

By 1929, the end of the nation's so-called Roaring Twenties, the shifts to service, and to a commercial, retail, and key wholesale center were largely in place.

The Chamber of Commerce began heavily promoting the city as a destination for tourists and as an automobile center that offered superior garages and hotels, excellent fishing, and was the perfect spot to head off for the woods or the seashore. The chamber also actively sought to bring conventions and meetings to town.

The shifts were also illustrated by numerous tenant changes downtown. In 1920, long-time wholesale firm Adams Dry Goods moved off Main Street to make way for Farrar Furniture Company. In 1921, Buckfield Drug Company opened with its "handsome new soda fountain" on the street level of the Stetson Building. Also on the first floor were a new shoe store and a music shop. The second floor included a new clothing store. Eastern Furniture Company continued to acquire space on Exchange Street for its showrooms, which had reached seventy-five thousand square feet.

In 1924, Sawyer Boot & Shoe Company, which traced its Bangor roots to the mid-1800s, took its 125-person workforce and manufacturing business to Freeport.

In the late 1920s, Freese's, the bellwether of Bangor retail, expanded yet again to provide four floors of merchandise in forty-eight departments, employing more than 250 people year 'round and upwards of 500 during Christmas. It was likely the city's largest employer and symbolized the fortunes of downtown Bangor for decades, for both good and bad.

Perhaps most telling of the new focus was Dollar Days, a shopping promotion designed to bring people downtown. Dollar Days included sales, special prizes, giveaway and other gimmicks. In 1924, record crowds descended on downtown, forcing stores like Besse Systems, a clothing store, to repeatedly lock its doors until customers inside could be cleared out to make room. People lined up outside some stores long before the doors opened, sometimes squabbling about who arrived first.

The business shift was even further illustrated in the first Chamber of Commerce-sponsored industrial survey released in 1929. In the combined Bangor-Brewer area, only seventy-eight manufacturing firms remained and only six had more than 50 employees. More than 65 percent employed fewer than 10 people. The only major manufacturer in the two towns was Brewer's Eastern Manufacturing Company, a manufacturer of lumber, pulp and paper. Eastern employed 783 people, representing roughly 42 percent of the twin cities' manufacturing jobs and nearly half of its payroll.

Overall, in the Bangor-Brewer area, only 5.6 percent of the population worked at industrial jobs, compared to 21.8 percent in Lewiston-Auburn and 24.2 percent in Biddeford. Furthermore, of the goods produced in Bangor, 36 percent were consumed in Bangor and 90 percent were sold within Maine, meaning Bangor goods were made for local consumption. Clearly, the days when Bangor was a national and international trade center were a distant memory.

Meanwhile, four hundred retail establishments operated in Bangor-Brewer with more than 30 percent of sales coming from out-of-town customers.

All this shifting meant that in the new downtown Bangor, shopping emerged as the new king. But its reign would be tested and abruptly interrupted on a dark day in 1929. On October 24, Black Thursday, the stock market crumbled and officially plunged the nation into its next transforming era — the Great Depression.

Chapter Nine

The Great Depression

R ev. Timothy H. Houlihan took to a Bangor pulpit on Sunday,
March 5, 1933, with a message for his Depression-weary congregation: Keep the faith ... in your bank.

Far from spiritual or philosophical guidance, this was street-level real-
ism. After all, there were reasons to panic. Like others across the nation
the previous day, Bangor residents found their banks shuttered. And
when Monday morning rolled around, all the doors would remain
locked. Millions of dollars were untouchable and, by and large, if you
didn't have money in your pocket, you probably weren't going to get any
from anywhere else.

The Maine banks were closed by state Bank Examiner Sanger N. Annis.
Annis followed the lead of other states that had moved to prevent the collapse of their banking systems. In the wake of state action, newly-inaugu-
rated President Franklin D. Roosevelt dramatically declared a national
"bank holiday," effectively shuttering banks for at least four days. Roosevelt
sought to shore up the nation's failing banking system and stem the financial panic sweeping the nation. Restoring confidence would not be easy. By
the time of the euphemistically-termed bank holiday, thousands of banks
had failed, costing depositors and investors millions of dollars. Fear of more
failures prompted a continued swarm of depositors to convert their deposits
into currency or gold, serving only to accelerate the downward spiral.

This was high drama for an America in her fourth, and perhaps worst,
year of the Great Depression, which exposed fundamental flaws in the
nation's seemingly strong 1920's economy and a weakness in banking laws.

The collapse wiped out billions of dollars of wealth. Millions of people became unemployed and hungry, schools closed for lack of money and towns went bankrupt.

The Great Depression lingered until the United States entered World War II roughly twelve years later. To varying degrees, economic and emotional trauma touched every town in America. Bangor was no exception.

America's Economic Disaster

In 1928, Herbert Hoover stood before Republican delegates to accept their nomination for president. He urged the nation to be optimistic: "We shall soon, with the help of God, be within sight of the day when poverty will be banished from the nation."[1] But, in little more than a year, poverty visited America as perhaps never before and never since.

Soup kitchens, breadlines and streets filled with homeless — a dramatic comedown for a nation seemingly so prosperous during the Roaring Twenties. The industrial revolution and mass production made affordable such products as consumer radios, automobiles and washing machines. Industrial era jobs gave many people the money to buy them. Installment credit made it easier for consumers to fulfill desires and worry about paying for it later. At the same time, the stock market soared to giddy heights, rising roughly 22 percent per year from 1923 to 1929. Middle-class people joined the wealthy to play a market they thought might rise forever. Buying on margin became popular, allowing investors to put down 10 percent and borrow 90 percent to buy stocks. Such a method works well when a market is rising, but when it falls, investors must pay back the borrowed money — money which they may not have. Low interest rates also fueled this roaring market, as did new companies that flooded the market with stock issues.

In the late 1920s, warnings about the dangers of a stock market "bubble" were brushed off by people heralding a new economy and a permanently high plateau of stock prices.

But ominously across the nation, agriculture struggled, as did railroads and certain other industries. Structural problems also existed. For one thing, commercial banks could use depositors' money to finance speculative ventures and underwrite investments. Big commercial banks were like financial department stores with no required separation of services or funds.

Furthermore, no insurance existed to protect deposits, meaning the life savings of each depositor was at the mercy of bankers and their investments.

The banking turmoil was felt most acutely in rural America, where banks failed at an alarming rate, eating away at confidence in the banking and financial system. During the 1920s an average of six hundred banks failed each year.

The increasingly volatile stock market finally began to crash and burn on October 24, 1929, "Black Thursday," leaving investors shaken. After two days of modest rallies on Friday and Monday, a follow-up wave of panic selling on "Black Tuesday" simply crushed the market. By mid-November the market was down some 40 percent and falling. From the pre-crash peak in September 1929 to the trough in July 1932, stock prices fell more than 80 percent. Many investors were wiped out. The Dow Jones Industrial Average would not return to its pre-crash high until 1954 — nearly 25 years later.

Although frightening and dramatic, Black Thursday was just the opening salvo to a grinding depression that caused an upheaval in the nation's banking system and acute distress for people across America for twelve years. Many factors conspired against a quick recovery. The Federal Reserve exacerbated problems by shrinking the money supply just when the country needed it to expand, plunging consumer demand and accelerating the collapse of businesses. The well-meaning but ill-advised Smoot-Hawley Tariff Act in 1930 set high protective tariffs on American goods that caused a sharp decline in foreign trade, only intensifying problems.

At the Depression's worst, thirteen to seventeen million people, or a quarter of the American workforce, were unemployed while many others were underemployed.

Nothing to Fear

Bank failures quickened following the stock market crash. In 1930, 1,350 banks failed; in 1931, 2,293 banks failed (costing depositors nearly $400 million); and in 1932, 1,453 banks failed. It would only get worse.

During the winter of 1932 and 1933, the banking system teetered on the edge of full-scale collapse. In November 1932, Nevada closed its banks after suffering devastating runs. In December, a major bank in New York failed. In February 1933, Michigan ordered a bank moratorium to calm people and right its ship. Other states, including Indiana, Maryland and Ohio, took similar actions in the following days. But panic only seemed to spread with each action.

Increasingly, banks could not meet the escalating demand for currency or gold. By March 4, 1933, all twelve Federal Reserve Banks were closed and banks in thirty-seven states, including Maine, were either closed or operating under severe restrictions.

Faced with such a crisis, the new president ordered the nation's banks to remain closed until at least Thursday, March 9. By then Roosevelt hoped to figure out a way to restore confidence and reopen them — not an easy task. The record was dismal.

In 1933, more than four thousand banks failed; meaning that a total of more than nine thousand banks failed between 1930 and 1933. Overall, nearly fifteen thousand banks failed between 1921 and 1933. Furthermore, total assets in all the nation's banks plunged 37 percent from 1930 to 1933. Assets in all state banks fell 44 percent.

Beyond obvious legislative needs, Roosevelt also recognized America's emotional trauma. In his inaugural address just days before the bank holiday, Roosevelt sought to both soothe the nation's fears and mentally prepare it for the struggle ahead.

He described the nation's economic situation by saying, "the means of exchange are frozen in the currents of trade; the withered leaves of industrial enterprise lie on every side; farmers find no markets for their produce, the savings of many years in thousands of families are gone."

And he moved to rally the American people: "This great Nation will endure as it has endured, will revive and will prosper. So, first of all, let me assert my firm belief that the only thing we have to fear is fear itself — nameless, unreasoning, unjustified terror which paralyzes needed efforts to convert retreat into advance."

A specially convened Congress hastily approved an emergency banking act that gave Roosevelt sweeping control over banking transactions, reopening healthy banks and dealing with failed banks. Roosevelt placed banks into three categories: solvent institutions in little danger of failing, weakened or insolvent institutions that needed to reorganize, and insolvent institutions that would never reopen. Healthier banks finally began to reopen on March 13.

The emergency banking act was simply a temporary measure to handle the crisis. In the weeks ahead Roosevelt pushed through an unprecedented amount of banking legislation that defined the industry for decades. Quite simply, this legislation created the modern banking and financial system.

In June 1933, Roosevelt signed the Banking Act of 1933, more commonly known as the Glass-Steagall Act. Among other things, Glass-Steagall prohibited commercial banks from underwriting securities or insurance and barred investment banks from accepting deposits. Furthermore — and over bitter opposition from some bankers — it established the Federal Deposit Insurance Corporation (FDIC), which provided a federal guarantee of bank deposits. Until Glass-Steagall, no deposits were guaranteed, which is why depositors lost millions during the Depression and the decades before that. Insurance coverage began January 1, 1934, initially guaranteeing up to twenty-five hundred per depositor, a move that effectively reestablished trust in banks.

Glass-Steagall created the Federal Open Market Committee, which allowed the Federal Reserve to determine monetary policy through the purchase or sale of U.S. Treasury securities. Future legislation fine-tuned and strengthened the role of the Federal Reserve. Glass-Steagall also allowed the Federal Reserve to set maximum interest rates on savings and time deposits and outlawed payment of interest on demand deposits.

Additional Depression-era legislation established the Securities and Exchange Commission to monitor the stock market and moved America off the gold standard. With new laws and protections in place, especially the FDIC, bank failures in 1934 dropped to barely sixty. The Depression would grind on and on, but the banking crisis was over.

The Bank Holiday in Maine

Maine reacted with relative calm to the crisis. The Bangor Clearing House Association, which represented all state banks in Bangor and Brewer, issued a statement on March 4 saying that Bangor banks had no choice but to suspend operations. "It should be emphasized that this situation is not due to local conditions, but to the general situation prevailing throughout the entire United States. With all the Federal Reserve banks throughout the country, all banks in the reserve cities and all stock

exchanges closed, it would obviously be impossible for banks in any local-
ity to continue to function during the present unsettled state of mind of
the people until some plan is formulated for relief on a national scale."[2]

The *Bangor Daily Commercial* weighed in with a front page statement on
March 6: "There should be no misapprehension about the real cause for the
bank holiday, which is to endeavor by reasoned and wise legislation to put
an end to the hysteria that has caused the hoarding of funds by many people and has materially lessened the value of banks to their communities."

The two Bangor daily newspapers worked hard during the Depression
to provide the impression, whether accurate or not, that for the most
part in Bangor, it was business as usual.

While Roosevelt's declaration of a bank holiday officially affected only
national and Federal Reserve banks, state banking authorities supported
his decision and followed suit. In Maine, Annis, the banking commissioner, became a virtual dictator over all state banks. His authority was made
perfectly clear in emergency banking legislation passed in Maine and outlined by the Associated Press: "Unlimited power over banking institutions
in the state was given to Gov. Louis J. Brann and Bank Commissioner
Sanger N. Annis today by an emergency bill which went through both
Houses of the Legislature without debate and with very little delay."[3]

On Tuesday, March 7, Bangor banks were authorized to reopen
Wednesday to make change, thus allowing some businesses to operate.
(Many businesses in Bangor also extended credit to customers during the
crisis.) Other restrictions were slowly lifted as well. By the end of the
first week, banks could release tightly restricted amounts of money to
meet payrolls and relieve "actual distress." However, banks could not
give out more than ten dollars to any person.

Finally, on Wednesday, March 15, banks in Bangor reopened, with
some restrictions. Savings departments of trust companies and all savings
banks still limited weekly withdrawals to ten dollars. Banks were also
instructed to guard against excessive money withdrawals by individuals
and permitted to deny withdrawals to anyone suspected of hoarding.

The reopening of banks after eleven days apparently did not cause a
great rush by Bangorians to withdraw money. Deposits actually exceeded
withdrawals on that first day, a day which one official called "just a
mighty good banking day."

Broad Street, 1942. Many of these storefronts were eventually demolished by Bangor's urban renewal program in the 1960s.

The *Bangor Daily News* proclaimed that hope and enthusiasm again walked the streets. Despite a heavy snowfall on March 15, the newspaper said that people crowded into stores to purchase items while depositing more than one million dollars in local banks. "It was a colorful throng that filled the streets. Cloaked and muffled away from wind and snow they wended happily on their way from store to store while leaders of the Bangor Chamber of Commerce and the Bangor Retail Merchants Bureau paused to pay them tribute."[4]

Chamber of Commerce Secretary Wilfrid I. Hennessey was also upbeat. He praised the city's banks and its residents for their actions: "Tonight more than ever before, all residents of Bangor should be proud of our community. Bangor has every reason for pride, contentment and satisfaction in the fact that every bank in our city opened for business today. This is a great record, as is apparent from casting an eye over the conditions today in many other cities less fortunate than Bangor."[5]

Indeed, while no Bangor bank failed, many other state banks were less fortunate. On March 15, only fifty-six national banks, trust companies and savings banks were authorized to reopen, roughly one-half of the banks operating in Maine. About two-thirds, twenty-two of thirty-two, savings banks, were allowed to open.

The following week, many Maine banks remained closed — some forever. In Portland, three banks failed, including the powerful and aggressive Fidelity Trust Company of Portland controlled by media mogul Guy P. Gannett and Walter Wyman of Central Maine Power. Portland's Casco Mercantile Trust Company and First National Bank also failed.

They were not alone. After closing for the bank holiday, Houlton Trust Company, Mars Hill Trust Company, Van Buren Trust Company and York County Trust Company remained closed (Houlton Trust would eventually reopen). Six other banks closed for good in May and June.*

Nearly all failures caused a financial loss to depositors. Although a significant percentage of deposits in failed banks were recovered, even that took a long time. For example, in 1946, more than thirteen years later, some closed banks still struggled to pay back customers. Savings depositors in Fidelity Trust Company recovered about 94 percent of their deposits, but Casco Mercantile depositors lost 25 percent and York County Trust savings customers lost 47 percent. That was far better than demand deposit (checking account) customers at York, who lost 69 percent.

Of savings banks, only Phillips Savings Bank experienced any significant problems. It scaled its deposits by 50 percent in April 1933 to stay alive, but Phillips was soon purchased by Franklin County Savings Bank and depositors' money was restored.

The banking crisis certainly left its mark on Maine. In 1930, there were thirty-two savings banks, forty-seven trust companies and thirty-six loan and building associations. Ten years later, there were the same number of savings banks and thirty-six loan and building associations, but the number of trust companies had dropped to thirty-one, a 34 percent decline. Meanwhile, the number of trust company branches and agencies dropped from sixty-five to fifty-two. National banks in Maine also failed, but no mutual savings bank in Maine failed during the 1930s. And in fact, even between 1900 and 1930 only two Maine savings banks failed:

*The six banks to close were: Augusta Trust Company, Danforth Trust Company, Gardiner Trust Company, Maine Trust & Banking Company, State Trust Company, and Fort Kent Trust Company. Also, the International Trust Company of Calais failed in 1932, while in late 1933, five new trust companies were opened.

Saco Savings Bank, because it over-invested in summer hotel property in Poland Spring, and Belfast Savings Bank.

Trust companies also suffered a temporary loss in customer faith. Total assets in savings banks climbed from $127 million in 1930 to $148 million in 1940, while assets in trust companies fell from $214 million to $127 million over the same period, a drop of 41 percent. As for savings deposits alone, the amount in savings banks climbed 11 percent, while the savings deposits held by trust companies fell 40 percent.

There were several key differences between the Great Depression and earlier depressions that wiped out savings banks as well as commercial banks. For one, the state tightened restrictions on savings banks after the earlier problems, particularly in terms of the types of allowable investments. Commercial banks faced no such restrictions. Furthermore, savings banks no longer tried to compete by offering high interests. The 7 percent interest rates of the 1870s had given way to rates of 2 and 3 percent or even lower in the 1930s.

Despite not closing any banks in 1933, one Bangor bank suffered problems: Merrill Trust Company. Merrill was probably Bangor's most aggressive bank, having already acquired thirteen banks by 1933, including four national banks in Bangor. But four years into the Great Depression, it was deeply troubled and needed to recapitalize and reorganize to survive.

The city's leading businessmen recognized Merrill's importance to the economy and perhaps even recognized the psychological benefit to the city of not losing a bank. Throughout late winter and early spring, businessmen, including rival bankers, worked to save the bank by raising capital through new stock and government aid. It worked. By May, leaders announced that only two hundred thousand dollars more was needed to bring the total raised to three million dollars, which would, in turn, leverage two million dollars from the Reconstruction Finance Commission, a Depression-era federal aid and finance program created by Hoover.

In addition to raising new capital, the bank also reorganized; all bank executives resigned and a new board of directors was chosen. Amazingly, the new executive board included executives of two rival city banks, Frank Silliman III, vice president of Eastern Trust, and Henry J. Wheelwright, vice president of Merchants National Bank. In 1936,

Wheelwright also became a trustee of Bangor Savings Bank. The reorganized Merrill Trust, which was incorporated in November 1933, became the biggest trust company in Maine by the mid-1940s.

Depression in the Pine Tree State

By all accounts, Bangor did not suffer as severely during the Great Depression as many other cities across America, nor even other cities and towns in Maine, but it did suffer, regardless of legend.

"State Aid to Paupers" in Maine doubled between 1933 and 1936, while the state's new Emergency Aid budget quadrupled, rising from $99,476 to $384,534. Aid costs and budget woes forced the state to slash the pay of all its workers.

Bangor's charity allocation nearly tripled between 1925 and 1935, rising from $53,612 to $150,612. To help deal with the financial strains, the city cut the pay of its employees by 12.5 percent.

City Manager James G. Wallace described the city's situation in 1932: "It was a year when our community severely felt the blight of business depression. It was a year when unemployment problems in Bangor became most acute. It was a year when demands upon the City Charity department were overwhelming."[6] In Bangor in 1932, nearly 104,000 meals were served at the almshouse and $11,397 was spent on groceries alone.

In 1933, the number of meals served at the almshouse increased to more than 116,000 while the city delivered more than seventeen hundred loads of wood to the poor and more than fifty-one hundred grocery orders. Despite that demand, the following year, Bangor's charity department stated, "The calls in this department during the past year were heavier than ever before."[7]

In 1935, there was no end in sight. The charity department reported, "The burden of the Bangor Welfare Department for the calendar year 1935 has been outstanding in the extreme."[8] The city also began to complain about a shifting attitude, saying that younger people were beginning to look down on "honest work" and were simply asking for aid instead. The city blamed this attitude shift on young people being raised in a new culture of aid and public relief.

Certainly, the last thing cities and towns wanted was people seeking more aid — towns couldn't pay existing bills. Problems were caused in large part by plunging tax revenues. In the years before a state income tax (not implemented until 1969), property taxes provided most revenue to towns and the state. As the Depression wore on, not only did tax delinquencies rise, but valuations plunged.

Bangor's total valuation fell by more than 9 percent from 1929 to 1935. The collective value of personal estates in Bangor (not including real estate) fell 27 percent from 1930 to 1940.

While the drop in valuations and tax revenues forced cuts and other hardships ("budgets pared to the bone," the city proclaimed), the decline in Bangor was less drastic than in some other Maine towns.

The total valuation of Penobscot County towns dropped nearly 14 percent during the Depression, while nearby Old Town at one point saw its valuation drop 22 percent. The coastal town of Eastport saw its valuation plunge 52 percent while Portland's valuation fell 35 percent.

Lack of money forced some towns to close public schools. And in some towns where schools remained opened, teachers' pay was as much as six months behind. Everywhere, town budgets were slashed. Some towns accepted food in lieu of taxes and then distributed the food to destitute residents.

Helping alleviate economic problems to some degree were various federal aid or New Deal programs that brought jobs, aid and low-cost loans through a variety of programs and agencies, such as the Civilian Conservation Corporation (CCC), the Works Progress Administration (WPA), the Farm Credit Administration (FCA) and the Emergency Municipal Finance Board. Hundreds of people in Bangor worked for federally-funded programs. City residents helped build sewers, repair roads, make clothes for the poor and improve parks.

Yet, despite its struggle, Maine remained staunchly independent and proud, never fully embracing Roosevelt's New Deal. Bred with the Yankee ideal of self-sufficiency, many saw accepting aid or going "on the town" as failure.

Journalist Lorena Hickok was sent around the nation by the Roosevelt Administration in 1933 to provide a picture of Depression-era life. She provided harrowing looks at parts of Maine and described the "typical Down East Yankees. Proud, reserved, independent. Shrewd, but honest. Endowed with all the good solid virtues on which this nation was founded.

Pretty much untouched by the moral and intellectual by-products of the American 'bigger and better' madness. Apt to be pretty intolerant of those who fail to live up to their standards. And, above all, thrifty."

She said federal aid was difficult to provide in most of Maine. "A 'Maine-ite' being the type of person he is, would almost starve rather than ask for help. In fact, his fellow citizens would expect it of him. It is considered a disgrace in Maine to be 'on the town.' At state headquarters in Augusta I was told that it was extremely difficult to get 'white collar' people for work relief projects in Maine because there are practically no 'white collar' people on relief. And the feeling in Augusta is that there must be thousands of this class in the state literally starving to death. But it is impossible to get at them. They won't ask for help, and it cannot very well be forced on them. And this attitude is quite general among the Yankee population."[9]

A similar attitude is exemplified by Arlene Proctor, a young woman who grew up in the mill town of North Vanceboro.

"Welfare was nonexistent," she told the *Central Maine Newspapers* in 1999. "The only thing that you could do was go to the town and become a 'Town Pauper.' This was a very disgraceful thing. One time the power company turned off our lights. My mother refused to go to town because people would know we needed help. So we used kerosene lanterns until we could afford to have the power turned back on.

"We really had to make our shoes last. We put cardboard in them when the soles wore out so we could make them last longer until we could afford a new pair. ... A lot of people would go barefoot during the warm weather to save on their shoes."[10]

As a result of Maine's reluctance to accept help, federal aid was distributed to only seven of sixteen counties in 1933, and most of it went to northern Aroostook County. Bangor's chief boast in 1932 was that it had not "had to ask for one dollar of federal aid for the families on its relief rolls." That didn't mean it wasn't needed, just that they didn't ask for it.

Given such attitudes, Maine received less aid than most states. Yet some places became so desperate that relief was accepted.

In Allagash, Hickok reported that 87 of 90 families were on relief. In Aroostook County, people needed help as potato prices collapsed. Potato prices in 1931 were one-third of the price in 1930 and for years farmers could not sell their harvest for even close to the cost of raising it.

In the mid-1930s, historian Richard Condon said, "Despite federal aid, people fell behind in mortgages, taxes, and store bills; more than 40 percent of the families in the town of Van Buren were fed and clothed by federal relief during the winters of 1936 and 1937."[11]

In addition, some twenty-seven Aroostook County towns were "practically bankrupt" and a federal field worker said that 19,206 individuals out of 43,484 people in those towns were on relief.[12]

In Bangor, aid figures alone do not fully illustrate the turmoil, given the reluctance to accept help and the difficulty (and sometimes reluctance) for towns to provide it. Furthermore, many people remember the Great Depression as a difficult time, but one filled with a pervasive spirit of neighborliness and person-to-person help. Such fundamental help does not show in statistics.

Non-city agencies also provided relief in Bangor. In 1938, the Bangor Welfare Society assisted 146 families, the local Red Cross assisted 799 service and ex-service men and their families, the local Salvation Army served sixteen hundred meals, provided fifty-four hundred nights of lodging to 2,189 homeless or transient men and helped 400 families with food and clothing.

At the city poorhouse, residents and other relief recipients raised food for meals and distribution to the poor. In 1941, even as recovery began, the city farm produced 2,326 pounds of pork, 97,481 pounds of milk and canned more than a thousand quarts of vegetables and fruit. The city also maintained a woodlot, largely worked by relief recipients, to distribute wood to the needy families.

One illustration of the demand for jobs came in August of 1933 when more than 1,500 people applied for fifty jobs at the new Sears, Roebuck & Co. store set to open in downtown Bangor. On a summer day, applicants not only jammed the store entrance but spilled into Harlow Street, waiting and hoping.

While the early 1930s were clearly the depths of the Great Depression, the nation suffered a massive relapse in 1937 after the market again collapsed.

As the Depression continued, Mainers reluctantly accepted more aid and federal intervention in social welfare and business, but still remained wary. Maine was one of five states to vote for Herbert Hoover in 1932,

Courtesy of Bangor Savings Bank
The teller line at 3 State Street in the 1940s. The men (from left to right) are: Edward Gibbons, Ray Sherman, Alvoid E. Cushman and Harold Nason.

one of only two states to vote against Roosevelt in 1936 and voted against him again in 1940, although this time by a slimmer margin.

Bangor Savings Bank Meets the Depression

Archly-conservative Bangor Savings Bank not only survived the economic depression, but it grew, a testament to both the bank's strategy and the restrictions placed on savings bank investments. During the first year of the depression, Bangor Savings Bank lost only 2.2 percent of its deposits. In the next sixteen years, the bank reported a decline in deposits only six times. The longest stretch of declines was from 1936 to 1938, but those declines were relatively slight. The largest loss in any single year was 4.3 percent in 1932, a decline that was much less severe than the disaster that struck the bank during the Depression of 1873 to 1878, and also less dramatic than the 8.7 percent drop during the Depression of 1893.

Most importantly for the people of Bangor, their deposits not only remained safe but collected interest throughout the period. Local depositors seeking safety moved their savings to Bangor Savings Bank and

198

Courtesy of Bangor Savings Bank

The staff at Bangor Savings Bank standing behind the teller line, July 1940. From left to right: Beryle Libby, unknown, Shirley Higgins, Alvoid Cushman, Edward Gibbons and Ray Sherman.

Penobscot Savings Bank during the period. Savings banks were always meant to be a haven for workingmen and women who could ill afford to lose a penny. In fact, the bank strictly enforced a cap on deposits, keeping it from accepting too much money. The bank realized it could not take all the funds people wanted to deposit, simply because it had no place to invest it. Deposits not earning interest were potentially devastating because the bank continued to pay dividends; thus all its money had to earn interest.

During the period from 1929 to 1945, the bank's total deposits increased 46.1 percent, to $11.56 million, while total assets increased 59.1 percent, to $13.99 million. The results were similar for most savings banks in Maine. Total industry assets rose 69 percent over the same period.

One reason was investment mix. Long-term Treasurer Walter Danforth and his protégé Harold L. Nason shifted the bank's assets dramatically during the Depression and World War II eras to ever more safe investments. State-approved investments were hard to find in the 1930s. Even so, Bangor Savings Bank remained more conservative than even its savings bank contemporaries.

In 1930, 11 percent of Bangor Savings Bank assets were invested in U.S. government bonds — a safe, but low-yielding, investment. The

Courtesy of Bangor Savings Bank

Staff of Bangor Savings Bank, 1940. Standing (left to right) are: Walter A. Danforth, Alvoid E. Cushman, Ray Sherman, Harold Nason and Edward Gibbons. Seated are (left to right) are: Shirley Higgins, Marsha Rideout, Helen Burton and Beryl Libby.

bank also made substantial investments in state, county and municipal bonds, railroad bonds and electric railway bonds. By 1936, the bank had invested 13 percent of its assets in U.S. Bonds, 30 percent in public bonds, 16 percent ($1.73 million) in cash on deposit, 13 percent in mortgage loans and 25 percent in public utilities.

The next four years represented a dramatic shift.

By 1940, U.S. bonds represented 51 percent or $5.98 million of Bangor Savings Bank's portfolio, with another 19 percent of its assets or $2.19 million in cash on deposit. By comparison, the savings bank industry as a whole had placed only 29 percent of its assets in U.S. bonds. Leading competitors such as Penobscot Savings Bank and Maine Savings Bank of Portland, the state's largest savings bank, had 27 percent and 29 percent, respectively, invested in U.S. bonds.

By June 1946, Bangor Savings Bank had increased its holdings in U.S. bonds to 71 percent or $12.76 million, while cash on deposit represented 15.7 percent, meaning 86.8 percent of the bank's assets were tied up in cash on deposit or U.S. bonds. The industry average was 78 percent. Such statistics indicate a move to ensure the safety of deposits. On the flip side, foreclosures were perhaps the most dramatic element in the bank's balance sheet, illustrating the problems faced by Bangor residents during the Depression.

By 1929, Bangor Savings Bank, which pledged to keep its money local, was increasing its mortgage loans, thus allowing people to buy homes. In 1932, the bank had $1.63 million invested in mortgages or roughly 16 percent of its assets. That year, two years into the Depression, its foreclosure account was a mere $17,817, representing at worst only a handful of houses. It is generally acknowledged that for various reasons the Great Depression hit Maine later than many places. Four years later, the bank's foreclosure account increased to $87,091 — a fivefold increase in four years.

By 1940, a decade into the Great Depression, the foreclosure account had swelled to $292,352, representing at least seventy-five houses and duplexes. Danforth and Nason were loath to sell these properties at great losses, if they could be sold at all during the 1930s. Their market value was significantly below book value. As a result, Danforth took the bank into what might be called the great "landlord era" and made the bank one of the largest landlords in Bangor. It rented and maintained apartments and houses throughout the city. And importantly for a struggling city, Bangor Savings Bank paid the property taxes and water bills and maintained the property.

The bank had a painter, plumber and other workers on staff or on call to handle the necessary work. For the do-it-yourselfers, the bank kept wallpaper, paint and other supplies behind the tellers. The tellers would simply pass what was needed over the counter when requested by customers.

For example, in May 1932, Bangor Savings Bank took possession of 365 Broadway, a house with a stone and brick foundation, a stove and one bath. Over the years, Bangor Savings Bank rented the house for eighteen dollars per month to an aviator and paid such costs as $4.60 per quarter for water, $1.52 for roof repairs and $54.22 for paint. The house was eventually sold for thirty-five hundred dollars; the terms included five hundred dollars down and a thirty-five dollars per month mortgage payment.

The story was the same all over town.

The bank took possession of 247 Forest Avenue in 1936. It rented the six-room house with hardwood floors, a hot air furnace and a brick foundation for twenty-five dollars per month before selling it in 1944 for thirty-two hundred dollars.

Despite holding some houses for years, not all appreciated in value.

At 141 Ohio Street, the bank began foreclosure in July 1940 on a mortgage originally dated 1924. The original valuation of the two family house was nine thousand dollars. In 1941, the bank valued the property at six thousand dollars, a 33 percent drop in seventeen years. It rented the house for twenty-five dollars per month, although expenses sometimes outweighed rental income. It sold the house in September 1945 for forty-five hundred dollars.

Rental income was helpful, but relatively small. In 1936, expenditures were $6,751.22 and revenues were $7,449. In 1940, net income was $9,126 and by 1945, rental income was $14,135.

In 1945, World War II ended, the economy was recovering and new loan programs made mortgages easier to obtain. The bank sold fifteen of its houses in 1944 and more in 1945. By 1946, the bank owned only $28,642 worth of houses, but had houses with a book value of $145,940 under contract. At one point, the bank had sold fifty-five houses for $195,455, an average sale price of $3,554. In short order, all houses were sold.

So, by the late 1940s, Bangor Savings Bank was nearly out of the rental business and back in the mortgage business.

World War II

The Japanese attacked Pearl Harbor Dec. 7, 1941, forcing the United States into World War II. The industrial effort required to fight the war finally lifted the nation fully from Depression.

Although unemployment had improved greatly by 1940, 10 to 15 percent of the Maine workforce remained unemployed. But by 1944, with the war effort in full swing, the Maine unemployment rate stood at a miniscule 0.6 percent. Only twenty-one hundred in Maine were considered unemployed that year, down from tens of thousands during the Depression. Most new jobs were directly tied to the war.

Bath Iron Works ramped up employment from about two thousand to more than twelve thousand people, including sixteen thousand

You Don't Fool Around With Red Tape!

... when you arrange a Home Loan at The Bangor Savings Bank. The entire process is streamlined to your particular needs. Your monthly payment (scaled to your income) reduces interest and principal together—and covers taxes. Of course you have prepayment without penalty, too.

Come in and talk it over.

BANGOR SAVINGS BANK

A Mutual Savings Bank
Savings - Mortgage Loans - Safe Deposit - Travelers Cheques

A SAVER CAN AFFORD TO DREAM

Back your plans with a savings program and you'll get the new car, handsome electric range or fur coat you want. As little as $1 opens your Savings Account here. Worthwhile dividends help pull up your total.

Serving local savers since 1852

BANGOR SAVINGS BANK

A Mutual Savings Bank
Savings - Mortgage Loans - Safe Deposit - Travelers Cheques

Courtesy of Bangor Savings Bank
Typical Bangor Savings Bank newspaper advertisements during the 1940s.

women, to build destroyers. New shipyards in South Portland employed upwards of thirty thousand people building "Liberty" ships and thousands more built submarines at Portsmouth Naval Shipyard in Kittery. At mills and factories throughout Maine, people cranked out shoes and uniforms and other goods for the war effort.

Some of those mills were in Bangor. But more importantly for the city, thousands worked to develop and maintain what became known as Dow Air Force Base, providing a critical boost to the local economy in the 1940s.

On the home front, people in Bangor dealt with food and gasoline rations and planted victory gardens to feed themselves. They held scrap drives and bond drives. German prisoners of war were even held in such places as Houlton and some worked for Great Northern Paper Company while others worked in the potato fields.

During the previous five years, the people of America had overcome the greatest economic depression in the nation's history and led the Allied forces to defeat Nazism and Fascism. Both Germany and Japan surrendered in 1945.

Courtesy of Bangor Savings Bank

Margaret B. Libby (left) and Frankie Lee Slade count money deposited by pupils from area schools as part of the Bangor Savings Bank School Savings program that started in the 1920s and taught children the value of thrift and the benefits of regular savings.

It was a costly victory. More than eight thousand men and women from Maine served during the war and more than sixteen hundred died. More than 110 Bangor men were killed. In Maine, as the war wound down, more than 580 Maine men were killed from January to April, compared to a total of 797 from 1942 to 1944. People were anxious for victory and peace.

Finally on a quiet August evening, workers at the *Bangor Daily News* scrawled a note in blue crayon on a white placard and placed it in the window. It said: "War Ends."

President Truman at 7 P.M. announced the Japanese had accepted terms of surrender.

Thousands of people surged into downtown Bangor. Church bells rang, whistles blew, fire alarms sounded. And thousands of cars, two and three abreast, circled throughout Bangor blasting their horns.

Fireworks, confetti, beer bottles, and flags were everywhere, while the high school band descended on downtown Bangor in joyous pandemonium. Businesses closed for two days.

"Bangor, always a city noted for restraint, let down its hair last night in one of the wildest demonstrations in its history. The sky was the limit and the ceiling was unlimited."[13]

The scene from Exchange Street to the Brewer bridge was "a series of happy, delirious, disjointed scenes of ecstatic happiness as the war-worn emotions of steamy-hot people burst forth after almost four years of worry and sorrow."[14]

And in short order the nation embarked on peacetime prosperity.

In Bangor, not only did the Depression and war end in the 1940s, but many other things changed from 1929 to 1945.

After nearly one hundred years, the city eliminated the mayor-council form of government and adopted a council-manager style in 1932. The final trip of the *Boston* in 1935 ended the era of steamship travel to

Courtesy of Bangor Daily News

The last steam train to serve Bangor arrives at Union Station in 1954. Following this run of locomotive No. 47, diesel replaced steam.

Bangor, while a fire destroyed *Bon Ton III*, ending the longstanding ferry service to Brewer.

City businesses continued to cut ice from the Kenduskeag to sell, while Dollar Days returned to downtown Bangor stores after a hiatus.

Meanwhile, a new pipeline reduced the number of tankers that came to Bangor. The waterfront more and more resembled a ghost town. Across town, Pan American Airways started service to what was then Godfrey Field in 1931 and air transportation became increasingly important.

After the war, the federal government announced it would keep Bangor's Dow Air Force Base open, a crucial move in continuing the city's post-war economic revival.

So with the Depression a memory, the war over and the wind once again at its back, Bangor headed into the next era of prosperity. The economic pop was evident at Bangor Savings Bank in 1946 when deposits jumped more than 31.5 percent, a percentage gain not seen since 1881.

Straight ahead were the glory days of the 1950s.

Chapter Ten

The Winds of Change

When Malcolm Jones went to work at 3 State Street in 1954 as a teller, both the venerable 102-year-old Bangor Savings Bank and downtown Bangor remained largely unchanged since being rebuilt following the 1911 fire. In many ways they were unchanged since the nineteenth century.

Downtown Bangor, once the lumber capital of the world and now the premier service and retail center of Northern and Eastern Maine, remained the heart and soul of the city. Its streets were jammed with cars. People crowded onto sidewalks to take care of banking, meet with lawyers, eat lunch or shop at Freese's, W.T. Grant, Sears, Standard Shoe and the many other stores.

Likewise, Bangor Savings Bank had certainly grown steadily in deposits, but it still operated from the same single location as it did in the late 1800s and it remained very much a mutual savings bank in character — archly conservative and basic. Savings banks still could not offer such products as checking accounts. Bank assets were dominated by low yielding U.S. government securities and the bank heavily promoted such services as safe deposit box rentals. Mal Jones, future bank president, increased the number of bank employees to just fourteen when he was hired.

Yet, the bank had begun to recognize that with the growing prosperity of America, people no longer squirreled away money solely for old age or emergencies. It promoted the idea of saving money for vacations or luxury items. "Once people saved principally for their old age, but today they save for just about everything," said Treasurer Harold L. Nason in 1952. He cited education, houses, automobiles and getting married as examples.[1]

In that vein, the bank opened its first Christmas Club accounts in the 1950s, allowing people to save money specifically to shop for Christmas gifts. The bank continued its school savings program, designed to promote thrift and, hopefully, gain new customers as pupils grew into adults. Nason said the school program imparted a saving mentality to students and pupils: "Thrift makes for better citizens and a better community," he said.[2]

Bank operations remained fairly basic. Jones and a co-worker periodically descended into the vault, took out boxes of government bonds and clipped off coupons for redemption. Employees still calculated account interest and mortgage interest by hand and kept ledger cards for each customer in giant cabinets behind the teller stations.

True to its origins, Bangor Savings Bank remained a safe haven for the city's working class men and women and its poorer residents. Many customers who probably could not open accounts elsewhere opened them at Bangor Savings Bank. Some of these retired woodsmen, old-time dock workers and other customers could neither read nor write. Some didn't have homes. They maintained their accounts and signed papers by simply marking their X in place of a signature. Jones and fellow teller Jimmy Shannon took turns serving as witnesses to verify the X-marked transactions that the other accepted at his window. Shannon knew most customers, so when someone came to deposit a social security check, Shannon gave Jones a nod if an X would suffice. The bank also maintained a fingerprint file for identification.

Jones took pride in these accounts, and the customers viewed the bank, in large part because of Harold Nason, as profoundly trustworthy. "Never did I lose a nickel doing business with any of those people," Jones said of the transient and sometimes mysterious old woodsmen who used the bank and sometimes lived in the seedy hotels around Exchange or Hancock Streets.

Not that it was always easy to service their accounts. After noticing a mistake on one account, Jones took his 1952 convertible and headed down to the hotels or bars where some of the men lived off and on because he knew the man was heading back into the woods the next day. He also knew he would meet some pretty rough characters.

"If they didn't know you or if they didn't want to see you, you couldn't find them," Jones said. "People covered for them. One time I was at a hotel and no one seemed to know this man I was looking for, and then finally I heard a voice from the shadows. 'Jones, what are you doing here?'"

He found the man, but he also learned a lesson: "I knew better than to park my flashy '52 convertible out front or go in with a necktie on."

The bank, already reigning as one of the city's oldest businesses, remained loyal to its customers and to its past.

For its 100th anniversary celebration in 1952, the bank held an open house from 5 P.M. to 9 P.M. to show off recent renovations. Among the bank trustees attending was Henry J. Wheelwright, grandson of founding trustee Joseph S. Wheelwright. The bank showed off the expanded lobby and the additional six hundred square feet of working space. To gain room, the bank reclaimed the buffer it had left on the east side of its property following the fire of 1911. The bank also dazzled visitors with its new mechanical posting machine.

While the 1950s were a time of reflection and general good times, the decade also marked the beginning of yet another transformation for both downtown Bangor and Bangor Savings Bank. By the mid-1970s both the bank and the city would be very different.

Harold L. Nason

Harold L. Nason reigned as a defining character at the bank for fifty-two years — more than twenty-seven of those years running the show — and an additional six years as a trustee.

Nason grew up in Kenduskeag and graduated from Bangor High School in 1919. He was hired as a bank messenger in 1923, when the bank staff totaled five people and assets were $7.3 million. Nason was promoted in 1934 at the depth of the Great Depression to assistant treasurer. When Walter A. Danforth died in July 1948, the bank promoted the forty-seven-year-old Nason to treasurer (then the equivalent of bank president).

Outside the bank, Nason followed the Bangor Savings Bank tradition of community involvement. He served as a Boy Scout leader, president of the Bangor Rotary Club, treasurer and director of the Bangor YMCA, trustee of Bangor Public Library, director of the Home for Aged Men

Harold L. Nason (1900–1991) joined Bangor Savings Bank in 1923, was named treas-urer in 1948 and named president in 1961. He retired as president in 1975 but remained on the board of trustees until 1981.

and commissioner of the Bangor Housing Authority. He married Helen Crowell and they had two sons.

In 1976, the city dedicated Nason Park Manor, a fifty-unit apartment building for senior citizens, in his honor.

Within the banking industry Nason served as president of the Maine Savings Bank Association and as a director of the National Association of Mutual Savings Banks. Physically, Nason was athletic and quick. He was an excellent basketball player who played on a traveling semipro team in Maine. He was a registered Maine Guide and knew well the rivers of Northern Maine

As treasurer/president, Nason was unquestionably old school — strict, tightfisted with money and rather humorless, meaning he was not always the easiest man to work for. "Harold Nason did not run a democracy at 3 State Street," said Malcolm Jones. One person long active in the industry remembered meeting Nason for the first time in the early 1970s and remained forever scared of him: "He was very intimidating."

It is said you didn't have conversations with Harold Nason — you listened. He sat out on the floor of the lobby where he could quickly scan the activities of his dozen or so employees during the 1950s and knew what they were doing — not knowing made him uneasy and the move to branches was not necessarily a comfortable one for him.

Nason operated a tight ship as he helped guide the bank out of the Depression and then ran it through the post-war growth of the 1950s, the changes of the 1960s and into the 1970s, by which time the whole concept of savings banks was changing radically.

His rules, combined with those of Assistant Treasurer Helen Burton, were legendary. Women could not wear pigtails nor could they drape sweaters over their shoulders or over the backs of chairs. They were to wear stockings. They were allowed no barrettes or other hair ornaments and skirt hems must always fall below the knees. Men, regardless of how hot it grew inside the non-air-conditioned bank, were required to wear suit coats and be clean-shaven. No one could place a pencil behind his ear — as Mal Jones found out when Nason charged toward his window to remind him he was not working at a grocery store.

Most of all, Nason was methodical and precise.

He arrived at the same time every day and wanted the blinds opened — all slats in the same direction — precisely at 9 A.M. In the same order and at nearly the same time every day, he came to work, sat down, polished his shoes, reviewed the cash balances and met with a trustee (for several years the trustee was Charles V. Lord). He talked with his wife precisely at noon and left for lunch, returned to the office precisely at 1:30 and read the Wall Street Journal precisely at 3 P.M. when the bank closed.

"You could set your watch by his routine every day," said Alice J. McInnis, the bank's executive vice president in 2002, who began her career at the bank in 1961.

No letter left the office without his signature and no one else held any significant power: "No one did anything that required a decision except him," Jones said. A man of few words, dismissal by Nason from a meeting was simply the turning of his chair. He was very straightforward: he either liked you or he didn't and you knew it. Yet, if not warm enough to be beloved by most staff, he was well respected. Alice McInnis said, "I probably got a better education from him than from anyone else in my life.

"In some ways, some people might have been pleased to see him go," she said. "But he really made an impression on me." Alice shed a tear when the man who hired her and impressed upon her the importance of meticulous attention to detail retired as president in 1975, after fifty-two years at the bank.

Beyond the walls of 3 State Street, Nason was viewed as a pillar of trust and honesty.

"Harold as a person was considered one of the finest gentlemen that ever was and a very astute and conservative banker," said G. Clifton Eames, former chair of the board of trustees. "He was very highly respected and a leading community citizen. He was also conservative in all ways: socially, politically and operationally."

Outside businessmen didn't always agree with him, but they respected him and he was "absolutely trustworthy and honest," Jones said. The bank grew slowly, but steadily, under his direction.

Nason served as treasurer for years under trustee Edgar M. Simpson, who joined the bank in 1930. Simpson[3] was elevated to president in 1936 and remained until 1953. He died a year later at the age of eighty-six. Simpson was followed by George F. Eaton[4] who served for about three years until his death. Insurance agent Donald S. Higgins[5] then served as president/chairman of the board from 1956 to 1971.

Among Nason's long time co-workers during his reign at 3 State Street was Helen Burton, the first female banking executive in Bangor and one of the first in Maine. Some considered Burton to be Nason's right-hand woman or even his enforcer. Nason sometimes sent her to address a situation, especially if it involved female employees. Yet, she

Television Comes to Maine

WABI-TV ushered in the television era when it became the first station not only in Bangor but also in Maine, going on the air January 31, 1953. Community Television Services, the station's parent company, had actually applied for a broadcasting permit two years earlier, but the Federal Communications Commission (FCC), buried by a flood of requests and struggling to manage the new medium, placed a two-year freeze on station construction. When the agency lifted the freeze in December 1952, WABI was one of the first to receive approval.

Despite winter weather, the station proceeded to build a 125-foot tower on top of Copeland Hill. Work began January 5 and was finished for the first local broadcast less than four weeks later. The first show aired was *Boston Blackie*, a detective drama about an ex-con turned private eye. The show, starring Kent Taylor and Lois Collier as his girlfriend, Mary, and Whitey the dog, was based on a radio program and popular movie series. WABI, a CBS affiliate, also aired such shows as *The Jack Benny Show*, *The Robert Montgomery Show*, *Foreign Intrigue*, *Biff Baker*, *USA*, *Playhouse 90*, *Your Hit Parade*. Then in March, the station broadcast the local boys' high school basketball tournament live, the first sporting event ever televised in Maine.

According to the *Bangor Daily News*, the original January 31 broadcast was a major event. Stores that previously saw sluggish sales of televisions were unable to keep up with demand after the announcement that a station was coming to Bangor. Local businesses took advantage of the excitement to push all their products. On the day of the premiere broadcast, more than a dozen advertisements, including three full-page ads, ran in the newspaper, all selling TVs. Meanwhile, other businesses like Cross Jewelers and the Bangor House Lounge tried to lure customers by proclaiming that they would have televisions airing the broadcast. And as a sign of the coming television age, P.E. Wards and Company of Dover-Foxcroft took advantage of the moment to advertise its stock of easy chairs, "for your TV viewing pleasure."
— Hoving

213

also served as a peacemaker and countered Nason's harder edge, saving Jones himself a couple of times from Nason's wrath.

Burton was born in the Aroostook County town of Linneus in 1897, but moved to Bangor at age four. She graduated from Bangor High School, then Gilman Business College before starting at Bangor Savings Bank as a secretary in 1923. She worked as stenographer and teller and also spent time in the loan department. In 1948, she was promoted to assistant treasurer. She remained the bank's top female executive for the next two decades. Like Nason, she was dedicated and seen as unquestionably trustworthy.

In Bangor, Burton became active in the Business and Professional Women's Club, the Woman's Choral Society and the Bangor Mandolin. She was a member of The Mother Church, First Church of Christ, Scientist in Boston and taught Sunday School at the Christian Science church in Bangor. She enjoyed sailing and traveling, and also spent years caring for her mother.

Both Nason and Burton started in 1923 and worked together for forty-six years until Burton retired in June 1969. "I hated to see her leave," Jones said.

After she retired, Harold Nason remained the lone executive from the bank's pre-Depression days.

Nason, like many Depression-era businessmen, came from a generation of men who were dedicated, took their work extremely seriously, and often identified themselves with their job or their company. For Nason, the bank was an extension of his person and retirement didn't come willingly or with any enthusiasm. As he prepared to leave, he gave his successor Malcolm Jones one overriding piece of advice and one sincere wish: "Now Mac, don't you let anyone take over this old bank."

After he retired, Nason sometimes walked down State Street, strolled past the bank and looked at the front window display. If it had been in place longer than he felt necessary, he might step inside the building, walk over to McInnis' desk and say, "Alice, I think it's time to change the display."

Mortgaging for the Future

One of the first important assignments Harold Nason gave Malcolm Jones in the 1950s was to find a way to improve the bank's liquidity. In other words: reduce bond holdings to generate cash for higher yielding investments. Nason initially wanted to recover any losses incurred by selling the bonds within three years.

Jones' task was a little easier because commercial banks had success-fully lobbied to have a federal tax imposed on savings banks. Some in the savings bank industry felt the tax would be disastrous, but Malcolm Jones claims it was the best thing that ever happened. With the new tax in place, the bank could sell its bonds at a loss and then write off that loss against taxes. This accounting method was not an option when banks didn't pay taxes.

Even before Jones started at Bangor Savings Bank, the bank worked to somewhat improve its bond position. By 1954, the bank had reduced its holdings in U.S. government securities to 55 percent of assets, down from 80 percent in 1946. That percentage was still considered too high, "an albatross around the bank's neck," according to Jones. When com-bined with cash, the two classes of assets in 1954 made up 64.4 percent of investments.

Driving asset changes were mortgage loans. Home ownership acceler-ated in the post-World War II era and then exploded in the 1950s with a flush economy and new loan programs. The existence of G.I. guaranteed loans, Veteran's Administration (VA) loans and Federal Housing Administration (FHA) insured loans allowed more working people to buy houses by loosening requirements to qualify for a mortgage. These pro-grams also reduced the risk to banks, thus making them more attractive. By selling its bonds, Bangor Savings Bank could generate more money to invest in mortgages, which provided a higher yield. In those days before truth-in-lending laws and other regulations, mortgage loans were not uni-form or standard from bank to bank. However, the government required standardized information for FHA and VA loans, which made them more uniform and, consequently, more saleable. In the 1960s, this development allowed the bank to dabble in the secondary mortgage market. The bank bought its first outside mortgages from Texas in the 1960s.

From 1946 to 1951, Bangor Savings Bank increased its mortgage loans from 5.1 percent to 15.6 percent of holdings and then to 44.2 percent by 1960. First mortgage loans grew from $17.4 million in 1960 to $38.2 million by 1965. In that year, mortgage loans represented 67 percent of bank investments, while cash plunged to 1.7 percent and U.S. securities to 12.9 percent, down from a combined 77.8 percent of assets in 1950.

Further illustrating the investment shift was the bank's income. In 1960, 40.7 percent of operating income came from bond interest and 54.4 percent from loans. In 1965, 75.9 percent of operating income came from interest on loans and only 20.5 percent was derived from bonds. In 1970, interest from loans represented 78.6 percent of operating income and bonds made up 17.2 percent.

Bangor Savings Bank was in the housing business — with good reason.

Statewide home ownership rose from 44 percent in 1940 to 62 percent in 1960 and then bumped up slightly to 63 percent in 1970, despite the state's economic woes in the 1960s.[6]

In the 1950s, the percentage of owner-occupied houses in Penobscot County was greater than the state average and the county also led the state in new housing units built.

In Bangor, 967 houses were built in the 1940s, and then construction of new homes jumped 50 percent in the 1950s to 1,452. The number of new houses built dropped to 1,008 in the 1960s, but that still represented healthy growth in new construction considering that it was achieved despite a large drop in population as Dow Air Force Base was shut down.

The bank's average account balance, which had slipped below the state average following the collapse of the lumber industry and the Great Fire of 1911, was rebounding as well. In 1957, the average account balance in Bangor Savings Bank was nearly 30 percent higher than the state average, $1,332 to $1,026, respectively.

Of course, the building and buying meant people needed mortgages. As in the past, most savings banks shifted their operations to reflect changes in society, developing a broader relationship with customers and adopting a more service-oriented focus. The need for retirement savings and emergency cash remained but they were not needed so desperately as in the days before pensions, social security, unemployment and other retirement and safety net vehicles. Greater personal incomes meant more disposable income to spend on wants as well as needs. Increased installment loans and credit cards enabled a new level of spending and people began splurging more on luxury and leisure items.

More than ever, America was a consumer nation.

Retail Mecca

Bangor in the 1950s was the region's retail mecca. Downtown streets were lined with stores such as Sears, F.W. Woolworth, W.T. Grant, Sleeper's and Standard Shoe. You could buy sporting goods at Dakin's or automotive parts at N.H. Bragg & Sons, a fixture downtown since the mid-nineteenth century. You ate lunch at the Newberry's or Woolworth's lunch counter.

The Saturday Evening Post visited the Queen City in 1951 and observed, "Bangor also supplies her outlying neighbors with banks, electricity and the very necessary somewhere-to-go. In that sense, she is the bastion of urban civilization on which this whole region does spiritually depend, the Paris of the north, where the arts have flowered and been preserved."[7]

The *Post* went on to say, "Contemporary Bangor is a rare and haunting city, drenched, at least during its balmy summers, with a mellow vintage beauty and supported by a stiff, stiff spine."

Courtesy of Bangor Daily News
The 1950s were the golden age of retail in downtown Bangor, especially during the Christmas season.

Some of the city's vintage beauty could be found at such places as the old Bangor House whose stuffed lobster au gratin and fish cakes, "apparently are composed of one part mashed potatoes, one part shredded codfish, and one part highly edible star dust."[8]

The brightest star in the downtown retail galaxy — as it had been for more than a half century — was Freese's, a sprawling 145,000-square-foot, multi-story department store. In the mid-1950s, it owned the city's only escalator, operated a popular lunch counter and employed upwards of six hundred people during the Christmas season, when Santa Claus annually enchanted the city's children. It ran a wired-gated elevator and the elevator operator shouted out floor numbers.

The store had powered through the past half-century after opening in a nineteen-by-sixty foot storefront in 1892. It expanded in 1929 on the eve of the Depression and then expanded again in both 1936 and 1939. Some said its acquisition of an adjacent building in 1919 set the stage for the retail dominance of Main Street.

Bangor Daily News editor Richard Shaw in 1995 reflected on Freese's, "In a city that thrives on memories, Freese's department store is perhaps the richest of them all; not a place, but an indelible presence of mind."[9]

"Going to downtown was a big event, it was just so exciting," said Regina Jones, who went shopping with her mother as a girl in the 1950s. "We didn't have the money to go all the time. When we did, my mother and I would call the taxi to take us downtown. We would get dropped off at Grant's to buy school clothes, we would get lunch at Woolworth's, a grilled cheese sandwich, and then go to Freese's."

She remembers Frawley's drug store with its soda fountain, Woolworth's with its candy-counter and Newberry's with its popcorn machine and fresh popcorn. And at Christmas time, she said, the cars rolled through Main Street bumper-to-bumper to look for parking spaces and gawk at the "incredible" light displays.

But even at its seeming height, events were unfolding that offered a foreshadowing of the looming decline of downtown retail. In 1957, Bangor lost local control of its lead department store when Freese's was sold to Gorin's of Boston, making Freese's part of a chain. Dow Air Force Base would shutdown, helping drive down the city's population from 38,912 in 1960 to 33,168 in 1970, the city's first decade-long decline since the 1870s.

Courtesy of Bangor Daily News

Freese's department store was the pride of downtown Bangor. The self-described "Fifth Avenue in Maine" was at one time the largest department store north of Boston. It opened in the 1890s and closed in 1985.

Furthermore, the upper levels of most downtown buildings were vacant save for pigeons. On some streets, city kids busted windows out of these upper floors and absentee landlords didn't seem to care.

Downtown continued to fray about the edges as sections of Broad Street and Exchange Streets grew increasingly seedy and run-down. The deterioration only increased during the 1960s.

"I can remember driving into that area and my father saying, 'Roll the windows up,'" said Timothy J. Cropley, an assistant vice president at Bangor Savings Bank. "It was like a skid row with people sleeping it off on the sidewalks. I can remember feeling happy when the 'scary' place was flattened."

Milkmen refused to deliver to certain areas around Hancock Street because while they were inside, drunks and vagrants would smash their bottles.

The Penobscot River grew so polluted by 1954 that the city abandoned its forty-two-year-old tradition of sending the year's first salmon to the president of the United States. And by the '70s, the river reeked, as pollution poured into the river in Bangor and from factories, towns and mills upstream. The otherwise glowing *Saturday Evening Post* article about Bangor in the 1950s described the Kenduskeag Stream, which flows into the Penobscot River, as an open sewer running through the heart of the city.

At the same time, two cultural developments were underway in the late 1950s and 1960s that proved sweeping in impact: the highway and the shopping center.

The Highway and the Mall

There is no way to overstate the impact of malls and highways on America's downtowns. The acres of easy and free parking and convenient locations proved irresistible to a nation increasingly obsessed with cars and saving time. Also, as women joined the work force, the convenience and extended hours offered by shopping malls became more and more important. The growth of shopping centers was aided by the simultaneous development of Eisenhower's interstate highway systems that enabled more people to easily reach places from greater distances. The push toward the suburbs, also aided by improved transportation, was yet another factor in the decline of downtown retail.

Shopping centers and malls typically sprang up near exits off the new limited access highways, which, for planning purposes, often crossed over vacant land (although in Bangor numerous houses were also taken by eminent domain). Vacant land was considered buildable land.

Also at this same time, passenger rail service ended in Bangor in 1960, thus closing Union Station, the downtown rail palace where rail lines met and passengers converged on the city. The Joshua Lawrence Chamberlain toll bridge opened in 1959, creating easier auto access to Bangor from towns across the Penobscot.

And so the automobile stood as the unchallenged king of transportation. All this meant lots of people driving around. In Bangor in the 1950s, concerns intensified about traffic congestion as most roads routed cars through downtown. For several years the city discussed a bypass to direct traffic around downtown.

Finally, twelve years after discussions began, a section of Interstate 95 opened in 1960. It was not yet the full highway connecting Bangor to Portland and beyond, but a four-mile stretch from Hogan Road to Odlin Road. An additional two and one-half-mile long "industrial spur" was built from Odlin Road toward Main Street near the new Bangor Auditorium. The limited access highway featured several interchanges, including exits at Broadway, Hammond Street and Hogan Road, making it accessible to nearly every part of Bangor.

Dedicated the same day was a twenty-four-mile stretch of highway from Augusta to Fairfield. Eventually, the two highway systems would link and connect Bangor and Eastern Maine to the nation's highway system. Towns not linked by the highway or those without adequate exits typically suffered. Construction was also underway north to Orono.

Whether anyone realized it at the time or not, the siting of the highway was crucial to the future because it essentially dictated where most retail, commercial and industrial growth would occur.

As if on cue, the Bangor Shopping Center opened on Broadway in October of 1961 near a highway exit. The combination provided unprecedented ease of access for shoppers from all directions.

Developers touted the Bangor Shopping Center (later known as Broadway Shopping Center) as a business that would "revitalize, bolster and strengthen the economy of the city which is primarily commercial."[10]

Few developments altered shopping patterns and affected the nation's downtowns as much as shopping malls and shopping centers which exploded onto the retail scene in the 1960s. The Bangor Shopping Center (later the Broadway Shopping Center) featured such stores as Zayre and was the first in Bangor.

The Bangor Shopping Center was not the modern, enclosed "mall-as-village-center development" that exploded in the late 1970s and 1980s, but a strip mall, a collection of stores that stood side by side and featured a giant common parking lot. Each store had a separate outside entrance. The center was built on a forty-acre site and offered more than twelve hundred parking spaces. The first stores included W.T. Grant, S.S. Kresge Company, Columbia Market and Zayre. Soon fifteen stores operated at the center. Success surpassed original expectations — and spawned imitators.

"It was really incredible," said Regina Jones, who frequented the shopping center as a young woman after shopping downtown as a girl with her mother. "Zayre department store is the one I remember best. It was all on one floor and so different from Freese's. I remember racks and racks of clothes. It was a totally new concept."

222

Clearly, not everyone at the time recognized the ultimate impact of shopping centers and malls when the Bangor Shopping Center opened. Norbert X. Dowd, executive secretary of the Bangor Chamber of Commerce, believed the impact on downtown would not be serious. "Anyone coming to Bangor to go to the new shopping center also will come into town."[11]

He was wrong.

As all major stores either moved to mall locations or recognized the benefits of a mall location by opening a second or third store, they siphoned off business and foot traffic from downtown.

"The Bangor Shopping Center was considered the most revolutionary idea to hit the retail community in Bangor since the beginning of time," said Alan Schiro, the third generation of his family to run Standard Shoe, which opened mall locations and kept its downtown store for years.[12]

In 1962, newspapers and other businesses tried to gauge the impact of the shopping centers on downtowns. By the mid-1960s a shopping center boom was underway in Penobscot County. In Bangor over the next few years, the Union Mall (now the Airport Mall) and Westgate opened with major anchors that included Woolco Department Store, Freese's and King's.

Many downtown stores began to struggle and staggered further with each mall opening and store defection. In the 1970s, F.W. Woolworth closed its downtown store, Sears pulled out and W.T. Grant closed. Smaller specialty stores remained, but the major draws were leaving fast.

A *Bangor Daily News* article in 1967 said, "While Bangor's Urban Renewal Authority still is searching for a major downtown department store, the two suburban builders apparently are on their way to adding over one quarter-million-feet of retail shopping space to the city's business community."[13]

Two years later, a planning consultant told the city its downtown was "composed of obsolete, inefficient, multi-storied buildings, vacant on their upper floors and increasingly so on ground floors."[14] The consultant's report suggested that downtown merchants were essentially driving customers to shopping centers. Some claimed that despite the warnings, downtown didn't properly react as more malls opened.

In 1992, former city councilor and mayor Paul Zendzian told *Down East* magazine, "When the Bangor Mall opened in 1978, a lot of people downtown were caught with their economic pants down. They hadn't made any capital investments in twenty years and they had no semblance of modern advertising."[15]

Finally in 1985, Freese's, reduced to a mere forty-five employees compared to the three hundred to six hundred in the bustling 1950s, shuttered its downtown store. By this time, the devastation of Freese's closing was more symbolic than actual.

The initial shopping center era culminated in 1978 when the Bangor Mall opened in a former cow field off the Hogan Road exit on Stillwater Avenue, bringing an unprecedented collection of retailers to the city all under a common roof [see page 258]. "The Mall" had emerged as a retail village, not unlike old Main Street itself — only fully climate-controlled and with lots of parking.

While the opening of Interstate 95 and the original Bangor Shopping Center may not have immediately killed major downtown retail, it certainly heralded the era that would drive it under. In its wake would come numerous aborted plans for revival, a failed downtown mall, and finally, a cluster of specialty stores.

On the other hand, major retail flourished in its new location at the outskirts of town. Development in those areas has never ceased and growth continues unabated today with new retailers, motels, and restaurants. Thus, even though the downtown suffered and the city lost some locally-owned stores, the malls and large retailers gave Bangor an even greater retail prominence in both Eastern Maine and the Canadian Provinces.

Bank Expansion

As the shopping center era began, one of the local businesses that immediately recognized the changing demographics and logistics was Bangor Savings Bank. While downtown streets were often congested in the 1950s, so was the Bangor Savings Bank lobby at 3 State Street. By 1961, the bank had more than twenty-three thousand customers. It had already enlarged its State Street offices by acquiring the Kenduskeag Building at 13–19 State Street. It built a new committee room and added working space for machines and desks. It also built a new parking lot on York Street, off Exchange Street, and started Friday night hours for customer convenience.

But with the downtown bypass and the shopping mall poised to siphon off thousands of people every day, the bank, while remaining committed to downtown, decided it was only logical to reach out to its customers by opening its first branch. That branch, one of only seven savings bank branches in Maine, opened in November of 1961 at the Bangor Shopping Center. As part of its grand opening ceremonies, the bank hosted an open house that drew five hundred invited guests and more than a thousand others. The bank handed out key chain thermometers and money clips as souvenirs. The *Bangor Daily News* described the two thousand-square-foot branch interior as a "cheerful but subdued pastel" of soft blue, orange and yellow. Branch hours were from 10 A.M. to 4 P.M. Monday through Friday, with additional hours on Friday night, and on Saturday from 9 A.M. to noon.

Opening the branch was an important decision by the bank as it wisely followed successful commercial and social trends by going to the people rather than forcing the people to come to it. Indeed, this was a key first move by savings banks in their four-decade evolution from stuffy banking businesses into aggressive retail businesses.

The bank offered Mal Jones the job of first branch manager, but he chose to stay at 3 State Street as internal auditor. He felt he could get more involved and remain more visible at the home office. That too was a consequential decision.

"By staying at the bank," he said. "I could stick my nose in a lot more places."

The Wrecking Ball Cometh

While the mall and highway ushered in the decline of downtown Bangor's retail business, the most dramatic physical change to hit Bangor since the Great Fire was not an unexpected event but a carefully designed plan to systematically lay waste huge chunks of Bangor: urban renewal (see page 228).

The first hint of the coming destruction was the razing of Union Station in 1961, an act still lamented four decades later. Although not actually part of the 1960s-era urban renewal craze, the glorious old station was the first building to fall. By 1964, city residents, hoping to remake an aging city core into a thriving modern city, voted to implement a much-debated Urban Renewal plan that would use millions of dollars from the federal government. Bangor staged the largest urban renewal project in New England. By the time the wrecking ball stopped swinging in 1974, it had razed fifty-two acres of both good buildings and bad, some historic and some rat-infested. Some of the destruction was needed. Mal Jones can remember fighting off cat-sized rats near the Bangor Savings Bank with an old cant dog (a logging tool).

No thought was given to historic preservation. Gone was the Penobscot Exchange Hotel, the Bijou Theater, City Hall, the entire Flat Iron Block on Broad Street and the historic Morse's Mill complex on the Kenduskeag. Wholesale firms were relocated to a new industrial park. And in contrast to the rapid rebuilding after the Great Fire, not much of significance was built for years.

Planting the Seeds of Reform

Newspapers in 1960 proclaimed that a great bank merger trend was under way. Although it would pale in size and scope with the mergers of

Courtesy of Bangor Daily News

A portion of the downtown area affected by the demolition tied to urban renewal in the 1960s. This photograph taken in 1975 shows the lack of development nearly a decade after the program began.

226

the 1980s and 1990s, the reason why consolidation was needed was much the same — growth.

One merger prompting such a proclamation was that of Canal National of Portland and York National of Saco into a forty-five million dollar institution. York and Canal were two of the state's oldest commercial banks, having opened in 1803 and 1826, respectively. As they would for years to come, bankers trumpeted the economies of scale and the increased services gained by creating a larger, merged company. Widgery Thomas, whose family had founded Canal 133 years earlier, said the York-Canal merger would allow the bank to offer more than a hundred banking services and increase lending capacity sevenfold.

Bankers also discussed the need to grow larger to pay for increasingly costly technology, such as equipment to handle new magnetic checking systems and computers.

At the time, Depositors Trust of Augusta was the state's largest commercial bank with assets of $90 million. According to some, this was simply insufficient. Chester G. Abbott, president of First Portland National, claimed Maine needed a bank with at minimum of one hundred million dollars in resources to provide Maine businesses with necessary financial sources.

While grumbling took place about big banks getting bigger, the race was on and, as of 2002, has not slackened.

Certainly the need for and the cost of technology was a real issue. Even Bangor Savings Bank, never at the forefront of technological innovation, introduced a new electronic data processing system in 1964 to speed up account transactions. Called the National Cash 390 system, the equipment was designed so that tellers could reduce the number of customer cards that needed to be manually pulled during window transactions by 50 percent. Furthermore, the new equipment automatically posted interest, principal payment, escrow for taxes and insurance premiums for mortgages, eliminating the need to calculate such amounts by hand. Account information was stored on magnetic tape for easy retrieval. At the time, Bangor Savings Bank maintained more than twenty-five thousand savings accounts, meaning hundreds, if not thousands, of transactions needed to be calculated and updated each day and fully updated every six months.

Bangor's Urban Renewal

Fires and floods, economic highs and lows, wars and local politics have left their marks on the city of Bangor. But nothing has been as enduringly destructive as the self-inflicted wounds of urban renewal, originally trumpeted as critical to the survival of Bangor as a vital economic hub of Eastern and Northern Maine.

In the 1950s, Bangor and other cities in America hungered for the federal dollars and credit tied to urban renewal programs. A potential $6.5 million was slated for Bangor and some viewed the federal funds as an opportunity to raze residential "slums" and target commercial "eyesores" — depressed properties deemed detrimental to Bangor's image as a modern and progressive city.

Urban renewal advocates decried downtown traffic congestion, lack of parking and vacant, crumbling buildings.

To gather support, advocates unveiled a model of Bangor that envisioned a metropolis liberated from the seedy hotels, beer parlors and urban squalor that had steadily eroded the downtown's marketability and collective self-esteem. The new downtown would be resplendent with broad tree-lined promenades, parks and plazas, free-flowing traffic and a tasteful blend of old world charm and modern glitz.

The *Bangor Daily News,* a champion of urban renewal, described the nineteenth century buildings sitting in the crosshairs of demolition as "looking like museum pieces not a business district." The newspaper encouraged voters to "convert Bangor into the modern business and tourist center it should be."

This image of a new Bangor did little to sway opponents. Real estate agents, business leaders and others were concerned with the impact on businesses that would be forced to move to the outskirts of town. Some also feared that demolition would wipe out the character of downtown Bangor. Opponents also worried about the absence of assurances that the proposals would ever come to fruition.

In 1964, city voters narrowly approved an urban renewal plan that would ultimately encompass a 52-acre swath of commercial real estate, including downtown landmarks and historic buildings.

In the months after the referendum was passed, developers rushed to peddle their vision of a futuristic Bangor. Proposals included a 22-story skyscraper, a 16-story luxury apartment complex, an 11-story intown hotel and a combination restaurant-condominium facility. However, before such buildings could rise, others had to come down.

So, in October of 1966, the death knell chimed for old, threadbare Bangor as the first bricks tumbled before the wrecking ball. Over time, demolition moved to both sides of Exchange Street from York Street to Washington Street. Sections of Hancock, Oak and Washington Streets and expanses of Broad Street, including the historic Flat Iron Block, to the Joshua Chamberlain Bridge were also razed. Gone were landmarks familiar to Bangor's logging past as well as other historical sites such as the Penobscot Hotel, the Bijou Theatre and the Silver Dollar Saloon. Gone were Bangor's old city hall and its clock tower at Hammond and Columbia Streets. All were erased by a sixties-era promise and a vision that within only a few short months would start to tarnish.

As early as the summer of 1967, urban renewal sentiment began to shift. The *Bangor Daily News* published nostalgic photo essays of the "blighted" blocks, and in its articles and editorials it began to question the pace and direction of the plan. The business community began to accuse city leaders and committee members of "dragging their feet." Some began to view plans as unrealistic and extravagant. Developers, only recently seeking opportunities to remedy Bangor's blight, now focused on another malady —

Bangor's remoteness. All the while, new shopping centers and a burgeoning airport redirected the city's focus.

By the end of the sixties, the *Bangor Daily News* assumed a position of cynical condemnation. Sarcastic headlines and scathing commentary accompanied regular reports on setbacks and failures: "What's New In Urban Renewal? Same Story: Wait Till Next Year." Echoing the sentiments of a community weary of failed promises, the newspaper said, "Urban Renewal failed to produce a new Bangor but did a capable wrecking job on the old one."

By 1971, less than a decade after its approval, Bangor's plan for urban renewal was pretty much dismissed as outdated. What had been applauded as Bangor's super highway to modernity had yielded little more than a footpath. A single-level shopping plaza, a bank building, a restaurant, an addition to Bangor Savings Bank's main office were built. Stillwater Park was revitalized into a middle-class area. However, the plan is remembered mostly for its failures. Today, "urban renewal" elicits shrugged shoulders from longtime Bangor residents who now lament exchanging much of downtown's nineteenth-century charm for parking lots and inconsistent architecture.

— Zelz

Despite some commercial bank mergers in the 1960s, the number of mutual savings banks in Maine stood at thirty-two in 1970, a number unchanged since the Great Depression. However, savings banks were slowly opening branches. They increased from seven in 1961 to twenty-four in 1970 (including a new Bangor Savings Bank branch in Belfast in 1964), and some savings banks itched for expanded powers.

Indeed, as pressure built to grow, savings banks felt squeezed by the state's Depression-era banking laws. Savings banks recognized that lifestyles and needs were rapidly changing and they looked longingly at the diverse service and investment options available to commercial banks. For one thing, more diverse investment options would reduce the savings banks' reliance on mortgage loans and thus make them less susceptible should problems hit that market.

Secondly, community banks wanted to offer additional services such as checking accounts, credit cards and personal loans to their customers to match consumer lifestyles. Lack of these services made it more difficult to attract new customers. Mal Jones clearly saw a problem developing at Bangor Savings Bank during the decade: the majority of the bank's deposit assets were held by customers who were in their sixties or older. While the bank successfully brought in some younger customers through mortgages, the bank was essentially barred from providing the services that young people demanded, so commercial banks were eating away business by offering one-stop shopping. However, one key weapon for savings banks was their ability (by law) to offer a slightly higher interest rate on savings accounts than commercial banks.

Another major development introduced by commercial banks in the early 1970s was the creation of bank holding companies, based on a strategy to acquire banks and thus establish de facto statewide branching. By 1970, four commercial banks, including The Merrill Trust Company and Eastern Trust and Banking Company (changed in 1972 to Northeast Bank and Trust), through their holding companies, controlled 45 percent of all deposits held by trust companies in Maine. Bangor-based Merrill had grown to $105.5 million in assets, nearly $14 million more than deposits held by Bangor Savings Bank. At one point in the early 1970s, the parent of Eastern Trust, Northeast Bankshare Association, operated thirty-four Northeast Bank offices, including First

Bank of Lewiston-Auburn, Guilford Trust Company, Lincoln Trust Company, Millinocket Trust Company and Peoples National Bank in Farmington and Westbrook Trust Company.

Meanwhile, into the 1970s, so-called thrifts — mutual savings banks and savings and loans associations — were barred by law from offering personal checking accounts or credit cards to customers, nor could they offer checking accounts to businesses or make substantial business loans.

One person who believed it was time for change was Gov. Kenneth Curtis, a reform-minded governor who successfully pushed through the state's first income tax in 1969. Curtis rose to power in the aftermath of what might be called the Muskie revolution. Democrat Edmund Muskie was elected governor in 1954 and his surging popularity resurrected the moribund Democratic Party. Republicans had largely ruled the state since the party was formed in the 1850s. Following Muskie's ascent, the Democrats could again challenge the Republicans and made Maine a two-party state.* In 1972, Curtis demanded action and appointed a commission to study banking reform.

Some savings banks were impatient. Androscoggin County Savings Bank in Lewiston blatantly attempted to force the checking account issue by opening up twenty-one checking accounts. That prompted a lawsuit by the state banking commissioner and led to a Maine Supreme Court decision in November 1970 that upheld the ban. The court said that while savings banks and commercial banks did compete in the lending market to a certain degree, checking accounts were not incidental to the savings bank business. The court added that savings banks were not meant to play a role in the operation of the nation's commerce, but were facilities through which a depositor could practice thrift. Despite the industry's new realities, savings banks struggled to shed this outdated definition.

Still, some savings banks remained reluctant to change. In the summer of 1972, the president of the Savings Banks Association of Maine, Roger C. Lambert, also president of Portland Savings Bank, pushed his case for reform to his fellow bankers. He told the association that the thrift industry needed statewide branching rights. Savings banks, he said, had one branch for every $19.5 million in deposits while commercial banks

*Not only did Maine become a thriving two-party state, it also elected Independent James B. Longley as governor in 1972 and Independent Angus King in 1994.

Sketch Club Paints Bank Into a Corner

By Peter Taber
Of the NEWS Staff

Faced with the bare facts, Bangor Savings Bank has pushed the panic button and called in its loan.

The loan involves a meeting room provided as a community service by the bank. The dispossessed lendee is the Bangor Sketch Club, a group of local professional and amateur artists. The bare facts are just that.

Apparently, when the bank's officers made the so-called Community Room available to the club for evening sketch sessions, it never occurred to them that the local artists might be interested in perusing the naked human form.

Imagine the shock waves that coursed through the 121-year-old banking institution when one evening an inquisitive janitor looked in and spied a young lady au natural, and went on to spill the beans to his superiors.

"We never made any secret of it," one of the sketch club members related. "I mean, we were discreet. We kept the door closed. But there was nothing unseemly. Everyone in the club is serious."

Said another member: "These are not sexual exhibitions. Just like a musician with his finger exercises, artists need to keep up on their anatomy. To draw from the figure is really quite a treat. Models are hard to get in this area."

Among the two-dozen-odd active members are a Superior Court Justice, a housewife, an accountant, an advertising agency manager, a physician's wife, and an investment broker."

None of these eminently respectable citizens is eager to rock the boat. Since the club has now found a new meeting place, the members for the most part are content to chuckle at the bank's consternation and forget about it.

Bangor Savings Bank president Harold L. Nason seems to already have forgotten everything.

Contacted Tuesday and asked about the sketch club's dealings with the bank, he stated, "They just made other arrangements."

When asked why the club had been asked to leave, he said, "They just made other arrangements."

Pressed still further and asked if nude models on the premises might have had anything to do with the bank's decision, Nason retorted, "My answer is, they just made other arrangements. That's all I can say."

Reprinted from the
Bangor Daily News
April 11, 1973

had one branch for every $5.8 million in deposits. He urged savings banks to offer services more aggressively and implored them to expand by opening the type of branches currently allowed by law.

"I think we should spend less time worrying about having exclusive territories as savings banks and work on more combinations so more money goes into the savings banks and not so much into the commercial banks," he said.[16]

Clearly some in Maine banking were poised for change and welcomed increased competition. In exchange, they were ready to abandon the security and insular environment they had long enjoyed.

Shifting Power at Bangor Savings Bank

Despite many restrictions, savings banks offered convenience wherever they could and promoted an increasing variety of loan programs. Bangor Savings Bank in the early 1970s offered mobile home financing, commercial lending, camp ownership, car financing and boat, snowmobile and home improvement loans — a clear shift from its former "put money away for a rainy day" philosophy. Further recognizing new lifestyles, Bangor Savings Bank offered a drive-up window and operated branches in Bangor and Belfast.

Growing as an important source of income were so-called other loans — any loan that wasn't a traditional mortgage. Other loans increased from a mere $144,418 in 1960, to $887,686 in 1965, to $3.2 million by 1970. The banks received a boost in this area in the 1970s when the state effectively shut down finance, or small loan, companies in the state. Some of that business then went to the banks.

By 1975, Bangor Savings Bank held $127 million in deposits and $139 million in total assets, but also watched competitors get much bigger. After slow growth in the 1960s, the bank posted annual deposit increases of 14.4 percent, 16.2 percent and 12.1 percent, from 1971 to 1973, respectively. It was the first three-year run of double-digit gains since the years 1888 to 1890. While bank assets had more than tripled from 1960 and 1975, growth still trailed the industry as a whole. The bank also watched net income drop for a few years, until rebounding in the 1970s. After hitting $453,695 in 1966, profits fell to $119,005 by 1971. They climbed again to $686,840 by 1975.

As an illustration of its position, in 1975, total assets in Bangor Savings Bank represented 8.3 percent of all savings bank industry assets in Maine, a decrease from 8.7 percent in 1968. Furthermore, its downtown rival, Penobscot Savings Bank, grew at a much faster rate. During the 1960s, Penobscot Savings Bank more than tripled its assets.

Amidst the industry changes and proposed legislation, trustees began prepping for change as well. In 1971, they promoted Malcolm E. Jones to executive vice president, making him the heir apparent to the aging Harold L. Nason, now in his seventies. Jones was also named to the board of trustees, becoming not only its youngest member but the first new member in a decade. Nason may not have enjoyed the idea of grooming a successor, but these were important times. Jones appreciated the fact that he had four years to prepare to take over.

As Jones prepared for the presidency, he faced a potential new banking landscape with greater competition and more opportunities. Times were certainly different, but he was ready. And as was the case with Nason for twenty-seven years, there existed no question who would call the shots at Bangor Savings Bank. As one trustee said in retrospect, "There is no question that Mal Jones ran the ship."

Chapter Eleven

A Banking Revolution

Shortly after becoming president of Bangor Savings Bank in the late fall of 1975, Malcolm Jones was in his office at 3 State Street when the telephone rang. It was Arnold T. "Arn" Gellerson, head of Piscataquis Savings Bank.

For some time, Jones had been trying, gently, to convince the aging Gellerson to merge his Dover-Foxcroft based bank into Bangor Savings Bank. His efforts were in vain and he knew he was just going to have to wait it out. "A.T. Gellerson didn't do anything until he was darn good and ready," Jones said.

Still, Jones had drawn up an agreement and had it waiting just in case the day came when Gellerson was in the mood to merge. This was the day. Gellerson told him, "I think we ought to talk about getting together."

In short order, Jones found himself, draft agreement in hand, racing toward Dover to work out a deal with Gellerson and push Bangor Savings Bank into a new county.

"It was a logical move for us and there would have been any number of people hawking that bank if word got out that it was available," Jones said. "I didn't want that to happen."

Neither Gellerson's decision nor his timing were surprising. Like many other small bankers in Maine he realized that new regulations had dramatically changed the industry for the first time in his career and that competition was going to intensify. The safety of a small savings bank's relative isolation and government protection was gone and, as a result, the technology and additional staff now needed to compete were going to get costly.

"He was very troubled by the new banking laws," Jones said. "There were a lot more regulations, a lot more disclosure, a lot more hoops to jump through and that wasn't his style. It was not going to be fun anymore."

The official merger on September 1, 1976, marked the first merger between two mutual savings banks in decades, a fact Jones discovered as he searched for precedent when trying to craft the deal.

The merger also signaled the start of a new era for savings banks in Maine. After forty-three years of mostly unchanged operational methods, savings banks suddenly were forced to confront competition. Those banks that decided to engage in the battle had to get bigger, sharper and more sophisticated, while those who chose not to engage would eventually have to merge or wither. Within ten years of the 1975 banking reform, the number of savings banks in Maine dropped from thirty-two — the same number as in 1932 — to eighteen, a 44 percent decline. The days of the old joke that claimed a banker lived a 3-6-3 life — pay out interest to depositors at 3 percent, take money in as interest on loans at 6 percent and be out on the golf course by 3 P.M. — were drawing to a close.

Within seven months of the Piscataquis deal, Jones also took over the tiny Eastport Savings Bank. The single-office bank was run for nearly fifty years by Ernest B. Quigley, who started at the bank in 1918 and increased the number of employees to two. When he retired at age eighty-seven, the bank had grown to four employees, had about seven million dollars in assets and competed against a branch of the powerful Bangor-based Merrill Trust Company.

"We had no trouble with earnings," Quigley said at the time, "but people want more services than a small bank can offer — we had essentially one type of mortgage and one type of savings account."[1]

Jones certainly recognized the shifts taking place.

"I like to think that things small can be viable, but that comes up against economic realities," he said about two months after the 1977 merger occurred. "Eastport Savings Bank didn't have the electronics or the staff to offer a full range of modern services, and couldn't afford them either."[2]

With those two acquisitions, Bangor Savings Bank had expanded from four locations — two in Bangor and one each in Belfast and Ellsworth — to eight, with new branches in Eastport, Dover-Foxcroft,

Greenville and Millinocket. The purchases helped push total assets from $161.8 million in 1976 to $231.9 million in 1978.

During the next decade, Jones looked at other banks as well. He checked out a bank along the coast because he wanted to push on to Mount Desert Island and he looked at one in Kennebec County because he coveted the Augusta market. But the only deal he found to his liking was the one-office Houlton Savings Bank. With that merger in 1981, Bangor Savings Bank made its first and only foray into Aroostook County.

With the first two acquisitions, Bangor Savings Bank essentially defined its Eastern Maine territory and then settled back to fill it in and learn how to run a bigger, more diverse company in a more competitive world.

Revolution

The events setting the stage for the competition and consolidation revolution in Maine banking came in 1975. That spring, a deeply divided Maine senate approved, after heated lobbying by commercial banks and savings banks, sweeping changes in Maine banking law. The changes not only modernized the state's banking industry, but were considered the most progressive banking reform in the nation.

The agent for change was the Governor's Banking Study Advisory Committee appointed December 1, 1972, by Gov. Kenneth M. Curtis shortly before he left office.

In 1974, the twenty-six-member advisory committee issued a comprehensive report addressing reform. Its subjects ranged from bank competition to regulatory oversight to capital investments as the advisory committee moved to rewrite what it called "outmoded regulations [that] have created inequities among these various institutions and inhibited free-market competition in the provision of financial services."[3]

The recommendations included broader powers for thrifts, including the ability to offer personal checking accounts and credit; statewide branching for all banks; permission to convert from a savings bank to a commercial bank or from a mutual bank to a stock organization; broader powers for the state banking commissioner; the commencement of interstate banking, providing that the other state granted the same opportunity to Maine banks; and increased latitude for savings banks to participate in commercial and consumer loans.

Through its recommendations, the committee sought to increase competition by placing all banks essentially on the same playing field, although keeping certain distinctions in place. It felt that greater competition would force banks to improve and then, the committee hoped, consumers would benefit from the wider range of banking choices that would result. The committee knew that modern consumers wanted one-stop banking. They didn't want to go to one bank for a mortgage, another bank for a checking account and maybe another for a savings account.

"This greatly increased the lending and consumer opportunities and was a benefit to consumers by opening up the marketplace to give the banks more powers and the consumer more choices instead of just confining the thrifts to a small niche," said Christopher Pinkham, current president of the Maine Association of Community Banks.

Additionally, the committee sought to increase oversight of the increasingly powerful bank holding companies, originally created in the 1960s largely to skirt prohibitions on statewide branching. By 1974, six bank holding companies in Maine controlled twenty-four banks and more than 70 percent of commercial bank deposits. Eight years earlier, there was only one holding company in Maine, controlling four banks and only 5 percent of commercial bank deposits.

There were macro-economic motives as well. Giving mutual savings banks more power would, hopefully, unlock some of the capital reserves they had built up over years of conservative management and push some of that capital out into the Maine economy in the form of loans. Meanwhile, the groundbreaking interstate banking laws were an even bolder attempt to inject new capital into Maine — the lack of which had been a persistent worry since the state was founded in 1820. As a safeguard, the proposed interstate banking law included a reciprocity provision — requiring that a state had to allow Maine banks to do business there before a bank from that state could come into Maine.* The advisory committee sought to ensure that out-of-state banks did not open new

---

*The reciprocity law was repealed in 1984 because it was seen as too restrictive, igniting a three-year frenzy of major bank acquisitions and ushering in the age of the regional megabank. However, the state replaced reciprocity with regulations designed to make sure out-of-state banks did not drain capital, but increased it. The state tracked investment through what it called a Net New Funds report.

banks or acquire Maine banks and then suck capital out rather than put it into the Maine economy. Since no other state allowed interstate banking in 1974, the effects of this law change would not be realized until 1983 when the first out-of-state acquisition occurred.

Given the intent and focus of the proposed laws, the most restricted banks — mutual savings banks and savings and loan associations — stood to benefit the most. Savings banks had tried to chip away at restrictive Depression-era statutes for several years with only minor success, so this was their big chance. The commission not only lumped bank reform into one comprehensive package but, importantly, comprised both thrift and commercial bank executives as well as non-bankers, promising that the reform package would carry broad support.

"The savings banks and the leadership of the savings banks, including Mal Jones and Bob Masterton (president of Portland-based Maine Savings Bank), were convinced if the savings banks were going to thrive and grow as institutions they had to have more authority to compete. On the one side they had the commercial banks and on the other side they had the credit unions," said Michael Healy, a former partner with Portland-based Verrill & Dana. Healy, now of counsel with the firm, served as chief lobbyist in 1975 for the Savings Banks Association of Maine (now the Maine Association of Community Banks). "The financial industry was going to go through consolidation and the savings banks needed to have the full powers to compete, otherwise they would not grow and they would get gobbled up."

Indeed, savings banks found themselves in a sometimes precarious financial position. Their only real investment option was residential real estate mortgages and the only significant way to acquire funds was through traditional savings deposits. In financial terms, they bought money short (deposits) and lent it long (mortgages). Since savings banks were locked into mostly long-term mortgage loans, they could not effectively adjust to sharp spikes in short-term interest rates, like those that occurred in the early 1970s.

The reform package wasn't perfect, even in the minds of many savings banks leaders, but since its passage was seen as critical to survival, savings banks decided to present a unified front.

"In '75 we campaigned hard," said Jones, who at the time was the executive vice president of Bangor Savings Bank. "As much as I did not want Portland banks moving into Bangor, I had to swallow hard to get the whole thing passed."

In addition to Masterton and Jones, Ralph "Woody" Hodgkins of Mid Maine Savings Bank and Roger C. Lambert of Portland Savings Bank helped lead the charge.

"The savings banks decided to support the commission's bill and not oppose any part of it," Healy said. "They felt if they went out and opposed a portion of it and then the commercial banks opposed a portion of the bill, that might kill it."

Public hearings began by 1974 and prospects initially seemed bright. Then consensus started to unravel as commercial banks began to raise objections. At one point, some legislators sought to keep the bill from being reported out of committee, claiming it needed further study — a move designed to effectively kill it.

Among the commercial bankers speaking against the bill was John Blatchford, executive vice president of the Merchants National Bank of Bangor. Blatchford told the Business Legislation Committee in May of 1975 that commercial banks felt the basic issue was "equality. We are willing to compete, and compete hard, if we are all treated equally."[4]

The crux of his argument was that federal law regulated interest rates and allowed savings banks to offer a slightly higher rate than commercial banks. Savings banks and consumer advocates, who also supported the changes, pooh-poohed such arguments. Basically, they said, commercial banks didn't want savings banks to have checking accounts, because they didn't want the competition. And since big commercial banks could already operate branches statewide through holding companies, they might not be eager to give the same option to thrifts. Ultimately, the committee chose to report out two bills. One, the majority report, backed the savings bank version, and the second, the minority report, was essentially the same but reduced the rate of interest that savings banks could offer to customers.

At a hearing in 1975, Rep. James Tierney (D-Durham) gave William Bullock of Merrill Trust his take on the situation in simple terms: "I understand your operation is very profitable now; obviously you don't want to change [the system]."⁵ Crunch time came in late spring. While the house of representatives supported the bill, its fate in the senate was tentative at best.

"It was very heated," Healy said of the lobbying campaign. "It was brutal."

A key vote — perhaps the key vote — was that of Sen. Howard Trotzky, a first-term Bangor Republican, who was lobbied hard by both sides, especially by his hometown bankers, Jones and Bullock. Trotsky was known as a man who looked at all sides and made up his mind late in debates.

Trotzky was a young man originally from New York City who became a Republican because he admired some of Maine's environmental leaders who were members of the party. Environmental causes were actually his passion and he gained some fame in the 1970s as an activist who successfully worked to ban log drives on the Kennebec River. He said he reluctantly ran for senate in 1974 because, as a local party leader, he could not find anyone else to run. After a long campaign, he upset Bangor's Frank Murray to win election. He served as chairman of the natural resources committee, which he desired, but also unexpectedly found himself front and center in a full-scale banking battle he knew little about.

"I was under more pressure on that bill than any bill I ever saw," said Trotzky, now a high school physics teacher.

On the day of a session, the telephone started to ring in the trailer where he lived during the legislative sessions in Augusta. It seemed the commercial bank lobby had reached his friends in Bangor to apply pressure. "The morning the bill was going to be in the senate, the telephone started to ring and the calls started to come in from Jewish people in Bangor, people in my synagogue, friends, people who had supported me and gave me money. That was the hardest part. The toughest call was from Max Striar, a businessman and a man who ran a foundation that supported a lot of Jewish organizations in Bangor and had supported me and had never asked for anything. He called and asked me to please vote for the commercial bank side. That was so tough, I had to tell Max, the one time he asked for something, why I was going to vote for the savings bank version of the bill instead."

Trotzky had decided he didn't think it was right to force savings banks to cut the interest rates because "that was going to hurt the little old ladies and the other savers in Maine."

On the first reading, June 12, 1975, the savings bank version passed by a fourteen to thirteen vote. However, bills must be read three times before being engrossed to become law, so there remained a chance for change.

In advance of a subsequent vote, Mal Jones' job was to trail Trotzky around the Statehouse and keep him away from any private conversations with commercial bankers or lobbyists. "I always said if I were a senator that day I would have come down a rope through the window to avoid the crowd in the hallways," Jones said. "It was packed."

Severin Beliveau, a lawyer with Preti, Flaherty, Beliveau, Pachios & Haley and a commercial bank lobbyist at the time, said that commercial bankers clearly wanted nearly all of the reform, but did "bitterly" oppose the introduction of checking accounts for savings banks. Although Beliveau, while agreeing that the reform did change banking forever, is not sure it lived up to its goal of bringing new capital into Maine.

On this day, Trotzky headed up to the Capitol Building where Jones was waiting by the chamber doors, but Bullock saw Trotzky first and the two stepped into a private office for an animated discussion on the upcoming vote. After that meeting, Trotsky brushed past Jones for the day's events and another round in the senate.

"What the man went through that day was a living hell," Healy said.

On a final reading, with the chambers packed, there remained one last chance for an amendment and everyone expected one to come.

Jones tells the story this way: "The next time the senate assembled, the results of the previous vote were read. Joe Sewall was president of the senate and he called out, 'Is that the sense of the senate?' He knew there was supposed to be a motion made from the floor so he holds the gavel aloft waiting for the motion to come that will delay or possibly kill the bill. But the guy who is supposed to make the motion was across the hall in another room listening to a house debate on a different bill. Finally, Sewall had to let the gavel fall. 'So be it,' he said. And that was it. I didn't quite understand what happened, so I leaned over to Mike Healy and I said, 'What just happened?' He looked at the faces of all the commercial bankers in the room and he said, 'I'll tell you later. Let's get out of here.'"

Gov. James B. Longley signed the bill in June 1975.

"The commercial banks took it for granted that they had the power to knock us down," Jones said, "but when it passed the senate by that one vote, well, that really threw them into trauma. After that, we were no longer afraid to flex our muscles."

And, with that, Maine banks, while still having some key differences and restrictions, were more alike then ever and consumers had more choices than ever.

Banking Superintendent Ralph G. Gelder praised the laws he helped craft, but reiterated that he felt banks should maintain clear distinctions. For example, he didn't think savings banks should be allowed to offer business checking accounts and wanted that right reserved for commercial banks. "It is my feeling that thrift institutions should stick to their traditional role of providing personal banking services," Gelder said.[6]

The new banking laws took effect on October 1, 1975. Roughly one month later, Malcolm E. Jones officially became head of Bangor Savings Bank. And for the next twenty years there were many in Bangor who would say that Mal Jones *was* Bangor Savings Bank.

Malcolm E. "Mal" Jones

Mal Jones was born in the tiny town of Athens, Maine, north of Skowhegan, on a farm that had been in his family since 1835. His father, Wallace, worked long days as a local millwright, so as a youth Mal Jones worked with his two brothers, one younger and one older, to keep the family farm running. They raised cows, pigs, horses and other animals and also tended a garden with potatoes, dry beans and other vegetables to eat all winter. They usually raised so much food that their mother, Clarice, grew disturbed when she had to pay more than five dollars a week for groceries.

On the day in 1941 that Pearl Harbor was bombed, plunging the United States into World War II, Jones was in the woods with his father learning how to handle a twitch horse. As for so many, World War II soon became personal. Jones' older brother, Vaughn, safely flew 50 or so bombing missions over North Africa in a Mitchell B25 and survived being shot down in Italy only to die on American soil when his plane crashed in Texas during a training flight in 1945. On his last visit home, Vaughn told Malcolm that when he returned from the war, he planned to buy the town's little country store. The two brothers had worked at the store once owned by their grandfather. Jones had his first job there when he was nine because the store owner felt he should have a little spending money in his pocket.

"If [Vaughn] had been successful in buying the store," Jones said, "I probably never would have left town."

Instead, Jones graduated from Somerset Academy in a class of four in 1947 and then attended the University of Maine at the urging of his father who, upon the death of his own father, was forced to quit school at sixteen to work in the mills. Jones studied business administration and took all the accounting classes he could before graduating in 1952. One of his fraternity brothers was future Bangor Savings Bank trustee and Bangor businessman David Fox.

After college — and one week after marrying Barbara Porter, a schoolmate from Athens — Jones left for Korea where he served in a unit that provided logistical support for the Eighth Army. Returning in 1954, Jones needed a job. His wife worked at Merchants National Bank in Bangor. Jones' choice of jobs came down to two options: Merrill Trust Company or Bangor Savings Bank. He asked his wife's boss for advice and was told to go with Bangor Savings Bank.

"I guess he felt my personality was best suited for Bangor Savings Bank and he was probably right," Jones said.

In any event, he never looked for work again.

"When he got out of college he could have gone to a commercial bank and probably been hired, but he had the idea that savings banks were sleeping giants," said Fox. "[He thought] If savings banks could get some of the activities that commercial banks had, then they had outstanding growth potential and that turned out to be true."

Jones started as a teller and all-around worker, shoveling snow from sidewalks, collecting mail, raising the flag and picking up supplies when necessary. Working long hours, he rose through the ranks, becoming assistant auditor in 1961, assistant treasurer in 1963 and vice president in 1968.

"Even before he became president he was a workhorse," said Fox. "He was probably there most every night working and he devoted himself completely to the bank."

Jones, a numbers man through and through, came up the ranks on the accounting side of the business and his ethic and outlook gained the trust of his boss, Harold Nason, also a bottom-line numbers man.

Malcolm E. "Mal" Jones. A legend in Bangor banking and business circles, Jones joined the bank in 1954 and was named president in 1975. He retired as president in 1995, after 41 years at the bank.

By the early 1970s, the board of trustees was pressing Nason, who was reluctantly set to retire at seventy-five, for a succession plan. Jones emerged as heir apparent. With the "strong" backing of Nason, the trustees — Chairman Donald S. Higgins, Martyn A. Vickers, Donald J. Eames, Charles V. Lord, George F. Peabody and Nason — named Jones

245

an executive vice president and put him on the board of trustees. That was a bold new move. Up until then, the only executive to sit on the board was the president. While waiting to take control, Jones was active in bank legislation, including the all-important reforms of 1975, and in deciding the future direction of Bangor Savings Bank. Nason was loosening his once iron-tight grip on decision making.

"A lot of people felt [Nason] had handpicked Mal, not necessarily in his own image, but because he knew Mal was the kind of person that would be needed to run the bank of the future," said Pinkham of the community banks association.

Jones became president in November of 1975. Over the next six years, he engineered the bank's friendly takeovers of Piscataquis Savings Bank, Eastport Savings Bank and Houlton Savings Bank, and then he retrenched. It was his practice to never do anything without fully testing it first.

"Anything he did was well-thought out and conservative," said Alice McInnis, the bank's executive vice president "His philosophy was that you can't be all things to all people, but you should do the things you do very well."

Jones attributes many of those tactics to his military service. "I learned from the army that you should never run your supply lines out too far," he said.

He also had, perhaps, a fear of failure.

"He was very astute at thinking out all of the things that could happen and foreseeing that this particular deal had this risk way down the road," said Clifton Eames, the trustee. "He worried about things to the point that he called himself a fatalist at one point."

But, clearly in addition to conservatism, Jones' trademark at the bank was his hands-on involvement. He was a people's banker, a roll-up-the-shirt-sleeves, unpretentious executive. He kept an eye obsessively focused on the bottom line and a fist clenched on the purse strings. He flashed an occasional sign of temper, but was also gregarious, a born storyteller and inspired loyalty.

Jones came to take the successes, failures and criticisms of Bangor Savings Bank personally. It is said by some that if a person didn't pay back a loan to the bank, Jones not only saw it as a hit to his bank, but as a personal insult.

"If anyone lived his business, Mal Jones lived his business," said Arthur M. Johnson, a former member of the board of trustees and former president of the University of Maine.

With his conservative bent and a motto of "keep it simple," Jones doggedly dug in to his business. He crunched numbers like an adding machine and considered a person's character when making a loan. It was said he usually knew when someone walked through the door whether they were going to get a loan or not.

For years, he reviewed nearly all commercial loans, met personally with applicants and visited sites. He might call applicants from his home on nights and weekends if necessary.

"Bangor Savings Bank knew businesses in that part of the state that many other outside banks just didn't understand," said Pinkham. "They always played to their strengths. People sometimes criticized Mal for being too conservative, but Mal stuck to what he knew best. The joke always was that Mal would go into a coffee shop for coffee and while he was there work out a deal on the back of a napkin at the table. He always tried to be practical."

Even though, relative to the industry, Bangor Savings Bank may have appeared glacial in its movements at times, it remained standing as other local banks in Bangor were gobbled up and as some others struggled or failed during the late 1980s and early 1990s — a testament to Jones.

"He ran a very sound bank," said James F. Jaffray, a trustee in the 1970s and 1980s. "It was just as strong as could be with a balance sheet that was as clean as a whistle — minimal problem loans and strong reserves. The bank came out of the banking problems of the 1980s smelling like a rose."

Among those taking advantage of Bangor's soundness was Snow & Nealley, a longtime Bangor manufacturing company.

In the early 1990s, Snow & Nealley was poised to file for bankruptcy when Nealley family members decided to return and try to rescue it. However, this was not only a time of turmoil for Snow & Nealley but one of great tumult in banking and in the economy in general. At a time when the company was trying to recover from tremendous debt and other problems, credit and bank flexibility were increasingly difficult to find in Maine. Family member David Nealley, now an investment advisor in Bangor, turned to the city's only locally-owned bank for help.

"The only bank willing to still look at us was Bangor Savings Bank and Malcolm," said Nealley. "He helped us get the financing we needed to get out of the hole and give the company a fighting chance. I think part of it was his business acumen and his people sense. Here is a family business that was run into a hole and near filing bankruptcy, but the family is willing to come back in and try to save it. So I think he said, 'Wait a minute. If they are willing to step up to the plate there may be something there.'"

Still, Jones remained tough. "He would come in and roll the sleeves up, light up a cigarette and talk to you about stuff that you thought had nothing to do with what you were there for and then he comes up with that one 'Columbo' question that cuts right to the point," said Nealley. "And you had better know the answer."

Snow & Nealley was just one beneficiary of the bank's position. Jones said he can still drive through town in 2002 and take pride in the institutions and businesses the bank helped save or grow like Husson College, which was on the verge of foreclosure in 1983, and the downtown Opera House, John Bapst High School and parts of West Market Square.

Jones worked hard and that included taking on the dirty work when necessary. "To compensate for his getting into the nitty-gritty, he worked weekends and nights, he worked all the time," Eames said. "He was really a very nose-to-the-grindstone person. Every little detail he would personally take responsibility for."

One rainy afternoon, someone working across the street from the main bank office called to say that the roof of 15 State Street was collecting water. The roof at 15 State Street — adjacent to 3 State Street — was flat and it had a skylight. If the water got too deep, it would start leaking through the skylight into the building. The bank president knew the roof from years of raising the flag. So he gathered his raincoat and rubber boots and headed for the roof. Jones was prepared, too, for the pigeons.

"I took a hoe with me because I knew what the trouble was. Some pigeons had died up there and when the water built up a little they floated over and plugged the drain. So I waded over — it was pouring and the water was almost up to my knees — and I hoed out the dead pigeons until the water started to drain again."

Jones sometimes took care of problems like that himself because he was not only hands-on, but loath to spend money unless he had a darned

The Bangor Savings Bank executive team, 1986. They are (from lower left): Malcolm Jones, Sally Burgess, Edward Youngblood, Ewen Farnham and Alice McInnis.

good reason. He might employ patchwork tape repairs on bank carpets, keep wobbly partitions in offices, and even drive off to discount stores to find the best deals, if necessary. Such luxuries as fax machines came late to his branches.

The Flood of 1976

What began as a typically wintry Groundhog Day in Maine whose worst casualty seemed to be school cancellations ended with the high drama of a Hollywood film.

In late January 1976, a weather system originating in North Carolina crept its way up the eastern seaboard to pummel Maine with a combination of ice, snow and freezing rain. Eighty mile per hour winds drove sheets of rain and snow, and, when combined with existing ground conditions, portended a perilous consequence. Within a day, that consequence would have a name: the Flood of 1976.

Employees of Bangor Savings Bank, Merrill Trust, Merchants National and Eastern Trust, all located on the banks of the Kenduskeag Stream, fidgeted and paced nervously as the Kenduskeag, jammed with ice, inched higher. From the veritable catbird seat of the 3 State Street South Annex, Bangor Savings Bank trustees were uncomfortably distracted as melting snow and weather conditions injected a rarely seen vigor into the churning waters. By late morning, bank tellers intuitively secured their drawers and, as if on cue, joined retail clerks, shop owners and business executives in a scramble for the Kenduskeag Plaza parking lots in hopes of rescuing their vehicles from the frigid waters of a flash flood. Pedestrians, now spectators, stood agape watching from streets and overpasses as the flood quickly consumed acres. The stream overpowered canal walls and fences to create an inner-city lake, one stocked not with salmon or bass but with Fords and Buicks.

By eleven-thirty, the stream reached its high water mark, pouring up to fifteen feet of water into the plaza and stranding nearly two hundred cars. Many floated from their parking spots, bobbed along for a short time and then sank. The *Bangor Daily News* reported that within fifteen minutes the waters crested, but the hand rails along the canal set the stage for still more drama.

A Bangor Savings Bank teller was among those who stampeded to the plaza in an attempt to rescue her car. She reached the automobile amidst the frenzy, but, confined by the frozen and rising torrent, was soon its prisoner. Forced to chase a shrinking air pocket, she had all but surrendered when she was rescued by an onlooker who dove into the icy waters, swam to her car, hauled her from the sinking vehicle, and with her, scrambled onto the car roof to await an approaching rowboat.

To prevent further disaster, bridges to Brewer were closed and power was cut to much of downtown. Police and rescue teams restrained crowds of gawkers while the Civil Defense's emergency broadcast system crackled updates and advisories over transistor radios. The storm that had caused fires and floods in Bangor also collapsed buildings in Eastport and Rockland and hammered parts of New Brunswick with 120 mile per hour winds.

The concentration of city banks along the stream made them particularly vulnerable and all suffered flooded basements. Bangor Savings Bank and Merchants National Bank were abuzz with activity well into the night as their pumps clanked away what remained of the Flood of 1976. And while the following morning's editorial cartoon made light of the Groundhog Day flood with a caption that read, "That wasn't my shadow … that was my reflection," the February fourth editorial reminded businesses, especially banks, of their vulnerability; "But when the bankers who run the banks along the Kenduskeag turn down a loan because of the risk, they might be reminded that their own institutions are subject to the same risks."

— Zelz

Courtesy of Bangor Daily News

The Flood of 1976, looking at the parking lot of Bangor Savings Bank.

The frugality didn't just save money, Jones claimed, but served to preserve the bank's image. He told people that if customers saw nice offices or "Taj Mahal" branches they would wonder why they were not getting a higher interest rate instead.

Even in non-bank matters, Jones was frugal. During the Flood of 1976 [See page 250], his old Chevy station wagon floated away from the parking lot. When a tow truck operator came by, Jones gave him twenty dollars to take his car to a heated garage to keep it from freezing up, which might have caused greater damage. Since his car was so old, Jones only received a few hundred dollars as an insurance settlement. Still, Jones took the settlement, bought the necessary new parts himself and then found a local school that would do the repair work as part of a class. He got his car back on the road and still got to pocket a little extra money. It was a good deal all round.

Finally, in 1995 Jones, now in his mid-sixties and facing yet more shifts in a banking world that seemed to change with ever-increasing speed, reluctantly stepped aside. It wasn't easy, and unlike Nason, he did not choose to groom a successor.

After twenty years at the helm and forty-one years at the bank, Jones had engendered deep loyalty among many bank employees, especially those who had started at a time when banking was a different business and worked with him for years. During his tenure, the bank had grown from one office with 14 employees to thirteen offices with more than 260 employees. Assets had risen from $25.2 million in 1954 to $687.2 million in 1995.

"I've known Malcolm for 26 years, and I consider him to be one of the best savings bankers in the state," said William C. Bullock Jr. of Merrill Merchants Bank in 1995. "He brought the bank into the 20th century."[7]

When Jones started, Harold Nason could sit and watch every action of every employee from his desk. But at the edge of the twenty-first century, no longer was the bank a family affair but rather a complicated, sprawling business with dozens of products that required an increasing number of specialized skills and a need to delegate authority.

Jones left a bank on solid financial ground, fattened with capital and poised for expansion — a bank ready to fill a statewide banking void if such an opportunity arose and someone pulled the trigger.

Such statewide ambitions were not necessarily for Jones.

"I was a hillbilly and I knew it," he said in 1995. "But as I used to tell my daughters when I'd pick them up at school in an old station wagon, 'You don't have to keep up with the Joneses. You are the Joneses and to hell with the rest of them.'"[8]

At his retirement party in the Bangor Civic Center, the bank staff presented Jones with a new pickup truck and said good-bye. There were more than a few watery eyes in the house.

Certainly most recognized that Mal Jones' retirement signified more than simply the passing of the torch. It marked the end of an era.

Settling In

In the early 1980s, Bangor Savings Bank stood at twelve branches with bank assets of $318.8 million. In 1980, net income surpassed one million dollars, up from to $686,840 in 1975.

With banking reform opening up opportunity and competition, Bangor Savings Bank also moved to establish the infrastructure to accommodate its measured growth.

Courtesy of Bangor Daily News

Five-year-old Heath McCourt opens his first savings account at the Brewer branch of Bangor Savings Bank in 1982.

The bank established its first marketing and sales division in 1977. It opened a new branch in Orono, installed new computers and introduced The Source as a marketing slogan to boost awareness that the bank offered more than basic banking services and to reflect its growth beyond Bangor. The bank offered its first credit cards in 1979 and began a man-

Courtesy of Bangor Savings Bank
In the early 1980s, Bangor Savings Bank unveiled The Source as a marketing slogan and logo.

agement trainee program to strengthen middle management in the early 1980s. Some moves were also designed to position the bank as a retail operation, which was the new thinking in banking.

"We developed more of a concern for the consumer," said Fox, the former trustee. "Many banks for a good many years took the position that you came to them and whatever they decided was something you were expected to accept. But in the 1970s we became more concerned with the customer."

Also in the 1970s, the bank brought in some outside trustees — including Johnson and Jaffray — to help sharpen the bank's focus and broaden its outlook. Unlike other trustees, Johnson, onetime president of the University of Maine, and Jaffray, a former senior executive with New York-based Citicorp, were not longtime Bangor businessmen.

"We were quite pleased to have those distinguished gentlemen," said Fox. "They brought to the board an outlook that we had not had in the fairly close-knit group." The trustee lineup in 1980 was: Chairman Martyn A. Vickers,[9] Nason, Gellerson, Jones, Fox, Eames, Arnold L. Veague, Johnson and Jaffray.

Moves were also necessitated by other changes. Deregulation of banking phased out some restrictions such as Regulation Q, a federal law that capped interest rates. Meanwhile, the industry saw the rise of money market accounts and other investment instruments that served as competition for the savings dollar. One development was that Fidelity of Boston began to advertise in Maine in the early 80s, bringing a powerful non-bank competitor into the market and ushering in the age of the mutual fund.

Also, the banking industry began to experiment with and then rapidly employ automated teller machines to extend their reach to customers, although Bangor Savings Bank did not move aggressively into ATMs until the late 1990s. It installed its first ATM in Dover-Foxcroft in 1987 and its second in the mid-1990s. The bank preferred that others test out such ventures and then react based on the results.

The increased investment options altered the bank's deposit mix. At Bangor Savings Bank, the amount of money held in money market accounts went from zero in 1981 to $82.6 million in 1985, surpassing regular savings deposits for the first time that year.

Also, in 1984, Bangor Savings Bank hired its first commercial lending officer, Walter "Bull" Durham. Initially, the department remained fairly limited in scope, mostly concentrating on commercial construction, projects secured by real estate or backed by a government loan program.

The early 1980s also saw significant financial problems caused principally by a disastrous increase in interest rates. The Prime Rate averaged 9.5 percent in 1978, 15.5 percent in 1980 and at times spiked above 20 percent in 1981.

In such an environment, thrifts suffered more than commercial banks because most were still dominated by thirty-year fixed mortgages, while commercial banks had more flexible loans and better short-term options, allowed them to adjust to interest rates more quickly.

Nationally, the mutual savings bank industry collectively reported operating losses of nearly $3.3 billion in the first three years of the 1980s.

During that period savings banks tried to move more customers into variable rate mortgages, which, while causing some concerns among consumer advocates, provided banks with more flexibility.

Given the various problems, Bangor Savings Bank reported its first loss under Jones, $1.5 million, for the year ending March 31, 1982.

The year-end loss was somewhat worse than necessary by choice. Jones said he realized the bank was probably going to report a loss so he wanted to clean up the bank's balance sheet by dumping some older investments.

He sold some bonds still left from the 1940s and 1950s as well as low-yielding preferred stock and booked a loss from those sales of more than $700,000. That loss allowed the bank to take some tax credits. Overall, the bank recovered taxes of $899,000 that year. Furthermore, the bank received about five million dollars from the sale of its securities and invested the money in higher-yielding investments.

The bank was also aided by consumer loyalty. Jones said that despite passbook accounts that paid only around 5 percent, many people kept their money in the bank instead of withdrawing it in favor of higher-earning options. In fact, regular savings accounts remained above one hundred million dollars during the period. Had customers shifted all that money to higher-yielding investments at the bank or withdrawn it all together, the bank's financial position would have been more greatly damaged.

While the loss was a difficult thing for Jones and the bank to face, the associated financial moves seemed to pay off. Interest rates eased and the bank reported a profit of $798,212 in 1983 and a profit of $2.4 million in 1984. It never looked back.

Mergers, Acquisitions and Out-of-State Banks

In the 1980s, the face of Maine banking changed dramatically. Banks grew larger and more visible; some presidents and chief executives assumed more public personas and even became celebrities, and regional megabanks arrived.

A surge in high-profile acquisitions in the mid-1980s culminated events that had started with reform in 1975. While the consolidation of smaller banks began in 1976, it was the 1980s, when laws were revised again, that finally brought about the interstate banking envisioned by reformers and dramatically changed the look and feel of Maine banking.

The number of state-chartered savings banks in Maine had fallen from thirty-two in 1975 to twenty by 1984 after remaining constant for forty-three years. The number of commercial banks dropped from forty-five in 1975 to twenty-six in 1984, a decrease of 42 percent. The number of state-chartered savings and loan associations dropped from sixteen to seven in 1984.

For commercial banks, the touchstone merger was Albany-based Norstar Bancorp's acquisition of Northeast Bankshare Association of Portland in 1983, marking the first acquisition of a Maine bank by an out-of-state bank.* Norstar then acquired Banc of Maine Corporation in

*Northeast Bankshare was the holding company that originally consumed the old Eastern Trust & Banking Company of Bangor.

1984. In other activity, Merchants National Bank of Bangor was purchased by Maine National Bank in 1982, Depositors of Augusta was bought by Key Banks Inc. of Albany, Casco Northern Corporation was purchased by Bank of Boston and Maine National Corporation was purchased by Bank of New England.

Making its first foray into Maine in 1986 was Fleet Financial Group of Rhode Island. That year the bank bought Merrill Bankshares, the parent of Merrill Trust of Bangor. The following year, Fleet merged with Norstar, thus combining the two largest commercial banks with a presence in Bangor and creating one of the largest banking companies in the nation, with twenty-five billion in assets.

The purchase of Merrill Trust removed from local ownership the last of the city's three commercial banks — Eastern Trust, Merrill Trust and Merchants National Bank — once known in Bangor as the "triangle" of banks for the way they controlled money in the city. Ultimately, the remnants of all three banks would come under the Fleet umbrella. The loss of Merrill Trust meant that at the time the only major longtime bank still based in Bangor and controlled by local ownership was the 134-year-old Bangor Savings Bank.*

Mergers and out-of-state acquisitions brought big banks to Maine. These banks, backed by out-of-state corporations, held assets unimagined in Maine only a few years earlier. By 1990, four of the six largest banks in Maine were owned by out-of-state corporations.

Thrifts were also changing. Prior to 1984, all thrifts were mutual institutions, meaning they were owned by depositors. Starting in 1984 with Maine Savings Bank, several thrifts converted to stock ownership, including Peoples Heritage Savings Bank. All did so in order to raise capital for expansion. The only way for a mutual savings bank to raise capital is through profits.

Meanwhile, Bangor Savings Bank stuck to its knitting even as it was increasingly outsized by its contemporaries. In 1987, it had $453.8 million in assets compared to Maine Savings Bank's $1.4 billion and Peoples Heritage Savings Bank's $1.5 billion. Across town, Fleet-owned Merrill Trust Company had $853 million.

*Despite similar names, Bangor-based Merrill Merchants Bank, created in 1992, has no connection to the old Merrill Trust or Merchants National Bank.

The Bangor Mall

For decades, herds of dairy cattle were the sole tenants of a sixty-acre parcel of green pastures near Bangor, an area now known for an entirely other type of green — the green of money. Up until 1975 the pasture sat within the triangle described by Interstate 95, Stillwater Avenue and Hogan Road in Bangor. For years, the pastoral atmosphere and rural setting had been slowly eroding until, finally, in August of 1977, the area surrendered to the rumbling noise of a bustling construction zone. After nearly a year of delays and site excavation, construction was underway for the Bangor Mall, slated to become Maine's largest shopping mall and promising to cement Bangor's preeminence as the retail destination for Eastern and Northern Maine residents.

An army of nearly two thousand predominantly-Maine-residing construction workers labored to complete the estimated thirty million dollar project by its official opening date of October 5, 1978. Sears Roebuck closed its downtown store of fifty years to become one of the mall's anchor stores, simultaneously ending one era while ushering in another.

The mall employed nearly fifteen hundred residents and, as the area's largest local employer, was embraced as the city's property tax cash cow. The mall initially featured more than seventy stores in 450,000 square feet of retail space and offered convenient parking for more than three thousand cars.

The momentum generated by enthusiasm for the new mall was slow to ebb. Expansion plans were quickly drawn for a third wing, a bank, a grocery store, restaurants, fast food chains and hotels which would spill out into the access road and beyond. The growth has never stopped.

In 1997, Bangor Mall announced an estimated $26.6 million expansion plan that would include a facelift for the existing site, 160,000 new square feet of retail space, and six additional acres of parking. The expansion, according to the *Bangor Daily News*, was aimed at bolstering the city's economic role in the regional economy while maintaining Bangor as the flagship community in Eastern and Northern Maine.

The expansion has also brought about the widening of roads, the construction of additional access ways, and even a new ramp and overpass to Interstate 95. It has also confirmed that the mall fulfilled its promise to solidify Bangor's position as a critical focal point to an increasingly viable regional economy.

— Zelz

So, of course, the question arose at Bangor Savings Bank: Should the bank convert to a stock-ownership institution?

Jones — perhaps harkening back to the advice of his old boss Nason who told him, "Now Mac, don't you let anyone take over this old bank." — was set against it.

But as investment bankers came calling and other banks inquired about acquiring Bangor Savings Bank, trustees encouraged Jones to at least examine the issue. So, Jones and Sally A. Burgess (now Sally A. Bates), senior vice president and treasurer, did so.

For Jones, conversion boiled down to two key points: control and capital. He felt that converting to stock ownership would likely mean a loss of local control and create a much greater chance of takeover by an out-of-state bank. Stock banks must ultimately answer to stockholders, thus executives are obligated to consider any offer and must have a good reason to tell stockholders why they said no, or face potential lawsuits. "If we had gone stock, we would have been gobbled up without questions," Jaffray said. "We would never have survived as an independent bank."

Jones also felt such a circumstance would hurt Bangor, which was already losing its other local banks, and possibly would hurt Eastern Maine.

"The respect that Bangor Savings Bank commands is in no small part due to the fact that it is so committed to the community," Bates said.

Secondly, the most legitimate reason to convert to stock ownership is to raise capital if there is a compelling reason and a good place to invest it. In Jones' mind, Bangor Savings Bank did not have a compelling reason. Thus, if there was no compelling need or place to invest, he felt, the bank would be forced to put the new capital to work in higher-risk investments. Some Maine banks encountered trouble partly for just that reason: They didn't have enough quality places to invest their capital, so they reached for more and more risky investments.

"It was such a trend," Bates said. "It was something that every bank needed to look at and if the investment opportunity had been different in our area it might have been appropriate. We looked at the opportunity to raise capital by going public, but we could not see a reasonable investment opportunity that would be safe."

The board, as usual, backed Jones.

"Mal was very successful in convincing us of the folly of converting even before any of the real damage started to happen to some of the banks that were converting," said Eames. "He could see they were struggling with the capital they had raised and were taking risks to place it and he was right. There was that fatalism again, he was looking down the road to see what might happen."

The issue continued to crop up, but never received serious discussion during Jones' tenure, in part because the bank was not looking to grow by acquisition or push into the more wealthy Southern Maine market.

"I supported Mal in resisting moving to Southern Maine," said Eames. "I thought like he did: 'Let's solidify what we have now in our market.'"

The acquisitions of Maine banks took a breather in 1987. The stock market crashed in October and soon the New England real estate bubble burst, plunging the New England region into a severe real estate recession. The good times were officially over and the big banking stories of the late 1980s and early 1990s took on a whole new aspect: failure.

Crash

The 1980s growth of banking was driven largely by aggressive acquisitions, commercial lending and real estate. Some people hoisted a few warning flags during the era but most were ignored.

Then as the economy came crashing down, the names of such bailout agencies as the Resolution Trust Company, RECOLL and the FDIC became as common in banking discussions and news stories as bank names. Horror stories sprouted up about the tactics that some of them took against debtors and troubled companies. Furthermore, as many banks reeled under a deluge of bad loans, a credit crunch soon visited the state.

"Calendar year 1990 was the most difficult year to face the Maine banking community since the Depression and bank holiday years of the early 1930s," wrote Maine Superintendent of Banking H. Donald DeMatteis in his annual report to the legislature. This affected people like Tom Minogue, an oil distributor from Lincoln who told a panel convened in Bangor, "You're bringing the consequences back to rural Maine of bad real-estate loans in Portland."[10]

In the early 1990s, Peoples Heritage Savings Bank teetered on the edge of failure but successfully worked through its problems to eventually become the biggest bank in Maine. Maine National Bank, tied to the spectacular failure of its parent, Bank of New England, was seized by the FDIC and ultimately taken over by Fleet.

By the end of 1992, either through acquisition or failure, these venerable Maine banking names had disappeared during the preceding decade: Maine National Bank, Maine Savings Bank, Depositors Trust, Merrill Trust, and Merchants National Bank. By 1996, Casco Northern was also gone, after Bank of Boston sold it to Key Bank.

Still, the most symbolic collapse for many thrifts and the general banking community in Maine was the dramatic failure of the 132-year-old Maine Savings Bank — a one-time symbol of Maine banking success.

Maine Savings Bank started in 1859, seven years after Bangor Savings Bank, as the Portland Five Cent Savings Bank. Over the years, it was the first to amortize loans in Maine, the first to offer a school savings plan, the first to branch into the suburbs, the first mutual bank to convert to stock and the first Maine bank to reach one billion dollars in assets.

Maine Savings was run by the dynamic, powerful and driven Robert T. Masterton, known in some circles as Maine's Mr. Banking and an undeniable force not only in Portland but the entire savings bank industry. Masterton built Maine Savings from five branches and about $150 million in assets when he took over in 1970 to twenty-eight offices and a billion dollars in assets by 1985. In 1984, the bank converted from a mutual savings bank to a stock bank raising forty-four million dollars to fuel its expansion plans through its parent, The One Bancorp.

Masterton's goal was to build The One from $822 million in assets in 1984 to five billion dollars by 1989. For four years, the plan was progressing and the splashy bank was the pride of Maine, particularly in 1987 when Masterton bought an out-of-state bank, Bank of Hartford. Next, The One bought a Massachusetts bank. Soon, The One reached $2.5 billion in assets and controlled more than fifty branches in Maine, Massachusetts and Connecticut.

However, instead of reaching its goal of five billion dollars by 1989, it stumbled headlong into the teeth of the real estate recession and suffered from its outsized ambitions and ill-advised loans, especially the condominium development loans it had made during the preceding few years. It began to hemorrhage money.

"[Maine Savings Bank] had been one of the most aggressive real estate lenders in Maine and the Northeast; when that market collapsed, the bank suffered substantial losses which ultimately depleted its equity capital," DeMatteis wrote in 1991.[11]

Compounding the crisis were the tragic health problems that beset Masterton. He was diagnosed with an inoperable brain tumor in 1987. He died May 16, 1988, at the age of fifty-seven.

Maine Savings would never be the same.

In the last quarter of 1988, the bank reported a small quarterly loss. It then reported a staggering loss of $144.7 million in 1989. In the following year, the bank worked out a recovery plan that called for it to slice itself in half by selling its non-Maine branches and divesting its investment subsidiary. Still, in 1990, the bank reported a loss of $90.4 million, plunging its net worth into negative territory. Maine Savings Bank was insolvent.

On Friday evening, Feb. 1, 1991, eighty-five FDIC regulators descended on Maine Savings bank branches, seized the bank, and by the time the branches reopened, its deposits were controlled by Fleet Bank of Maine.

Simply put, it was the largest and most costly bank failure in Maine history.

"[When Maine Savings failed] I was deeply concerned," said Jones. "I believed it reflected badly on our industry and was worried that people would begin to get worried about all the other savings banks."

Also keeping a close eye on the collapse of Maine Savings was P. James Dowe Jr., president of Bath Savings Institution.

Dowe, who would become president of Bangor Savings Bank in 1995, took over as head of Bath Savings in 1986 and began to transform the sleepy bank as he spread it out along the Maine coast in the very shadow of Maine Savings.

When Maine Savings fell, Dowe said, "I wanted to read everything I could about why they failed. I wanted to know what happened so we could be humble about what we were doing and so we didn't take the same path."

More than a decade after the collapse of Maine Savings, Dowe still carries an old *Maine Times* article that chronicled the mistakes made and

Bank Robberies

No profession is immune from potential dangers or hazards. Whereas some threats are preventable, others can only be minimized by identifying vulnerabilities and taking appropriate steps. Robbery has always been the Achilles heel of the banking industry, and tension, nerves and anxiety contribute to an explosive atmosphere with potentially life-threatening consequences. Despite being romanticized by movies and fiction thrillers, bank robbery presents real threats to the financial services industry; and the industry has gone to great lengths and great expense to protect its employees, customers and assets.

For more than 130 years, Bangor Savings Bank remained free from armed robbery. That run was abruptly ended in October of 1982, when a shotgun was leveled at a Hogan Road branch teller. Without any further violence, the robber departed almost as anonymously as he had entered, fleeing on foot to the Bangor Mall. With the aid of video surveillance and attention to security protocol, the thief was identified within days and captured. He and three accomplices were tried and convicted.

Lightning may never strike twice in the same place but obviously bank robbers do. On a Friday evening in February 1989 the Hogan Road branch was hit again. Confronting a single teller, the bandit brandished no weapon and, according to witnesses, made his getaway in less than sixty seconds. Lightning also struck twice for law enforcement, as this thief, too, was nabbed by the authorities, tried and convicted.

During the 1998 restoration of the 3 State Street lobby, customers were directed next door to bank at 15 State Street. Despite its temporary nature, the facility was still equipped with surveillance and security devices. The appearance of impermanence, however, may have seduced a pair of gunmen with a false sense of security. On the morning of February 5, 1998, they struck Bangor Savings Bank. Brandishing weapons and threatening employees and customers, the two took their booty and made a getaway in a stolen van. Life on the lam was fleeting for the two culprits. Both were arrested within five days and were eventually tried and convicted.

— Zelz

263

the troubles that beset Maine Savings because of miscalculations, hubris and the economy. At least every year, he takes out the article and rereads it as a cautionary tale.

"I am not picking on Maine Savings Bank," he says, "but there is a lesson there and we have to remember it."

Bangor Savings Bank

Meanwhile, Bangor Savings Bank rode out the financial storm of the late 1980s and early 1990s like it was tepid bathwater.

"We may have looked really slow, maybe even stupid, to some people, but some of the people and businesses who thought Bangor Savings Bank was slow and stupid are not around anymore," said Bates, the former senior vice president and treasurer.

From 1990 to 1992, the bank reported annual profits of $3.1 million, $4.5 million and $5.1 million, respectively, and watched assets grow from $553.6 million to $628.7 million. It picked up some business as the only remaining locally-controlled bank in Bangor that offered personal service at a time when more and more banking decisions were being made out of state.

There was a growing feeling that the failures and consolidations of Maine's historic banks into a handful of major players had created a growing void that needed to be filled. Thus, some saw an opportunity on the horizon for a local bank.

Indeed, some newspaper stories began to question the commitment of some out-of-state banks. As early as 1989, big commercial banks began pulling out of some rural areas and concentrating in the more wealthy southern part of Maine. As a result, Bangor Savings Bank was reaching deals with companies that were cast aside by troubled banks and with companies that otherwise couldn't get credit in an increasingly tight market.

"Banks were being much stricter with their underwriting guidelines because of the FDIC and because they got burned when the market crashed," said Jack DeCamp, senior vice president of commercial lending. "If customers didn't meet banks' new, very stringent guidelines, or if they weren't the best quality deals, then other banks didn't want them. Bangor Savings could be more patient with them because we understood them, we were a community bank and wanted to help."

The percentage of bank assets in Maine controlled by out-of-state ownership peaked in 1991 at 46.8 percent. By 1995, that dropped to 37.1 percent as some out-of-state banks either failed or pulled out altogether.

Clearly, commercial business was available for Maine banks, of which Bangor Savings Bank was now one of the biggest, that were willing to mix it up and take even small risks.

By 1993, the three largest Maine-based banks were Peoples Heritage Savings Bank, Bangor Savings Bank and Camden National Bank. Peoples, Bangor and Camden collectively controlled assets of $3 billion, of which 67 percent was controlled by fast-growing Peoples.

Fleet Bank of Maine, Key Bank of Maine and Bank of Boston-owned Casco Northern had assets of $3.1 billion, $2.4 billion and $1.1 billion, respectively. The statistics also show that the four big Portland-centered banks had collectively assets of $8.6 billion, versus Bangor Savings Bank's $633 million making it a distant fifth in size, but the state's biggest bank not headquartered in Portland.

As these events unfolded into the mid-1990s, Doug Brown, founder of Doug's Shop 'n Save, a leading Bangor businessman and a long-time member of the board of Fleet Bank and its predecessor Merrill Trust, would occasionally run into Bangor Savings Bank Chairman G. Clifton Eames.

Brown knew the bank well, watched the state's business world closely, and regularly surveyed the landscape. He would say to Eames, "Clif, you know your bank is a sleeping giant. When you pull up your sleeves and decide to really go at it, you can be one of the largest banks in the state and a very important bank in this state. There is a need out there."

And indeed, after nearly 150 years of filling the basic needs of Bangor area residents, the sleeping giant seemed ready to stir.

Chapter Twelve

Fleet of Foot, Eye on the Future

It is easy to pinpoint the date of Bangor Savings Bank's transformation from financial role player to statewide force — April 3, 1998, the day the 146-year-old bank inked a deal that eventually brought twenty-eight Fleet Bank branches under its control, gave Bangor Savings a presence from Eastport to Kezar Falls, and placed its branches in thirteen of sixteen Maine counties.

Before that spring day, Bangor Savings Bank was undeniably vital to Bangor and most of Eastern Maine. And it was methodically developing an increasingly sophisticated financial infrastructure. Yet, when the "important" Maine banks were discussed or written about in the press, they were usually banks headquartered in downtown Portland. Jim Dowe, Bangor Savings' chief executive officer since 1995, and the bank's board of trustees[1] set out to change that. As the number of community banks dwindled and as out-of-state banks either left Maine or withdrew from parts of the state, they saw a void — and an opportunity.

The Fleet deal was just the largest salvo in the bank's unexpectedly quick strike. Within a span of just months from late 1997 through early 1998, Dowe led an effort that tripled the number of bank branches, invigorated the commercial lending department (including opening the bank's first lending office in Portland in 1998), acquired a Portland-based brokerage firm, and created an insurance subsidiary — clear and decisive steps toward his goal of making Bangor Savings Bank a Maine-based, statewide financial services company. Its new size would also give it the financial heft to assist nearly any business in Maine.

"We will be the bank that understands Maine from an economic perspective, a social perspective and a political perspective and we will have the financial capacity to address the needs of the people of Maine," Dowe said shortly after announcing the Fleet deal.[2]

It was no idle boast.

After more than a century of mostly measured, at times imperceptible change, the bank's transformation certainly came more quickly than anticipated and did not occur without a short-term price. Earnings sagged in the aftermath of the Fleet deal, and the mutual savings bank struggled both to digest its acquisitions and adjust to its new size and mission.

After all, these were the boldest moves in the bank's history and the biggest since Mal Jones acquired two savings banks to expand the bank's territory in the mid-1970s.

But regardless of the short-term disruption, Dowe, with his upbeat vision of "what could be," was dramatically placing his stamp on the venerable Bangor Savings Bank. The farm boy from Turner and the first top executive hired from outside the company in nearly eight decades had teamed with trustees to untether the bank from its regional mindset and set its course for a statewide future.

P. James "Jim" Dowe Jr.

Jim Dowe was born in Augusta in 1948 and then grew up in the rural town of Turner. His mother, Peggy, was an elementary school teacher and his father, Paul, worked nearly four decades for the University of Maine Cooperative Extensive Service, an agency providing assistance to farmers and agricultural projects in Maine.

Like his predecessor Mal Jones, Jim Dowe was born and raised on a farm. The family's first love was horses, but they also raised sheep, beef steer and seemingly "every animal known to man" at some time on their eighty-or-so acre farm. Dowe, a long-time 4H-er, traveled to county fairs throughout Androscoggin, Sagadahoc and Oxford counties during the 1950s and 1960s, participating in agricultural competitions such as showing sheep and beef cattle and riding in equestrian events.

Most of Dowe's neighbors depended on agriculture for their livelihood. "That was what Turner was in those days, principally agricultural, so most of my friends were doing the same thing I was, only more so," Dowe said.

Dowe worked on the family farm in the midsummer sun and rose on winter mornings before school to tend the animals. Each fall he worked at local apple orchards. His father expected him to work and earn money.

"Looking back, I think probably the reason my dad did it was so that I would learn how to work," he said. "It was a valuable lesson. And it is not one that is always easy to impart."

Courtesy of Bangor Savings Bank

Maine native P. James Dowe Jr. became president and chief executive officer of Bangor Savings Bank in 1995 after serving as president of Bath Savings Institution. He has guided the bank through its statewide expansion.

After graduating from Leavitt Institute in the mid-1960s, Dowe attended the University of Maine at Orono, graduating with a degree in education in 1972. While attending college he married his high school sweetheart, Susan James, who grew up in nearby Auburn.

With no specific career goal in mind, but with the general idea that he would eventually pursue a career as a coach and teacher, Dowe, while still a college student and newlywed, found himself working at a Livermore Falls ski shop in the early 1970s putting in the hours to buy food, pay for school and cover other expenses.

One day Woodbury "Woodie" Titcomb, head of Lewiston-based Northeast Bankshare Association, walked into the ski shop. Titcomb came in with his family and spent time talking while looking at equipment. He didn't particularly know Jim Dowe that well, but he struck up a conversation and the two men seemed to hit it off. Titcomb asked the young man straight out: "Is this what you are going to do for the rest of your life?"

In short order, Dowe interviewed with Titcomb and, after graduation, started work in Northeast's fledgling management trainee program. He was immediately hooked on banking.

"The people I was connected with were people I respected and wanted to learn from. That opportunity really intrigued me," Dowe said. "And I had an instant affection for the business. I found it was in my blood."

Dowe was tutored under Titcomb, a veteran of the First National Bank of Boston and a man whom Dowe admired for his experience and sophisticated approach to banking. As part of the small management trainee group, Dowe sat in on board meetings and learned the business at the bank's highest levels. He also spent time working on commercial lending and special analysis projects and even washed Woodie's car a few times.

Dowe stayed at Northeast Bank for more than two years, leaving when management changed. He then worked for the old Peoples Bank of Lewiston as a branch manager and again worked on special projects, mostly on the commercial side.

When Dowe left Peoples, he temporarily left banking and worked as an account manager for Xerox Corporation. He liked the job, but when he realized that the next step up would force him to leave Maine, he decided that that was something he just didn't want to do. He planned to live and raise his family in Maine.

So, by the late 1970s he was back in banking, working for Androscoggin County Savings Bank and working under Hanson E. Ray, another positive influence who ran "a wonderful bank." Again, Dowe was heavily involved in the commercial side of the bank and special projects. "He gave me an opportunity to grow and to be challenged. I learned a lot from him," Dowe said. "He was a lifelong banker and very conservative, yet progressive at the same time."

It was Ray who tried to force Maine into giving savings banks the power to offer checking accounts in the early 1970s by simply issuing them to a handful of his customers. The bank was sued by the state banking commissioner and ordered to close the checking accounts, but the bank's actions helped move the checking account issue forward.

In 1986, Dowe became president of Bath Savings Institution, a traditional, eighty-seven million dollar savings bank with offices in Bath and Damariscotta. "Our strategy was pretty simple, we wanted to go down to the edge of Portland and then fill in back to Damariscotta," Dowe said. "And we wanted to diversify."

In his first chief executive job, Dowe instinctively developed certain management practices. For example, he hired a strong support team. "The thing I learned at each stop along the way is that there is no substitute to having great people work with you. My view has always been that you identify the great people that are there, give them the opportunity to do what they do better than you, and then you find out where the gaps are and recruit talented people to fill them. This creates a vibrant atmosphere and an opportunity for success. These are the type of people who seize opportunities and have the confidence to get things done."

At Bath, he did just that.

"As I look back on Bath, the bank is still run basically by the people I hired while I was there," he said. "We hired some very talented people."

It was a philosophy he eventually brought to Bangor Savings Bank.

"Jim, I think, is very good at identifying and recruiting the right kind of people for the team and then he relies on them to deliver," said G. Clifton Eames, the former Bangor Savings Bank chairman who helped hire Dowe. "He is not going to go to the chief financial officer and get into the nitty-gritty detail of every line item."

271

Among those Dowe hired at Bath was Glen Hutchinson, who rose to bank president. "Generally, he had a positive outlook here," Hutchinson said. "He was able to see what could be."

And "what could be" at Bath was a bank with a bigger role.

Under Dowe, Bath Savings bolstered its commercial operations, established a trust company subsidiary and pushed out along the state's mid-coast.

"Jim changed the culture of the bank and brought in some very good people," said Christopher Pinkham, president of the Maine Association of Community Banks. "He took a sleepy little bank and made it a strong player. They started to diversify and spread out. He had the foresight to see that the bank was going to get tripped up if anything happened to BIW [Bath Iron Works] or the base [Brunswick Naval Air Station] during any of the rounds of base closures or other government cutbacks."

The success at Bath Savings Institution did not go unnoticed.

One person taking note was Arthur M. Johnson, a trustee of Bangor Savings Bank, who was also active in economic development organizations and a former president of the University of Maine. Johnson, who lived on Southport Island near Boothbay Harbor, admittedly was one of Bangor Savings Bank's more enterprising trustees. He was a strong believer in the need and value of community banks, but he also felt the bank should look harder at the Southern Maine market and he strongly encouraged strategic planning and strategic thinking, all things he felt were evident in Dowe's work.

Meanwhile, by the early to mid-1990s, Bangor Savings Bank was itself preparing for change and trying to develop a succession plan as Malcolm Jones approached retirement with no heir apparent on staff.

Trustees knew basically the type of leader they wanted for the bank.

"We wanted a successful banker with CEO experience, a progressive thinker and a visionary type of person, not someone happy with the status quo, but also not someone who was going to move us too far too fast," Eames said. And they were somewhat biased toward a leader with Maine connections.

Johnson, who had watched Dowe develop at Bath, felt Dowe fit the bill. "I felt he was the right guy, because he came from a bank with the same philosophy and because I knew the kind of bank he operated,"

Johnson said. "He did the things I thought were important and he was what I would call 'suitably aggressive.' He had expanded Bath Savings in the right direction, but still had done so slowly."

Johnson described Dowe as personable and friendly, but also somewhat quiet. Dowe was also heavily involved in the community and in banking organizations — activities considered important by Bangor Savings Bank.

Dowe, however, was happy in Bath. His family liked the city and he was reluctant to make a career move.

"It was a complicated decision to leave Bath," Dowe said. "Bath is a wonderful place. We loved it there. We had two daughters go through Morse High School and a son who would go there. I didn't have any reason to want to leave." He discussed the opportunity with Susan and they decided to stay put.

Then, purely by chance, Dowe, who sometimes worked at his branches to stay in touch with customers, was filling in as branch manager in Damariscotta one day when Johnson walked into the bank to take care of some other business. "I went into the branch and Jim was there that day," Johnson said. "I basically told him, 'Jim, we are down to the last vote, if you are interested at all, you had better let us know.'"

In Johnson's opinion, "[Bangor Savings Bank] was the obvious thing for him to do." And this time, Dowe reconsidered the significance of the opportunity and realized that he'd have to leave Maine to find a similar one — just as when he was with Xerox, that was not something he or Susan wanted to do.

"Their mission there was to do more of what we were doing for the middle-coast of Maine, but all over Maine," Dowe said. "It was an institution that had the capacity to serve the entire state of Maine. It had size, it had capital, it had a tremendous reputation and an enlightened board. There was a sense that the future was in being able to serve this entire grand state of ours and serve it in a way that is broader than just traditional banking."

So, on a clear day in the summer of 1994, Jim Dowe, Arthur Johnson and Clifton Eames sat in Johnson's Southport living room, looked across Sheepscot Bay, and discussed the future of Bangor Savings Bank and Jim Dowe. They basically wanted to know Dowe's philosophy and in turn they told him they felt Bangor Savings Bank was both poised to grow and needed to grow and that he was the man to steer it.

It seemed a perfect fit. As they headed off from Southport that day, although there remained the need for Jim and Susan to visit the folks in Bangor, Dowe was poised to become the new captain of the ship.

An Expanded Mission

Jim Dowe officially became president of Bangor Savings Bank on July 1, 1995, replacing the legendary Mal Jones. For the first time in nearly eighty years, the president of Bangor Savings Bank was not intimately steeped in the bank and its existing culture. For this institution, any leadership change was a rare occurrence. Dowe was just the fourth new leader in seventy-seven years. There was at least some anxiety at the bank as people waited to see what the new guy was going to do.

Dowe brought to the bank the same basic commitment to community banking and community in general as Walter A. Danforth (treasurer, 1917–1947), Harold L. Nason (treasurer and president, 1947–1975) and Malcolm E. Jones (president, 1975–1995) before him. But certainly, he brought a new operating style.

Dowe was generally more casual — perhaps for the first time ever, the bank's leader could be seen around the office without a jacket. In that vein, Dowe enjoyed skiing and riding motorcycles. Not long after he came to Bangor Savings, he took a 505–mile motorcycle trip along the back roads of Maine with a group of bikers that included Gov. Angus King and former Maine Chief Justice Daniel Wathen. He might also spend a summer day rowing on the ocean and spend winter nights in gymnasiums of Eastern Maine watching his son play basketball for Bangor High School.

Dowe is also generally inclined, more so than his predecessors, to make bold moves when necessary to fulfill the bank's mission. And he is inclined to delegate more authority to his management team, a must because of the bank's size, mission and new complexity.

"He brought some fresh ideas," said Alice McInnis, an executive vice president who has worked for the last three bank presidents. "But all the presidents I have worked for have been very consistent in their commitment to the bank."

Bangor Savings Bank President P. James Dowe Jr. (left) and G. Clifton Eames, former chairman of the board, on State Street. Eames and Dowe helped guide the bank through acquisitions and statewide expansion in the late 1990s.

Dowe is known as an optimist, as Hutchinson of Bath and others pointed out. "He is full of enthusiasm," said David Carlisle, current chairman of the board. "The world needs optimism."

Optimism is fine, but Dowe also inherited a financially solid bank, providing him with the capital — more than ninety million dollars — and the borrowing capacity to make strategic moves without issuing stock or draining reserves.

Statistically, in 1995 the bank stood at $687 million in assets and $599 million in deposits. Its thirteen branches were mainly clustered in Eastern Maine, ranging as far south as Belfast and as far northwest as Greenville. The bank had added only one branch, and that was in Bangor, since acquiring Houlton Savings Bank in 1981. Still, in 1995 it stood as the second largest savings bank in Maine behind Peoples Heritage Savings Bank,* with its $2.4 billion in assets, and fourth overall

*Peoples Heritage Bank has since converted to a national charter, making Bangor Savings Bank the largest state-chartered bank in Maine.

in Maine behind Fleet, with $3.1 billion in assets, and Key Bank, with $3.6 billion. The three largest banks were all stock banks, while Bangor Savings Bank remained a mutual.

Important pieces of infrastructure were also being put in place. Jones had opened a three million dollar operations center in 1993 that brought workers together from five scattered sites. A trust department was started in 1989 and the framework to ramp up the commercial operation was in place. The bank had become increasingly active in commercial lending following the upheaval and bank failures of the early 1990s. The majority of the bank's loans, however, were still tied to real estate. The bank operated only one ATM.

Dowe wasted little time in pushing the bank forward. He quickly opened a branch in Unity, which he billed as the gateway to expansion south and worked to expand the bank's image.

In 1996, he distributed an annual report with the theme, A Case of Mistaken Identity, reflecting his belief that many people mistakenly still thought of Bangor Savings Bank as simply a savings bank and did not recognize its other financial products and services.

Secondly, he retired The Source as a marketing slogan and logo and replaced it with a new, more symbolic Bangor Savings Bank logo. According to the bank, the logo's green symbolizes the state's vast forest resources; the blue suggests the timeless beauty of lakes, rivers and ocean; and the ellipse represents both the bank's capacity to expand to meet customer needs and the historic role of Bangor Savings Bank in Maine banking.

Dowe's expansion plan accelerated in 1996, when the bank learned that Fleet might want to shed some of its branches. Suddenly, here was an opportunity that came faster — and was larger — than anyone could have predicted a year earlier. It was an opportunity that also meant taking more risk than usual.

"The times have called for more aggressive actions," Clif Eames said in 2002. "Competitive pressures require that you can't stay still. The bank worked with consultants from CIBC World Markets and quickly hammered out a deal to acquire thirty-one Fleet branches spread from Rumford to Castine to Jonesport. (Regulators later required Bangor Savings to remove three branches from the deal in Piscataquis County claiming they would give the bank an excessive concentration in certain local areas.)

Bangor Savings was moving fast. It would complete the deal in only a few short months and then convert all branches by August.

The bank was not just working on the Fleet deal but moving along parallel tracks to offer customers other services and become a financial services company. In the spring of 1997, the bank formed

Courtesy of Bangor Savings Bank
The new Bangor Savings Bank logo unveiled in 1996.

Bangor Insurance Services to put the bank in position to offer insurance products to its customers. In November, it teamed with Sargent, Tyler & West of Brewer to offer those insurance services and then the bank sold its first policy in February 1998.

Within a month of announcing the Fleet deal, the bank announced it was buying Portland-based Livada Securities, a twenty-nine-year-old brokerage firm that managed investments of two hundred million dollars. Bangor Savings Bank would open a Livada office in Bangor and bring brokerage services to most of its branches.

There were important reasons for these moves, reflecting industry trends. First, banks were increasingly looking to provide diversified services to fend off non-bank competition, much as savings banks had in 1975 when they felt they needed checking accounts to compete. Secondly, as competition for loans and mortgages heated up and depositors took advantage of their many investment options, banks sought fee-based services such as insurance and brokerage commissions as part of a complete strategy.

"The market is going in a direction that is knocking down the barriers between banking, insurance, and securities," said Donald Groves, chief bank examiner at the time.[3]

While the purchase of Fleet branches and Livada generated great enthusiasm at the bank, it also created more of a struggle than anticipated. Undeniably, the deal forced the bank to take a financial hit. Bank profits dropped from $8.8 million in 1998 to $1.9 million in 2001, although in 2002, the bank began to realize the benefits of its larger size and scope and reported much improved earnings.

"Jim is looking to make Bangor Savings Bank 'Maine's bank' and is putting emphasis on building our image and our infrastructure for that purpose," Eames said. "In the long run, building that base is going to support a statewide and locally-owned community bank. To get there, he is willing to risk dropping the margins somewhat on what we all expect will be a temporary basis."

The spring and summer of 1998 were certainly a whirlwind for the employees of Bangor Savings Bank. The bank deals increased staff from 280 to more than 500 in less than one year. Completing what the bank called Project Black Bear took tremendous dedication and work by employees — the bank closed on the Fleet branches and opened them as Bangor Savings Bank branches in a stunningly short eighty-nine days. The necessary background work included the assimilation and evaluation of employees, the integration of computer systems, the switching of accounts and checkbooks, and the welcoming of thousands of customers and accounts. Jim Dowe and various staff members went on road trips to visit every branch.

Looking back on the bank's growth from fourteen branches to forty-two branches and the addition of new insurance products and brokerage services, Dowe and other leaders believe they could have moved a little slower. They recognize in hindsight that they could have consolidated certain branches more quickly, could have challenged regulators to keep some of the branches the bank was unable to purchase and could have streamlined some human resource functions such as hiring and evaluating talent which proved a heavy burden.

"In hindsight, you can always do things a little smarter," Dowe said, but he added that, fundamentally, the bank leaders stand behind the moves.

"We paid a price for what we did," said Dowe. "There is no question. The investment we made was at a cost and we have paid a price. But now we are seeing that investment pay off. We did the right thing and now is the time and opportunity for us to benefit."

David Carlisle,[4] who replaced Eames as bank chairman in 1999, said the moves position the bank well for the future. "It hasn't yet benefited the bank in terms of a contribution of earnings," Carlisle said. "But from the standpoint of forming a starting point it was the right thing to do. If you had to do it all over again, I might change a few things, but I certainly

Courtesy of Bangor Savings Bank

Bangor Savings Bank's acquisition of 28 new branches in 1998 pushed the bank into many new communities, such as Machias shown here, and expanded its reach virtually statewide.

279

G. Clifton Eames Learning Center

Bangor Savings Bank has long supported education and professional development, ranging from leadership and product education to health and elder care.

Today's competitive financial services industry demands that professionals remain current with trends and tuned to the needs and expectations of the modern, financially savvy customer.

As part of the bank's commitment to hiring and enhancing the careers of its employees, the bank completed the G. Clifton Eames Learning Center in June of 1999. The learning center is named after the bank's former chairman, long-time Bangor businessman and important community leader. For years, Eames ran N.H. Bragg & Sons, a company started by his ancestors in the 1800s.

The Eames Learning Center in Bangor is an eighty-seat state-of-the-art facility. Internet access and tabletop ports for laptop computers allow ongoing delivery of software education to employees throughout the organization. Two high-resolution beam projectors and corresponding drop-down screens can enhance the presentations of external development consultants and, of course, those on the Bangor Savings Bank team who frequently share their expertise.

The Bangor Savings Bank Foundation

Since opening in 1852 as a place for the city's poor and daily laborers to save money, Bangor Savings Bank has remained committed to community banking and community service. Philanthropy is an integral component of its identity and its mission. Over the years, the bank has supported the arts, academic institutions, and service and civic organizations.

Then, recognizing the ever-increasing statewide needs, trustees created the Bangor Savings Bank Foundation in 1997. The Foundation has allowed the bank to formally advance its philanthropic agenda. By identifying education, social and civic services, culture, the arts and health as a focus, the Foundation, through irrevocable contributions of bank earnings, has targeted a broad range of objectives in pursuit of a better future for Maine. In the same spirit of community, Bangor Savings Bank shares its research, direction and advice with others looking to support the greater community.

Through the Foundation, philanthropy remains as much a part of the Bangor Savings Bank future as it has been a part of its past.

— Zelz

wouldn't second-guess the decision. It has allowed the bank to grow and increase the deposit base and get into some communities. And even though that was expensive, it was not nearly as expensive as it would have been to open new banks in all those areas."

Former Chairman Eames, a veteran of Bangor business as well as trustee of Bangor Savings Bank, helped usher in nearly all of the changes that took place in the late-1990s. "He was a real chairman," Dowe said. "He asked the tough questions, he worked to challenge the rest of the board to think

Courtesy of Prentiss & Carlisle

David M. Carlisle became Bangor Savings Bank Chairman in 1999.

deeply, and once the decisions were made, he was there to support them."

And Eames, now retired as both trustee and head of N.H. Bragg & Sons, looks with pride at the bank. "To a person today," Eames said, "and despite the less-than-stellar results of the last couple of years, there isn't anyone who would say we didn't do the right thing for the future of Bangor Savings Bank."

Further banking reform

Following the banking reform of 1975, dramatic consolidation took place, further deregulation opened the marketplace to even more competition and opportunity, and out-of-state banks roared into Maine. In addition, the number of non-bank competitors such as mutual fund companies and mortgage companies increased and cut into the traditional bank business.

Technological change has been dramatic as well. After banks conducted banking operations basically the same way for more than 150 years, the last twenty years of the twentieth century saw the advent of ATMs, telephone banking and finally Internet banking, allowing customers to make most transactions from their home via their computer. This is a long way from the old days of 9 A.M. to 3 P.M. banking.

Still, consolidation may be the most visible change. The combined number of savings banks and commercial banks in Maine dropped from seventy-four in 1972, shortly before banking reform, to thirty-four in 2001. The number of savings banks alone dropped from thirty-two to eighteen (which include two federally-chartered savings banks) during the same period. Meanwhile, the number of branches of all banks, including credit unions, reached 540 in 2001. When you add bank home offices, the number of banking locations soars to more than 650.

State reform came again in 1997 with the state's Universal Bank Charter, the most dramatic and progressive bank reform since 1975. The Universal Charter essentially eliminated all differences between types of banks and effectively broadened bank powers by making it easier for them or their holding companies to offer brokerage and insurance services.

Furthermore, the Universal Charter provided for new types of ownership (such as limited liability partnerships), streamlined some regulations and certain application processes, eliminated restrictions on operating hours, eliminated lending and deposit restrictions on thrifts (including a prohibition against paying interest on demand deposits), and created new types of banks such as merchant banks and uninsured wholesale banks.

"The Universal Bank Charter is a bold, new state initiative that enhances the state chartering system by providing our financial institutions with the powers and flexibility to satisfy the ongoing needs of Maine businesses and consumers, as well as making Maine an attractive place for financial institutions to locate their offices and operations centers," Gov. Angus King said at the time.

The state's Universal Charter came even as various pieces of reform legislation worked their way through the federal government, ultimately including the repeal in 1999 of many of the old restrictions created by the Glass-Steagall Act during the Great Depression.

Meanwhile, Peoples Heritage Bank has continued to grow through its new holding company, Banknorth Group, and expand into other states. And Bangor Savings Bank has edged closer to becoming the state's second largest bank through the growth of Bangor Savings Bank into a $1.32 billion bank and the continued contraction by out-of-state banks. Neither Fleet Bank nor Key Bank report their Maine assets, but both have declined dramatically from their mid-1990s heights.

Deposits held by Fleet and Key in 2001 were $1.17 billion and $2.13 billion, respectively. Their total loans were $1.16 billion and $1.39 billion, respectively. Bangor Savings Bank held $1 billion in deposits and had $1.1 billion in outstanding loans.

This changing landscape provided a commercial opportunity for Maine banks. In 2001, overall commercial lending growth in Maine was flat. However, while community banks saw an 11 percent increase in loans, out-of-state banks saw a drop of 19 percent, continuing a trend. Out-of-state banks have watched their share of outstanding commercial loans in Maine drop from 45 percent in 1997 to 27 percent in 2001.

Meanwhile at Bangor Savings Bank, from 1995 to 2001, commercial loans, excluding commercial mortgages, increased nearly sixfold, rising from $11.3 million to $65.7 million. Commercial mortgages have increased from $137.1 to $167.3 million or 22 percent during the same period. As part of its strategic plan for growth, the bank has built relationships with an increasing number of important Maine companies.

"If you are a Maine company, with only a very few exceptions we can do virtually anything you need," Dowe said. "That was our goal, that was our plan and we have arrived at that."

Visions of a Downtown Revival

Starting in the 1980s, the city watched as growth in the Bangor Mall area dramatically expanded. New exits from Interstate 95 have been added to alleviate traffic congestion and new "big box" stores, so-called because of their mammoth size, opened their doors. By 1998, the development of the Bangor Mall area helped boost the percentage of retail purchases made in Bangor to more than 50 percent of all Penobscot County retail purchases. Unfortunately, this growth simply bled downtown of its retail base until the city center was a mere shell of its former self. Only in the mid-1990s did the downtown show visible signs of shaking off the doldrums that began in the early 1960s and lifted only sporadically over the past forty years, despite numerous studies and revival efforts.

In 1981, *Down East* magazine visited the Queen City to evaluate its prospects for revival, but even a generally positive article described the downtown as one "marred by ubiquitous parking lots and vacant commercial sites."[4] Those were the scars of urban renewal.

At that time, there was hope that the economic boom underway in Southern Maine would soon shift north, but it didn't happen. Major projects and grand economic development plans locally and in the region either fizzled or never got off the drawing board. Meanwhile, economic heavyweights in the area continued to decline and the city continued to debate its ill-fated urban renewal project. The great hope of the Sunbury Mall in downtown gave way to the stark reality of vacant storefronts.

"In the long run, I think we'll see that Urban Renewal did a lot of good for the city," Merle Goff, who served as city manager from 1966 to 1976, said in 1982. "But there's no denying the adverse results. Some of those buildings shouldn't have come down. We just didn't have today's historic preservation values in the sixties."[5]

One criticism of urban renewal is that it hampered any attempt by the city to emerge as an historic attraction. There is no question many great names of the past are largely a memory. Among those that have vanished are W.T. Grant, which closed its Central Street store in 1976, and Freese's, once the "Fifth Avenue of Maine," which closed its downtown store in January 1985. Although greatly diminished in size and import by this time, the announcement that Freese's would close saddened many and "there wasn't a dry eye in the place," according to one employee.[6]

Shopper Charlotte Brophy said, "What little bit of money I have, I want to spend downtown where I earned my living. I'd like to see it built up, not torn down. Bangor will never be the same."[7]

Meanwhile, Standard Shoe closed its downtown store in 1995 and then closed its last Standard Shoe store in 1998, ending that ninety-year-old local family business. Also long gone were such downtown stores as Senter's, Sears, F.W. Woolworth and Mammoth Mart.

In fact, nearly all of the historic names were gone, except Bangor Savings Bank, which continued its commitment to downtown by restoring its branch at 3 State Street in the late-1990s and opening new corporate offices on Franklin Street.

Then by the mid-1990s, signs of life emerged on several fronts in Bangor and hopes began to bud for many more. In historic West Market Square, The Grasshopper Shop of Maine, a clothing and gift store, operated in the Wheelwright & Clark Block near such other businesses as The Whig & Courier Pub and Boyd & Noyes jewelry store.

Courtesy of Bangor Daily News
Main Street in downtown Bangor, 1996, looking toward intersection with Hammond Street.

Cadillac Mountain Sports took over part of the old W.T. Grant build-ing, while Rebecca's gift shop and G.M. Pollack & Sons jewelry store operated along with clusters of specialty stores on Main Street. Some condominiums and new upper-story apartments opened to lure new resi-dents to parts of downtown.

At the same time, the city began to look better.

Also reawakening was the old Freese's building. In 1995, part of the store was converted to senior citizen housing. In 2001, the Maine Discovery Museum opened with three floors of interactive exhibits. The museum billed itself as the biggest children's museum north of Boston. During the dedication ceremony, Congressman John Baldacci, a Bangor native, proclaimed, "You're restoring the heart of Bangor."[8]

Even more symbolic, and perhaps most important to a sustained revival has been the reclamation of the Penobscot River and the Bangor waterfront, once the source of the city's grandeur. After the city's lumber industry died in the early twentieth century, pollution slowly turned the river into an abandoned, reeking stream and the waterfront itself simply rotted. Recognizing the problems and the potential, the city began to acquire tracts of waterfront land, clean up contamination left by railroads and other industrial users, and devise plans and concepts to revive a waterfront long dormant.

That work is starting to pay dividends. In 2000, Bangor was honored by the U.S. Department of Housing and Urban Development (HUD) for its Penobscot Riverfront Development Project, a project that prepared and cleaned land for potential development from the Veterans Memorial Bridge off the lower end of Main Street to the downtown area.

The waterfront development plans are grand, but largely still conceptual. The plans include hotels, marinas, a conference center, office building, retail sites, a Maine products pavilion, docks and a museum. Local businessman Christopher Hutchins has pledged up to three million dollars to build an amphitheater.

Given the momentum, some people have already returned to parts of the waterfront. The Sea Dog restaurant has opened on the river as has a new park. The Maine Shakespeare Festival now takes place on the riverfront each summer and the National Folk Festival is set to begin a three-year run in Bangor starting in the summer of 2002.

Elsewhere, the city is discussing options for a new Bangor Auditorium and Civic Center. City Councilor David Nealley, whose ancestors helped found Snow & Nealley in the 1800s, sees a need for regional support for some major projects, but believes Bangor is pulling out of its "lull."

"The bulk of the work has been done in the 1990s," he said. "It is sort of interesting that people don't see work beginning until there are some buildings up. When there is an amphitheater or a hotel or some restaurants and pavilions down there, then the rest of the community will say something is happening down there. But all that important infrastructure work, shoring up the bulkheads and cleaning up the waterfront, that type of slow grunt work is largely done."

The Twenty-first Century

In the toddler years of the twenty-first century, Bangor and Bangor Savings Bank are considerably changed from their nineteenth-century days. They both have seen the heyday of lumber, survived the devastation of the Great Fire, and watched the glory of the 1950s downtown retail, the far-reaching effects of urban renewal and the rise of the shopping mall.

And they have also witnessed a virtual revolution in banking with the number of banks dwindling from more than 150 to less than 40 and as operations have changed from 9 A.M. to 3 P.M. to twenty-four-hour access via the Internet. The simple passbook has been replaced by a dizzying array of investment and savings options. Bangor Savings Bank itself has watched bank after bank come and go in the city even while it has remained at the same location now for 112 years.

What hasn't changed is

Courtesy of Bangor Daily News
Bill Frederick of Lougee & Frederick's Inc. Florist hangs a Christmas wreath outside Bangor Savings Bank's historic offices at 3 State Street in 1986.

that Bangor Savings Bank remains vital. Now it serves an increasingly large community of people and businesses that span the width and breadth of Maine, while the Queen City remains an essential economic and social force in Eastern Maine. From the Bangor Mall to Eastern Maine Medical Center, the city's largest employer, to the University of Maine in nearby Orono, the city of Bangor continues to serve a sprawling geographic region.

In the future as in the past, Bangor will serve as the economic catalyst for a region and perhaps even a state. As such, it will remain as it was in the 1840s when Thoreau traveled up the river to find a thriving city at the edge of a great region and wrote, "There stands the city of Bangor . . . like a star on the edge of night."

287

Bangor Savings Bank Board of Trustees, 2002. Standing (left to right) are: Charles E. Hewett, Kenneth A. Hews, Calvin E. True and Robert A. Strong. Seated are: James H. Goff, P. James Dowe Jr., David M. Carlisle, Martha G. Newman, and Gary W. Smith.

Jim Dowe, as is his nature, can see a modern version of the same greatness. It is hard to say where Bangor and Bangor Savings Bank[9] will be or what they will look like in twenty-five or fifty years. There is no question that banking will continue to change and evolve. Consolidation will continue, financial services will continue to meld into banking organizations. Bangor Savings Bank will continue to look for expansion opportunities and one day soon will probably expand into all the counties of Maine — but always with one eye on its 150-year legacy.

"We want to create something here," Dowe said. "We want to unselfishly look ahead. We want to really say 'what can we do now so that someone we don't know today will have the same opportunity to work or do business with a Maine-based, independent financial institution twenty-five years from now.' We want to do what we can to make sure that Bangor Savings Bank is still here to serve the people of Bangor and the people of Maine."

Epilogue

In my office, on the wall directly across from my desk, is a picture of founder and Bangor Savings Bank's first president, Elijah Hamlin. I look at that picture often, and can't help but think of how much has remained constant since Elijah's time, and yet how much has changed. I feel privileged to be the most current addition to an amazingly short list of Bangor Savings Bank presidents. Each of us — with the support and leadership of bright and dedicated Trustees and equally talented employees — has been faced with the daunting but very special task of constantly "refounding" this company. Over and over again, through recessions, depressions and economic booms, war and peace, natural disasters, and regulatory evolution, Bangor Savings Bank has reinvented itself to meet the challenges of the time and the needs of its customers. And yet the core principles and mission have remained constant — whether voiced or not. Think first about the customer, stay relevant for the times, and look to the future. Remain true to the mission, but dare to be bold in the process of reinvention. *That* has been the secret of our survival for 150 years.

So on this, our sesquicentennial anniversary, we have written *Here for Generations: The Story of a Maine Bank and its City*, this history from before our founding in 1852 to 2002. We wanted to capture the facts and circumstances surrounding our long and prosperous "life," not only to tell our story, but also to discover and record the lessons that were learned as the story unfolded, so that we, and others, may learn from them.

It turns out that the lessons from our history validate our approach to our future. Be thoughtful, but bold. Understand what you want to accomplish, and go for it. Remember why you exist, and whom you owe that existence to. Find and value good employees who care about their customers and their company. Select leadership that is tuned in to the times, while looking to and preparing for the future. Give back in so many ways that you lose track. And finally, when decisions need to be made, be aware of all of this, and then make those decisions based on what you believe to be the right thing to do. It is what Elijah did, and what the leadership of the bank has been doing ever since. It is why we have been successful, resilient, and remained relevant. It is why we have been Bangor Savings Bank for 150 years, and why we can say with confidence that we will be here for Maine for a long time to come. I hope you enjoyed our story.

P. James Dowe Jr.
Bangor, Maine
April 2002

Appendix

Petition to Create Bangor Savings Bank

To the Honorable Senate and House of Representatives, of the State of Maine in Legislature assembled.

The undersigned, citizens of Bangor, in the county of Penobscot, State of Maine, pray that you would grant them and their associates an act of incorporation for a Savings Bank to be located at said Bangor with such powers and privileges, and subject to such provisions & restrictions, as are usual with such institutions, and as to you may seem fit and proper.

Bangor, Dec. 29th, 1851

E.L. Hamlin
Albert Holton
Samuel H. Dale
George R. Smith
Michael Boyce
A. Thompson
T.W. Baldwin
Henry A. Wood
Jabez True
Albert W. Paine

Text of Original Bank Charter

State of Maine.

In the year of our Lord one thousand eight hundred and fifty two.

An Act to incorporate the Bangor Savings Bank.

Be it enacted by the Senate and House of Representatives in Legislature assembled, as follows:

Section 1. E.L. Hamlin, Albert Holton, J.S. Wheelwright, Samuel H. Dale, George R. Smith, Michael Boyce, A. Thompson, T.W. Baldwin, Henry A. Wood, Jabez True, Albert W. Paine and such others as may associate with them, are hereby constituted a body politic and corporate, by the name of the Bangor Savings Bank, and by that name may prosecute and defend suits at law; and may have and use a common seal, and all deeds, grants, conveyances, covenants and agreements, made by their treasurer or any other person under their authority and direction pursuant to the by-laws of the corporation, shall be good and valid, and said corporation shall have power to make any by-laws for the convenient management of their concerns, not repugnant to the laws of the state.

Section 2. Said corporation shall be capable of receiving from any person or persons, disposed to avail themselves of the advantages of said institution, any deposit or deposits of money, and to use and improve the same for the purposes herein provided.

Section 3. All deposits of money received by the said corporation, shall be used and improved to the best advantage, and the net income or profit thereof shall be by them applied and divided among the persons making such deposits, their executers, administrators or assigns, in just proportion, and the principal of such deposits may be withdrawn at such reasonable times and in such manner, as the said corporation shall direct and appoint.

Section 4. Said corporation at their first and afterwards at their annual meetings, shall have power to elect by ballot, any person or persons they may deem proper, as members of said corporation.

Section 5. Said corporation shall meet at Bangor, at such time in the month of July annually, and at such other times, as the society, or the president thereof may direct, and any five members of said corporation, the president or vice-president, treasurer or secretary being one, shall form a quorum: and the said corporation, at their meeting in July annually, shall have power to choose a president and all other officers as to them shall appear necessary; which officers, so chosen, shall continue in office one year and until others are chosen in their stead; and the treasurer and secretary shall be under oath to the faithful performance of the duties of their offices respectively; and the said treasurer shall also be required, before entering upon the duties of his office, to give bond to said corporation, in such sum as they may require, with sufficient sureties to be by them approved, for the faithful performance of said duties.

Section 6. The first meeting of said corporation may be called at such time and place in Bangor and by such one of the persons named in the first section of this act, as a majority of all the persons named in the said first section may direct, by giving notice thereof in any public newspaper printed in the city of Bangor, fourteen days before such meeting.

Section 7. The powers granted in this act may be enlarged, restricted or annulled, at the pleasure of the Legislature.

Section 8. This act shall take effect from and after its approval by the Governor.

In the House of Representatives February 10, 1852.
This bill having had three several readings, passed to be enacted.

G.P. Sewall Speaker, In Senate, February 11, 1852.
This bill having had two several readings, passed to be enacted.

Noah Prince President
February 14, 1852. Approved
John Hubbard.

Secretary's Office
Augusta Feby 26, 1852

I hereby certify that the foregoing is a true copy of the original deposited in this office
John G. Lawyer
Sec'y of State.

Bank Presidents

Until the 1960s, the title given to the chief executive of the bank was treasurer. The official title was then changed to president.

Albert Holton	1852
John Patten	1865
Samuel D. Thurston	1876
James Crosby	1893
John L. Crosby	1894
Everett F. Rich	1908
Walter A. Danforth	1917
Harold L. Nason	1948
Malcolm E. Jones	1975
P. James Dowe Jr.	1995

Chairmen

Until the 1960s, the title given to what is now called the chairman of the Board of Trustees was president.

Elijah L. Hamlin	1852
George W. Pickering	1863
Charles Hayward	1877
Joseph Wheelwright	1890
Samuel F. Humphrey	1895
Charles V. Lord	1903
Frederick H. Appleton	1905
Charles H. Bartlett	1913
Edgar M. Simpson	1936
George F. Eaton	1953
Donald S. Higgins	1956
Martyn A. Vickers	1972
G. Clifton Eames	1989
David M. Carlisle	1999

Board of Trustees

When Bangor Savings Bank was founded in 1852 it had five officers and an additional 19 trustees. The total number remained 24 until the late 1860s when the number of trustees was cut to five. The exact start date of some early trustees is not known and they are indicated by listing the year by which it is known they sat on the Board of Trustees.

*Elijah L. Hamlin	1852	Joseph W. Low	by 1861
*Isaiah Stetson	1852	Joseph Bryant	by 1861
*Samuel H. Dale	1852	J.C. White	by 1861
*Albert Holton	1852	Lemuel Bradford	by 1861
*Joseph S. Wheelwright	1852	A.D. Manson	by 1862
Thomas W. Baldwin	1852	Hollis Bowman	1863
William A. Blake	1852	James Littlefield	1863
Michael Boyce	1852	A.G. Wakefield	1863
Samuel Farrar	1852	Daniel Sargent II	1863
John Burt Foster	1852	F.M Sabine	1864
Charles Hayward	1852	George K. Jewett	1865
Samuel F. Hersey	1852	J.W. Humphrey	1865
Leonard March	1852	N.H. Dillingham	1865
Franklin Muzzy	1852	James Patten	1867
Albert Ware Paine	1852	Charles Stetson	1867
Waldo T. Peirce	1852	William B. Hayford	1875
Nathan Pendleton	1852	John S. Ricker	1878
George W. Pickering	1852	Samuel F. Humphrey	1886
Amos M. Roberts	1852	James Adams	1886
George R. Smith	1852	Charles V. Lord	1887
Arad Thompson	1852	William H. Strickland	1890
Jabez True	1852	Moses Giddings	1891
John Winn	1852	Frederick H. Appleton	1895
Henry A. Wood	1852	George Varney	1903
John Bright	by 1856	Arthur F. Stetson	1905
Thomas A. Taylor	by 1856	Matthew Laughlin	1907
Joseph C. White	by 1856	Erastus C. Ryder	1908
Solomon Parsons	by 1861	Walter L. Head	1910
James B. Fiske	by 1861	Charles H. Bartlett	1911

Board of Trustees (*continued*)

* The Bank's original officers

Bangor Savings Bank Total Assets

1855	$29,021
1860	$71,636
1865	$319,818
1870	$1,474,484
1875	$2,393,900
1880	$1,034,333
1885	$1,794,749
1890	$3,178,668
1895	$3,311,453
1900	$4,410,165
1905	$5,452,062
1910	$6,183,431
1915	$6,504,519
1920	$6,755,218
1925	$7,718,912
1930	$8,807,100
1935	$10,879,393
1940	$11,812,868
1945	$13,990,433
1950	$21,302,061
1955	$28,370,214
1960	$39,443,293
1965	$57,022,117
1970	$82,767,051
1975	$138,977,591
1980	$271,405,894
1985	$393,895,969
1990	$553,572,694
1995	$687,190,793
2000	$1,241,640,000
2002	$1,336,954,000

Bangor Savings Bank Branch Locations ~ 2002

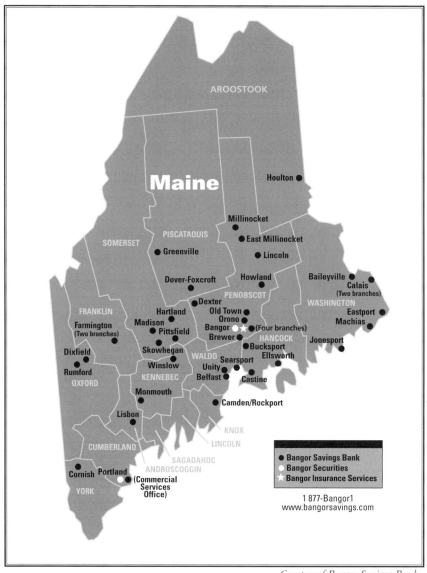

Courtesy of Bangor Savings Bank

This map shows locations of all Bangor Savings Bank offices as of May 31, 2002.

Bangor Map

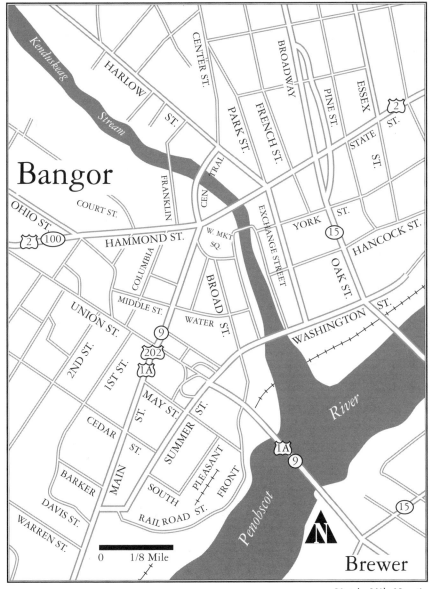

Map by Mike Nasuti

A street map of downtown Bangor, 2002.

State of Maine

Proclamation

WHEREAS, Bangor Savings Bank was chartered as a Maine mutual savings bank on February 14, 1852, and is one of Maine's oldest companies operating under its original name and ownership; and

WHEREAS, Bangor Savings Bank, having begun operations in rented offices at West Market Square in Bangor, Maine, under its first president, Elijah L. Hamlin, brother of Hannibal Hamlin, Vice President of the United States in the first term of Abraham Lincoln; and

WHEREAS, Bangor Savings Bank having rebuilt its offices following the great Bangor fire of 1911 at 3 State Street, Bangor, Maine, and operated from this historic facility unto this date now operates from 45 locations throughout the State of Maine and on the web at www.bangorsavings.com; and

WHEREAS, Bangor Savings Bank's mission is "a timeless commitment to Maine and all who love her"; and

WHEREAS, Bangor Savings Bank has changed and prospered in service to the people of Maine so that today with more than 500 employees, Bangor Savings Bank has become a contemporary provider of comprehensive consumer and commercial banking products including trust, insurance, and investment services for more than 100,000 households and businesses within the State; and

WHEREAS, Bangor Savings Bank established and endowed The Bangor Savings Bank Foundation as a permanent philanthropic institution to provide strategic contributions in support of educational, social and civic, cultural and arts, and health and wellness initiatives in Maine communities; and

WHEREAS, Bangor Savings Bank for 150 years with its trustees, corporators, officers, and employees has faithfully discharged its duties to the public and set an example of leadership, business enterprise, corporate responsibility, community service, and the true spirit of Maine.

NOW, THEREFORE, I, ANGUS S. KING, JR., Governor of the State of Maine, do hereby proclaim February 14, 2002 as

BANGOR SAVINGS BANK SESQUICENTENNIAL DAY!

throughout the State of Maine, and urge all citizens to recognize this important event.

In testimony whereof, I have caused the Great Seal of the State to be hereunto affixed GIVEN under my hand at Augusta this twenty-eighth day of January in the Year of our Lord Two Thousand and Two.

Angus S. King, Jr.
Governor

Dan A. Gwadosky
Secretary of State
TRUE ATTESTED COPY

300

Endnotes

Chapter One: The Birth of Bangor

1   Tribal names and territories are presented based on information from the Smithsonian Institution and historian Dean R. Smith: "Eastern Abenaki," *Handbook of North American Indians, Vol. 15* (Washington: 1978). Other sources use different names depending on the era and whether following the early French or English naming convention. The early French broke the Wabanaki into four ethnic groups, according to Bruce J. Bourque: *Twelve Thousand Years: American Indians in Maine* (Lincoln: Nebraska: 2001). They were: Souriquois, mostly in what is now Nova Scotia and New Brunswick, later known as the Micmac; the Etchemins, mostly located in Eastern Maine from the St. John River to the Kennebec, later known by the French as the Maliseet and the Canibas (Kennebec) tribes; the Almouchiquois, located west of the Kennebec and a group usually hostile to the Souriquois. The name Almouchiquois translates to "dog people." In addition, the French later added a fourth name, Abenakis, and that name that soon came to cover all four ethnic groups.

2   For further descriptions of Champlain's journeys, consult Samuel Eliot Morison: *Samuel de Champlain: Father of New France* (Boston: 1972) and H.P. Biggar: *The Works of Samuel de Champlain in Six Volumes* (Toronto: 1922).

3   *I am convinced.* Biggar, *The Works of Samuel de Champlain*, p. 285.

4   In 2002, the Penobscots own roughly sixty thousand acres of land, including more than 180 islands in the Penobscot River. The center of the Penobscot Nation is located at Indian Island in Old Town. The Penobscots acquired thousands of acres of land in the 1980s following a lawsuit filed jointly with the Passamaquoddy tribe that had sought 12.5 million acres or more than two-thirds of Maine. That lawsuit hinged on the Indian Nonintercourse Act of 1790 which prohibited the sale of Indian lands without approval by Congress. The Indians and their lawyers argued that treaties and deals signed in 1796, 1818 and 1833 were invalid. In a negotiated settlement reached in 1980, the Penobscot, Passamaquoddy and Maliseet tribes were awarded $81.5 million, a portion which was used to acquire thousands of acres of land and a portion which was set aside for aid and economic development.

5   *old damn.* James B. Vickery, *Bangor, Maine: An Illustrated History 1769-1976* (Bangor: 1976), p. 16.

6   *By much effort.* Jacob McGaw, "Notices of Bangor from its Settlement in A.D. 1769 to the End of 1819" (Collections of the Maine Historical Society), p. 24.

7   *We are here.* Vickery, *Bangor*, p. 16

8   *A British officer.* William D. Williamson papers.

9   *So also.* McGaw, "Notices," p. 39.

10   *Could your honors.* Alan Taylor, *Liberty Men and Great Proprietors* (Chapel Hill, North Carolina: 1990), p. 72.

11   *inhabited by poor people.* Taylor, *Liberty Men,* p. 73.

12   Taylor, *Liberty Men*, p. 133.

13   While important in the town's early history, James Budge was also a troubled man. He was apparently fond of drink and a little dangerous, so his wife had him put in jail. Rev. Lemuel Norton, who brought prisoners food at the Castine jail, described Budge: "He was a man of strong intellectual powers, rather a good scholar, and something of a poet; wrote a great deal, made some excellent poetry–but rum, that demon rum, which destroys its thousands every year, destroyed him, got the mastery over him, and probably ruined him for this world and for that which is to come." John E. Godfrey, "The Annals of Bangor, 1769–1882," *History of Penobscot County, Maine with Illustrations and Biographical Sketches* (Cleveland: 1882), p. 538.

14   *I went to Bangor.* Godfrey, *The Annals of Bangor*, p. 545.

15   *Soon after I came.* Godfrey, *The Annals of Bangor*, p. 546

16   *It fell upon.* McGaw, "Notices," pp. 60-61.

17   *the black death.* Joseph W. Porter, editor, "Rev. John Sawyer and Family, And Kimball Families of Bangor" *Bangor Historical Magazine: A Monthly* (June 1891), p. 274.

18   *a plague. Voices*, p. 53.

19   *Against all obstacles. Voices*, p. 53.

Chapter Two: The Rise of American Banking

1   *The whole tendency.* Eastern (Portland) *Argus*, May 26, 1837.

2   *An Experiment. Bangor Daily Whig and Courier*, May 30, 1837.

3   The most complete secondary account of Maine's early banking is provided by Walter W. Chadbourne: *A History of Maine Banking, 1799–1930* (Orono, Maine: 1936). Some statistics presented in this text

are taken from his account, and supplemental statistics and raw data are gleaned from state banking reports and Bangor Savings Bank records.

4   *The Castine Bank.* Everett Birney Stackpole, "State Banking in Maine." *Sound Currency* (May 1900), p. 78.

5   *The Boston Alliance.* Chadbourne, *A History*, p. 44.

6   *That some of.* Whig and Courier, Dec. 8, 1836.

7   *representations were made.* Godfrey, *The Annals of Bangor*, p. 602.

8   *Bangor was a little village.* Godfrey, *The Annals of Bangor*, p. 602.

9   *One would think.* Godfrey, *The Annals of Bangor*, p. 602.

10   *Bangor banks.* Edward Wesley Potter, "Public Policy and Economic Growth in Maine, 1820–1857, Ph. D., diss., University of Maine, 1974, p. 223.

11   *Massachusetts investors.* Potter, "Public Policy," p. 272.

12   *Wage worker.* Franklin H. Ornstein, *Savings Banks: An Industry in Change* (Reston, Virginia: 1985), p. 16.

13   *nurtured by.* Ornstein, *Savings Banks*, p. 16.

14   *It is not by.* Weldon Welfing, *Mutual Savings Banks: The Evolution of a Financial Intermediary* (Cleveland: 1968), p. 10.

Chapter Three: Elijah Livermore Hamlin.

1   *divided the honor.* E.O. Jameson, *The Choates in America 1643-1896* (Boston: 1896), p. 192.

2   *a welcome visitant.* Whig and Courier, July 20, 1872.

3   *Of Sheriffs.* Franklin H. Andrews, *The Hamlin Family: A Genealogy of James Hamlin of Barnstable, Massachusetts* (Iowa: 1902), p. 197.

4   *I have trained them.* Charles E. Hamlin, *The Life and Times of Hannibal Hamlin, by his Grandson* (Cambridge: 1899), p. 13.

5   *From this day.* Hamlin, *The Life and Times*, p. 13.

6   *I was a very.* Reginald H. Sturtevant, *A History of Livermore, Maine* (Lewiston, Maine: 1970), p. 50.

7   *patient and devoted.* Hamlin, *The Life and Times*, p. 13.

8   Metallak, known as The Lone Indian of the Magalloway, was a member of a band of Abenaki who lived in the upper Androscoggin and was a well-known guide. He died in New Hampshire in 1847, reputedly at the age of 120. The birch bark map he made for Elijah Hamlin is on display at the Hamlin Memorial Library and Museum at Paris Hill.

9   *hell fire.* Clarence A. Day, *Ezekiel Holmes: Father of Maine Agriculture* (Orono, Maine: 1968), p. 19.

10   *Now remember.* Andrews, *The Hamlin Family*, p. 345.

11   *If you want.* Hamlin, *The Life and Times*, p. 30.

12   *The town came. The Story of Bangor: A Brief History of Maine's Queen City* (Bangor: 1999), p. 37.

13   *All Maine was looking.* Charles E. Clark. *Maine: A Bicentennial History* (New York: 1977), p. 107.

14   *In addition.* John Arndt, "The Solid Men of Bangor: Economic, Business and Political Growth of Maine's Urban Frontier 1769–1845" (The Florida State University, 1987), p. 163.

15   *The assertions that. Whig and Courier*, Aug. 23, 1836.

16   *I therefore. Whig and Courier*, Aug. 23, 1836.

17   *evident that the bank.* Stackpole, "State Banking in Maine," p. 82.

18   Neal Dow, known as The Father of Temperance, played a major role in the history of nineteenth-century Maine. He was a leading temperance reformer nationally and helped bring Prohibition to several states. In Maine, he led the battle to enact the Maine Law in 1851 which restricted the sale of alcohol. It was the first Prohibition law in the United States. Prohibition remained a powerful political issue in Maine into the twentieth century.

19   *and its putrid corpse. Eastern Argus*, June 27, 1848.

20   *Mr. H. Portland Advertiser*, May 30, 1848.

21   *Among all the men. Whig and Courier*, May 30, 1848.

22   *I will do for you.* Elijah Hamlin to Hannibal Hamlin, April 5, 1850, Hamlin Papers

23   *so choked. Mayor's Address: And the Annual Reports of ... Made to the City Council of Bangor, 1852*, p. 8.

24   *The common idea. Mayor's Address 1852*, p. 7.

25   *The real progress. Mayor's Address 1852*, p. 7.

26   *A putrid mass.* Scroggins, *Hannibal: The Life of Abraham Lincoln's First Vice President* (Lanham, Maryland: 1994), p. 130.

27   *He left a glorious. Eastern Argus*, June 26, 1856.

28   *he has enrolled. The Machias Union*, July 1, 1856.

29   *You and I.* Hamlin, *The Life and Times*, p. 302.

30   *Didn't they howl. Oxford Democrat*, Jan. 25, 1885.

31   *About twelve o'clock.* Louis C. Hatch, *Maine: A History, Vol. II* (Somersworth, New Hampshire: 1919), p. 422.

32   *had enough.* Richard W. Judd, et al, *Maine: The Pine Tree State from Prehistory to the Present* (Orono: 1995), p. 350.

Chapter Four: The Founders

1   Details on the lives of each founder were drawn from a variety of sources, including obituaries that appeared in the *Bangor Daily Whig and Courier* and federal census records.

2   *was one of.* *Whig and Courier,* Feb. 4, 1875.

3   *lightening campaign.* H. Draper Hunt, *Hannibal Hamlin of Maine: Lincoln's First Vice-President* (Syracuse: 1962), p. 116.

4   *The naturalness.* Hunt, *Hannibal Hamlin,* p. 118.

5   *This terminates our.* Hamlin, *The Life and Times,* p. 416.

6   *To tell you.* Hannibal Hamlin to Samuel F. Hersey, Hamlin Papers.

7   *Gen. Hersey died.* John E. Godfrey, *The Journals of John Edwards Godfrey, Vol. 2,* (Rockland, Maine: 1979), p. 204.

8   *No more.* *Whig and Courier,* Feb. 15, 1875.

9   *energetic and innovative.* James B. Vickery, *Made in Bangor: Economic Emergence and Adaptation, 1834-1911* (Bangor: 1984), p. 8.

10   *I was therefore.* Franklin Muzzy, *Critical Early Years in the Life of Franklin Muzzy* (Minneapolis, 1827), p. 16.

11   *not worthy.* Muzzy, *Critical Years,* p. 21.

12   *These, together.* Muzzy, *Critical Years,* p. 24.

13   Carol Toner. "Franklin Muzzy: Artisan Entrepreneur in Nineteenth-Century Bangor," *Maine Historical Quarterly* (Fall 1990), p. 70.

14   *continued to espouse.* Toner, "Franklin Muzzy," p. 70.

15   *He had a high.* *Whig and Courier,* Nov. 5, 1873.

16   *from becoming.* Toner, "Franklin Muzzy," p. 85.

17   *We know dear Caroline.* Franklin Muzzy to Caroline Muzzy, September 14, 1845, Muzzy Papers.

18   *I feel utterly lost.* Caroline Muzzy to Franklin Muzzy, January 23, 1853, Muzzy Papers.

19   *While in the.* *Whig and Courier,* Nov. 5, 1873.

20   *His habits.* *Whig and Courier,* Nov. 5, 1873.

21   *He was one.* *Whig and Courier,* Oct. 28, 1895.

22   *Thus ended.* *Whig and Courier,* Sept. 29, 1876.

23   *My old friend.* Godfrey, *The Journals, Vol. 2,* p. 270.

24   David C. Smith, *A History of Lumbering in Maine 1861–1960* (Orono: 1972), p. 196.

25   *swift work.* *Whig and Courier,* Dec. 8, 1871.

26   *The insurance agent.* Godfrey, *The Journals, Vol. 2,* p. 72.

27   *Apparently Roberts.* Arndt, *The Solid Men*, p. 110.

28   *His was an example.* Elnathan Duren, "Personal Reminiscences by Elnathan Freeman Duren, Sec. 1864–1907," *Fiftieth Anniversary of the Bangor Historical Society 1864-1914* (Bangor: 1914), p. 61.

29   *In the morning.* Godfrey, *The Journals, Vol. I*, p. 216.

30   *In the spring. Report of the Joint Select Committee on the Defalcation of Benjamin D. Peck, late Treasurer of the State of Maine* (Augusta: 1860), p. 38.

31   *The run upon.* Elijah Hamlin to Hannibal Hamlin, Jan. 6, 1860. Hamlin Papers.

32   *It seems that.* Elijah Hamlin to Hannibal Hamlin, May 24, 1858, Hamlin Papers.

33   James H. Mundy, *hard times, hard men: Maine and the Irish 1830–1860* (Scarborough: 1990), p. 40.

34   *was in a very.* William E.S. Whitman and Charles H. True, *Maine in the War for the Union* (Lewiston: 1865), p. 335.

35   *a man of. Whig and Courier*, August 13, 1898.

36   *pecuniary embarrassments. Whig and Courier*, Dec. 13, 1862.

37   *zealous advocate. Whig and Courier*, Jan. 9, 1890.

38   *Onward the shouting.* R.H. Stanley and George O. Hall, *Eastern Maine and the Rebellion* (Bangor: 1887), p. 82.

39   *Following the death.* Mundy, *Presidents of the Senate* (Augusta: 1979).

40   *attacked by a hemorrhage. Whig and Courier*, Dec. 12, 1861.

41   Arndt, *The Solid Men*, p. 183.

42   *another of the old. Bangor Daily News*, Jan. 21, 1907.

43   *It came rushing. Whig and Courier*, April 3, 1846.

44   *The saddest most. Whig and Courier*, April 3, 1846.

45   *The whole river. Whig and Courier*, April 3, 1846.

Chapter Five: Widows, Orphans and the Daily Laborer

1   *When Thomas Hobbs.* Mundy, *hard times, hard men*, p. 31.

2   *there will come a feeling. Whig and Courier*, May 10, 1852.

3   *One of the most. Whig and Courier*, May 10, 1852.

4   *That these institutions. Annual Report of the Bank Commissioners of the State of Maine, 1861*, p. 93.

5   *They constitute a safety. Annual Report of the Bank Commissioners of the State of Maine, 1856*, p. 96.

6   *the notable defects.* Chadbourne, *A History of Banking*, p. 99.

7   *The time may soon arrive. Voices*, p. 134.

8   *very angry. Bangor Daily Commercial*, June 21, 1889.

9   *its heavenly color.* Stewart H. Holbrook, *Holy Old Mackinaw: A Natural History of the American Lumberjack* (New York: 1938), p. 27.

10   *a women who lied.* Wayne E. Reilly and Richard R. Shaw, "In Search of the Real Fan Jones," *Down East* (April 1988), p. 42.

11   *Ladies of the night.* Reilly, *Down East*, p. 42.

12   *Fan Jones she runs.* Reilly, *Down East*, p. 78.

Chapter Six: A Financial Crisis

1   *transformed into fairy. Whig and Courier*, Oct. 19, 1871.

2   *What this state needs. Address of Governor Chamberlain to the Legislature of the State of Maine, January 1870*, p. 9.

3   *as the great achievement.* Charles W. Tuttle, "Hon. John Alfred Poor, of Portland, ME," *New-England Historical and Genealogical Register and Antiquarian Journal* (October 1872), p. 360.

4   *redeeming his native.* Edward C. Kirkland, *Men, Cities and Transportation: A Study in New England History 1820–1900* (Cambridge: 1948), p. 206.

5   *though not yet.* Kirkland, *Men, Cities and Transportation*, p. 206.

6   *The weather was bad.* Neil Rolde, *Maine: A Narrative History* (Gardiner: 1990), p. 190.

7   *the deserted village.* Laura E. Poor, *The First International Railroad and the Colonization of new England: Life and Writing of John A. Poor* (New York: 1892), p. 31.

8   *with more extended.* Clark, *Maine*, p. 98.

9   *Let village, and city.* John A. Poor, "Remarks of John A. Poor, Upon the European and North American Railway (1851), p. 8.

10   *Had Mr. Poor.* Laura E. Poor, *The First International Railroad*, p. 75.

11   *the hitherto hostile.* Kirkland, *Men, Cities and Transportation*, p. 221.

12   *weld the trade.* Kirkland, *Men, Cities and Transportation*, p. 472.

13   *The fact that they. Eighteenth Annual Report of the Condition of the Savings Banks of the State of Maine, 1874*, p. 6.

14   *Depositors must be aware. Whig and Courier*, Jan. 3, 1878.

15   *Should the depositors. Bangor Daily Commercial*, Jan. 3, 1878.

16   *So many savings banks. Bangor Daily Commercial*, Jan. 4, 1878.

17   *The undersigned. Whig and Courier*, Jan. 25, 1878.

18   *appears to represent. Mayor's Address. Also, the Annual Reports of the Several Departments and the Receipts and Expenditures for the Municipal Year 1876-'77*, p. 7.

19   *The continued depressed state. Mayor's Address, 1876–'77*, p. 118.

20   *We are informed. Whig and Courier*, January 4, 1878.

21   *A Well Known Merchant. Whig and Courier*, Aug. 15, 1876.

22   Sis Deans, *His Proper Post: A Biography of General Joshua L. Chamberlain* (New Jersey: 1996), p. 95-97.

Chapter Seven: The Fall of King Lumber

1   *Bangor appeared.* Judith S. Goldstein, *Crossing Lines: Histories of Jews and Gentiles in Three Communities* (New York: 1992), p. 38.

2   *The twin monsters. Bangor Daily News*, March 22, 1902.

3   *quickly took on.* Clark, *Maine*, p. 138.

4   *As the price.* Smith, *A History of Lumbering*, p. 253.

5   *ownership of the land.* Smith, *A History of Lumbering*, p. 175.

6   *The Times had changed.* Fannie Hardy Eckstorm, *The Penobscot Man* (Boston: 1904), p. 190.

7   *the long-expected.* John E. McLeod, *The Great Northern Paper Co.* (1978), p. 6.

8   *would mean.* Smith, *A History of Lumbering*, p. 269.

9   *And at the same.* Clark, *Maine*, p. 139.

10   *the lumber trade.* W.F. Blanding, editor, *Bangor, Maine: Industries and Resources 1888* (Bangor: 1888), p. 21.

11   *The police. Bangor Daily Commercial*, April 3, 1914.

12   *fell upon. Bangor Daily News*, April 3, 1914.

13   *Twenty-five years. Bangor Daily Commercial*, April 3, 1914.

14   *A sailor would. Bangor Daily News*, January 25, 1921.

15   *Once she. City of Bangor Mayor's Address, 1876–'77*, p. 20.

16   *This port.* Blanding, *Bangor, Maine*, p. 24.

17   *the only half-safe.* Bill Caldwell, *Rivers of Fortune* (Portland: 1983), p. 185.

Chapter Eight: From the Ashes

1   *Shacks sprung up. Bangor Daily News*, July 1, 1911.

2   *Many fires. Bangor Daily News*, May 3, 1911.

3   *The vault. Bangor Daily News*, May 3, 1911.

4   *an eye out. Bangor Daily News*, May 6, 1911.

5   *The news. Bangor Daily Commercial*, May 16, 1911.

6   *The Trustees. Bangor Daily News*, Sept. 29, 1911.

7   *a decided ornament. Bangor Daily Commercial*, Jan. 3, 1912.

8   *It is splendidly.* The *Industrial Journal,* December 1913, p. 11.

9   *Civic Improvement. Bangor Daily News,* May 30, 1911.

10   *Impractical plans. Bangor Daily Commercial,* May 29, 1911.

11   *block after block. Chamber of Commerce Journal of Maine* (September 1915), p. 181.

12   *a growth. Chamber of Commerce Journal of Maine* (September 1915), p. 181.

13   Charles H. Bartlett was born in Bangor in 1858. He went to prep school at Phillips Exeter Academy before attending Harvard College and Harvard Law School, where he was a member of the Hasty Pudding Club. He was admitted to the bar in 1883. During his career, he served as president of the Penobscot Bar Association and was a member of business clubs, including the Tarratine Club and the Rotary Club. He was a member of the Unitarian Church. His wife, Virginia Hight Bartlett, died in 1890, only five years after they were married. They had one son, Charles D. Bartlett.
Bartlett also helped organize Eastern Maine General Hospital and served as a trustee. He also served as a director of the Maine Central Railroad and First National Bank. He served as president of Bangor Savings Bank from 1913 until his death in February 1936.

14   *There had been enough. Bangor Democrat,* Sept. 27, 1853.

Chapter Nine: The Great Depression

1   *We shall soon.* Federal Reserve Bank of Boston, *Closed for the Holiday: The Bank Holiday of 1933* (Boston: 1999), p. 3.

2   *It should be. Bangor Daily Commercial,* March 4, 1933.

3   *Unlimited power. Bangor Daily Commercial,* March 7, 1933.

4   *It was a colorful. Bangor Daily News,* March 16, 1933.

5   *Tonight more than ever. Bangor Daily News,* March 16, 1933.

6   *It was a year. Annual Report of the City of Bangor, Maine for the year ending December 31, 1932* (Bangor: 1932), p. 7.

7   *The calls. Municipal Activities, 1934* (Bangor: 1934), p. 12.

8   *The burden. Municipal Activities, 1935* (Bangor: 1935), p. 15.

9   *A Maine-ite.* Richard Lowitt and Maurine Beasley, *One Third of a Nation: Lorena Hickok Reports on the Great Depression* (Urbana, Illinois: 1981), p. 36.

10   *Welfare was non-existent. Central Maine Newspapers,* Oct. 29, 1999.

11   *Despite federal aid.* Judd, *Maine,* p. 519.

12   *practically bankrupt.* Judd, *Maine,* p. 523.

13 *Bangor, always a city. Bangor Daily News*, Aug. 15, 1945.

14 *a series of. Bangor Daily News*, Aug. 15, 1945.

Chapter Ten: The Winds of Change

1 *Once people. Bangor Daily News*, Feb. 14, 1952.

2 *Thrift. Bangor Daily News*, Feb. 14, 1952

3 Simpson was a Bangor lawyer who was born in Massachusetts and moved to Maine as a young man. He studied at Lincoln Academy and graduated from Bowdoin College in 1884. He moved to Bangor in 1910, worked as professor at the University of Maine Law School, and was a partner in the firm of Ryder and Simpson. In addition to serving as trustee and president at Bangor Savings Bank, Simpson served as legal counsel for Eastern Trust and Banking Company and the Bangor Building and Loan Association.

4 George F. Eaton was born in Brewer in 1892. He graduated from Bowdoin College in 1914 and earned a law degree from the University of Maine in 1916. He married Elizabeth Gale Littlefield in 1917. Eaton was the founder and senior partner with the law firm of Eaton, Peabody, Bradford and Veague in Bangor, and was involved with numerous businesses and organizations including spending thirty-three years as a trustee of Eastern Maine General Hospital. He also served in World War I, attended Hammond Street Congregational Church and served on the city council. He died in October 1956.

5 Donald S. Higgins was born in Brewer in 1897. He graduated from Bowdoin College in 1919. He worked as a general agent for Travelers Companies for fifty years. In addition to serving as president of Bangor Savings Bank, Higgins was a director of Merchants National Bank and president of the Bangor Loan and Building Association. He served on numerous other boards and held posts including: director of Eastern Maine Medical Center, trustee of Bangor Theological Seminary, and president of the Bangor Chamber of Commerce. He was an active Mason and attended the Brewer Methodist Church. He married Marian P. Harvey.

6 While greatly exaggerated, the liberal magazine *The Nation* (June 22, 1963) presented America with a grim picture of Maine in 1963. Author William Ellis called Maine "a state gasping for breath, bogged down in the muck of supreme depression — a state dedicated seemingly to the humiliation of its own people. Substandard living conditions are widespread."

7 *Bangor also supplies.* George Sessions Perry, "The Cities of America: Bangor, Maine," *Saturday Evening Post* (March 10, 1951).

8   *apparently are.* Perry, Saturday Evening Post (March 10, 1951), p. 97.

9   *In a city.* Bangor Daily News, Feb. 4, 1995.

10   *revitalize, bolster.* Bangor Daily News, April 12, 1961.

11   *Anyone coming.* Bangor Daily News, August 21, 1962.

12   *The Bangor Shopping.* Bangor Daily News, June 28, 1984.

13   *While Bangor's Urban Renewal.* Bangor Daily News, Oct. 30, 1967.

14   *composed of obsolete.* Bangor Daily News, June 29, 1969.

15   *When the Bangor Mall.* Down East magazine (January 1982), p. 13.

16   *I think we.* Portland Press Herald, Sept. 17, 1972.

Chapter Eleven: A Banking Revolution

1   *We had no trouble.* Maine Sunday Telegram, June 5, 1977.

2   *I like to think.* Maine Sunday Telegram, June 5, 1977.

3   *Outmoded regulations.* Report of the Governor's Bank Study Advisory Committee, 1974, p. 3.

4   *We are willing.* Bangor Daily News, May 23, 1975.

5   *I understand.* Maine Times, May 9, 1975.

6   *It is my feeling.* Portland Press Herald, October 9, 1975.

7   *I've known.* Bangor Daily News, May 27, 1995.

8   *I was a hillbilly.* Bangor Daily News, May 27, 1995.

9   Martyn A. Vickers was born Oct. 18, 1906 in Brownville Junction. He graduated from Catholic University in 1929 and earned a medical degree from Georgetown University in 1933. He was a doctor in Bangor for more than fifty years and was active in numerous medical associations. He served as chairman of Bangor Savings Bank from 1972 to 1989 and also served as president of the Bangor Public Library Trustees, chairman of the Bangor School Board, and as a director of Husson College. He attended St. Mary's Catholic Church.

10   *You're bringing the.* Bangor Daily News, April 3, 1991.

11   *{Maine Savings Bank}.* The Status of Maine's Financial Institutions, January 15, 1991 (Augusta), Introduction.

Chapter Twelve: Fleet of Foot, Eye on the Future.

1   In 1995, bank trustees were: G. Clifton Eames, chairman; Gary W. Smith, vice chairman; James H. Goff; Kenneth A. Hews; Malcolm Jones; Martha G. Newman; Robert A. Strong; and Calvin E. True. Arthur M. Johnson, a former trustee, still served on the search committee.

2   *We will be.* Maine Sunday Telegram, April 26, 1998.

3   *The market is. Bangor Daily News*, Dec. 1, 1997.

4   *marred by.* Gloria Hutchinson, "Bangor on the Penobscot: City
      Awaiting Renaissance?" *Down East* magazine, (January 1982).

5   *In the long run.* Hutchinson, *Down East* magazine (January 1982).

6   *there wasn't. Bangor Daily News*, January 10, 1985.

7   *what little bit. Bangor Daily News*, January 11, 1985.

8   *you're restoring. Bangor Daily News*, Feb. 12, 2001.

9   The Board of Trustees in 2002 is: David M. Carlisle, chairman; Gary
      W. Smith, vice chairman; P. James Dowe Jr.; James H. Goff; Charles
      E. Hewett; Kenneth A. Hews; Martha G. Newman; Robert A. Strong
      and Calvin E. True.

Selected Bibliography

Address of Governor Chamberlain to the Legislature of the State of Maine, January 1870. Augusta, 1870.

Andrews, H. Franklin. *The Hamlin Family: A Genealogy of James Hamlin of Barnstable, Massachusetts.* Exira, Iowa: Published by Author, 1902.

Appleby, Bruce. "Uncle Solon and Them Steers." Bachelor's thesis, Bowdoin College, 1960.

Atack, Jeremy and Peter Passell. *A New Economic View of American History from Colonial Times to 1940.* New York: W.W. Norton & Company, 1994.

Arndt, John Christopher. "The Solid Men of Bangor: Economic, Business and Political Growth of Maine's Urban Frontier 1769–1845." Ph. D diss., The Florida State University, 1987.

Bailey, Dudley P. *The Maine Savings Banks and the Late Crisis.* New York: The Banker's Magazine and Statistical Register, 1880.

Bangor Board of Trade. *The City of Bangor in 1883: A Condensed Historical and Descriptive review.* Bangor: Bangor Board of Trade, 1883.

Bangor Historical Society. *Fiftieth Anniversary of the Bangor Historical Society: Proceedings at the Bangor Public Library, Wednesday, April 8th, 1914.* Bangor: Bangor Historical Society, 1914.

Bangor, Maine: A City of Progress. Bangor: C.H. Glass and Company, 1912.

Bangor Savings Bank. *Rounding Out a Century, 1852-1952.* Bangor: Bangor Savings Bank, 1952.

Banks, Ronald F., editor. *A History of Maine: A Collection of Readings on the History of Maine 1600-1970.* Dubuque, Iowa: Kendall/Hunt Publishing Company, 1969.

Banks, Ronald F. *Maine Becomes a State: The Movement to Separate Maine from Massachusetts, 1785-1820.* Somersworth, New Hampshire: New Hampshire Publishing Company, 1973.

Biggar, H.P. *The Works of Samuel De Champlain in Six Volumes.* Toronto: The Champlain Society, 1922.

Blanding, Edward Mitchell. "Bangor, Maine." *New England Magazine* (April 1897).

———. *The City of Bangor: The Industries, Resources, Attractions and Business Life of Bangor and its Environs.* Bangor: Edward Mitchell Blanding, 1899.

Blanding, W.F., editor. *Bangor, Maine: Industries and Resources, 1888.* Bangor: Bangor Board of Trade, 1888.

Bourque, Bruce J. *Twelve Thousand Years: American Indians in Maine.* Lincoln, Nebraska: University of Nebraska Press, 2001.

Bygone Bangor. Bangor: Bangor Publishing Company, 1976.

Caldwell, Bill. *Rivers of Fortune.* Portland: Guy Gannett Publishing Co., 1983.

Chadbourne, Walter W. *A History of Banking in Maine, 1799–1930.* Orono, Maine: University of Maine Press, 1936.

Chase, Edward E. *Maine Railroads: A History of the Development of the Maine Railroad System.* Portland: The Southworth Press, 1926.

Chase, Henry. *Representative Men of Maine.* Portland: The Lakeside Press, 1893.

Clark, Charles E. *Maine: A Bicentennial History.* New York: W.W. Norton & Co. Inc., 1977.

Clark, Charles E, James S. Leamon and Karen Bowden. *Maine in the Early Republic: From Revolution to Statehood.* Hanover, New Hampshire: University Press of New England, 1988.

Cobb, Margo. *If These Walls Could Talk.* Bangor: YMCA Bangor-Brewer, 1999.

Coe, Harrie B., editor. *Maine: Resources, Attractions, and Its People.* New York: The Lewis Historical Publishing Company Inc., 1928.

Day, Clarence. *Ezekiel Holmes: Father of Maine Agriculture.* Orono, Maine: University of Maine Press, 1968.

Deans, Sis. *His Proper Post: A Biography of General Joshua L. Chamberlain.* Kearny, New Jersey: Belle Grove Publishing, 1996.

Dibner, Martin. *Portrait of Paris Hill.* Paris, Maine: Paris Hill Press, 1990.

Doty, C. Stewart. *Hard Times: The Farm Security Administration in Maine's St. John Valley, 1940–1943.* Orono: University of Maine Press, 1991.

Dunnan, Nancy. *Banking.* Englewood Cliffs, New Jersey: Silver Burdett Press Inc., 1990.

Eckstorm, Fannie Hardy. *The Penobscot Man.* Boston: Houghton, Mifflin and Company, 1904.

Ellis, William S., "The Trouble with Maine" *The Nation* (June 22, 1963).

The European and North American Railroad Co., its Charter, Organization, Condition, Means and Prospects. Cambridge: Press of John Wilson and Son, 1869.

Federal Reserve Bank of Boston. *Closed for the Holiday: The Bank Holiday of 1933.* Boston: Federal Reserve Bank of Boston, 1999.

Foner, Eric and John A. Garraty, editors. *The Reader's Companion to American History.* Boston: Houghton Mifflin Company, 1991.

Godfrey, John E. *The Journals of John Edwards Godfrey, 3 Vols.* Edited by James B. Vickery. Rockland, Maine: printed by Courier-Gazette Inc., 1979.

————. "The Annals of Bangor, 1769-1882." *History of Penobscot County, Maine with Illustrations and Biographical Sketches.* Cleveland: Williams, Chase & Co., 1882.

Goldstein, Judith S. *Crossing Lines: Histories of Jews and Gentiles in Three Communities.* New York: William Morrow and Company Inc., 1992.

Grant, Philip A. Jr., "The Campaign of 1834 and the Bank Question" *Maine Historical Society Newsletter* (Fall 1972).

Green, Nancy H. and Clarence H. Prisko. *History of Columbia and Columbia Falls.* Cherryfield, Maine: Narraguagus Printing Co., 1976.

Greenleaf, Moses. *A Survey of the State of Maine.* Portland: Shirley and Hyde, 1824.

Hamlin, Augustus C. *The History of Mount Mica of Maine, U.S.A. and its wonderful deposits of matchless tourmalines.* Bangor: A.C. Hamlin, 1895.

Hamlin, Charles Eugene. *The Life and Times of Hannibal Hamlin, by his Grandson.* Cambridge: Riverside Press, 1899.

Hamlin, Simon Moulton. *The Hamlins of New England.* Portland: The Moser Press, 1936.

Hassinger, Amy. *Finding Katahdin: An Exploration of Maine's Past.* Orono: University of Maine Press, 2001.

Hatch, Louis Clinton. *Maine: A History.* Somersworth, New Hampshire: New Hampshire Publishing Company, 1919.

Herbert, Richard A. *Modern Maine: Its Historic Background, People and Resources.* 4 vols. New York: Lewis Historical Publishing Company, 1951.

History of the Land Grant to the European and North American Railroad. Portland: State Chamber of Commerce and Agricultural League, 1923.

Holbrook, Stewart H. *Holy Old Mackinaw: A Natural History of the American Lumberjack.* New York: The MacMillan Company, 1938.

Hunt, H. Draper. *Hannibal Hamlin of Maine: Lincoln's First Vice-President.* Syracuse: Syracuse University Press, 1969.

Hutchinson, Gloria, "Bangor on the Penobscot: City Awaiting Renaissance?" *Down East* (January 1982).

Jameson, E.O. *The Choates in America, 1643-1896.* Boston: Alfred Mudge & Son, 1896.

Judd, Richard W., Edwin Churchill and Joel W. Eastman. *Maine: The Pine Tree State from Prehistory to the Present.* Orono: University of Maine Press, 1995.

Judd, Richard W. *Aroostook: A Century of Logging in Northern Maine.* Orono, Maine: The University of Maine Press, 1989.

Kirkland, Edward C. *A History of American Economic Life.* New York: F.S. Crofts & Company, 1932.

———. *Men, Cities and Transportation: A Study in New England History 1820–1900.* Cambridge: Harvard University Press, 1948.

Knox, John Jay. *A History of Banking in the United States.* New York: Bradford Rhodes & Company, 1900.

Lashbrook, Lawrence G. "Work Relief in Maine: The Administration and Programs of the WPA." Ph. D diss., University of Maine at Orono, 1977.

Leading Business Men of Bangor, Rockland and Vicinity. Boston: Mercantile Publishing Company, 1888.

Leighton, Levi. *Centennial Historical Sketch of the Town of Columbia, from 1799 to 1896.* Cherryfield, Maine: Narraguagus Printing Co., 1974.

Lowitt, Richard and Maurine Beasley. *One Third of a Nation: Lorena Hickok Reports on The Great Depression.* Urbana, Illinois: University of Illinois Press, 1981.

McCulloch, Hugh. *Men and Measures of Half a Century.* New York: C. Scribner's Sons, 1888.

McLeod, John E. "The Great Northern Paper Company." Orono: University of Maine at Orono, Special Collections, 1978. Photocopy.

McGaw, Jacob. "Notices of Bangor from its Settlement in A.D. 1769 to the End of 1819." Unpublished manuscript, Maine Historical Society, Portland.

Meader, Everett L. "The Greenback Party in Maine, 1876-1884." Master's thesis, University of Maine, 1950.

Morison, Samuel Eliot. *The Oxford History of the American People.* New York: Oxford University Press, 1965.

———. *Samuel de Champlain: Father of New France.* Boston: Little, Brown and Company, 1972.

Morton, A. C. *Report on the Survey of the European and North American Railway.* Portland: Harmon and Williams, 1851.

Mundy, James H. *Second to None: the Story of the 2d Maine Volunteer Infantry: The Bangor Regiment.* Scarborough, Maine: Harp Publications, 1992.

———. *Hard men, hard times: Maine and the Irish 1830–1860.* Scarborough, Maine: Harp Publications, 1990.

———. *Presidents of the Senate of Maine.* Augusta: Secretary of the Senate of Maine, 1979.

———— *Speakers of the Maine House of Representatives.* Augusta: Clerk of the House, 1981.

Muzzy, Franklin. *Critical Early Years in the Life of Franklin Muzzy told by Himself.* Minneapolis: Harrison and Smith Co., 1827.

Myers, Margaret G. *A Financial History of the United States.* New York: Columbia University Press, 1970.

Noyes, Edward A. "Discount Banks of Maine" 1896.

Ornstein, Franklin H. *Savings Banks: An Industry in Change.* Reston, Virgina: Reston Publishing Co., 1985.

Paine, Albert W. *History of Mt. Hope Cemetery, Bangor, Maine.* Bangor: O.F. Knowles & Co., 1907.

Paine, Albert W. *Paine Genealogy, Ipswich Branch.* Bangor: O.F. Knowles and Co., 1881.

Pike, Robert E. *Tall Trees, Tough Men.* New York: W.W. Norton & Co. Inc., 1967.

Poor, John A. "Remarks of John A. Poor, Upon the European and North American Railway," 1851. (Collection of the Portland Public Library.)

Poor, Laura E., editor. *The First International Railroad and the Colonization of New England: Life and Writing of John Alfred Poor.* New York: G.P. Putnam's Sons, 1892.

Potter, Edward Wesley. "Public Policy and Economic Growth in Maine, 1820–1857." Ph. D., diss., University of Maine, 1974.

Reilly, Wayne E. and Richard R. Shaw. "In Search of the Real Fan Jones" *Down East* (April 1988).

Ring, Elizabeth. *Maine in the Making of the Nation, 1783–1870.* Camden, Maine: Picton Press, 1996.

Robbins, Donald H.W. "Benjamin! You're in a Peck of Trouble! The Story of Benjamin D. Peck." Unpublished Manuscript by Donald H.W. Robbins, 1985.

Roberts, C.P., editor. *Knowles' Bangor Business Almanac for 1875 with Historical Sketches of Bangor and its Business Enterprises.* Bangor: O.F. Knowles & Co., 1875.

Rolde, Neil. *Maine: A Narrative History.* Gardiner, Maine: Tilbury House, 1990.

———— *An Illustrated History of Maine.* Augusta, Maine: Friends of the Maine State Museum to Commemorate the 175th Anniversary of Statehood, 1995.

Scroggins, Mark. *Hannibal: The Life of Abraham Lincoln's First Vice President.* Lanham, Maryland: University Press of America, 1994.

Shaw, Horace H. and Charles J. House. *The First Maine Heavy Artillery, 1862–1865.* Portland: 1903.

Shaw, Richard R. *Bangor Volume II: The Twentieth Century.* Dover, New Hampshire: Arcadia Publishing Corp., 1997.

Shettleworth, Earle G. Jr. "Benjamin Deane Imprinted his Design on City." *Bygone Bangor.* Bangor: Bangor Publishing Co., 1976.

Shorey, Henry A. *The Story of the Maine Fifteenth.* Bridgton, Maine: Press of Bridgton News, 1890.

Simonton, William G. Jr. "Maine and the Panic of 1837." Master's thesis, University of Maine at Orono, 1971.

Smith, David C. *A History of Lumbering in Maine 1861–1960.* Orono, Maine: University of Maine Press, 1972

Snow, Dean R. "Eastern Abenaki." *Handbook of North American Indians, Vol. 15.* Washington: Smithsonian Institution, 1978.

Souvenir of Bangor, Maine: photo-gravures. Bangor: J. D. Glynn, 1895.

Stackpole, Everett Birney. "State Banking in Maine." *Sound Currency* (May 1900).

Stanley, R.H. and George O. Hall. *Eastern Maine and The Rebellion: Being an Account of the Principal Local Events in Eastern Maine During the War.* Bangor: R.H. Stanley & Company, 1887.

The Story of Bangor: A Brief History of Maine's Queen City. Bangor: BookMarc's Publishing, 1999.

Sturtevant, Reginald H. *A History of Livermore, Maine.* Lewiston, Maine: Twin City Printery, 1970.

Taylor, Alan. *Liberty Men and Great Proprietors: The Revolutionary Settlement on the Maine Frontier, 1760–1820.* Chapel Hill, N.C.: The University of North Carolina Press, 1990.

Thompson, Deborah. *Bangor, Maine 1769-1914: An Architectural History.* Orono, Maine: University of Maine Press, 1988.

Toner, Carol N. *Persisting Traditions: Artisan Work and Culture in Bangor, Maine, 1820–1860.* New York: Garland Publishing Inc., 1995.

Tuttle, Charles W. "Hon. John Alfred Poor, of Portland, ME," *New–England Historical and Genealogical Register and Antiquarian Journal* (October 1872).

Unger, Irwin. *The Greenback Era : A Social and Political History of American Finance, 1865–1879.* Princeton, N.J.: Princeton University Press, 1964.

Vickery, James B., editor. *An illustrated history of the city of Bangor, Maine, formerly the plantation of Conduskeag or Kenduskeag in ye country of*

Arcadia on the river named Penobscot, containing narratives of ye ancient sites and persons. Bangor: Bangor Bi-centennial Committee, 1976.

————. Made in Bangor: Economic Emergence and Adaptation, 1834-1911. Bangor: Bangor Historical Society, 1984.

Voices From the Past: Bangor, First Hundred Years. Bangor: Juniper Press, 1978. (Reprint of *The Centennial Celebration of the Settlement of Bangor — September 30, 1869,* 1870.

Wait, George W. *Maine: Obsolete Paper Money and Scrip.* Wisconsin: Krause Publications, 1977.

Washburn, Israel. *Notes, Historical, Descriptive, and Personal of Livermore, in Androscoggin (formerly Oxford) County, Maine.* Portland: Bailey & Noyes, 1874.

Welfling, Weldon. *Mutual Savings Banks: The Evolution of a Financial Intermediary.* Cleveland: The Press of Case Western Reserve University, 1968.

Wescott, Richard R. "A History of Maine Politics 1840-1856: The Formation of the Republican Party." Ph.D. diss., University of Maine at Orono, 1966.

————. *New Men, New Issues: The Formation of The Republican Party in Maine.* Portland: Maine Historical Society, 1986.

Whitman, William E.S. and Charles H. True. *Maine in the War for the Union: A History of the Part Bourne by Maine Troops in the Suppression of The American Rebellion.* Lewiston, Maine: Nelson Dingley Jr. & Company, 1865.

Williamson, William D. *The History of the State of Maine; from Its First Discovery, A.D. 1602, to The Separation, A.D. 1820, Inclusive.* Hallowell, Maine: Glazier, Masters & Company, 1832.

Wood, Richard G., *A History of Lumbering in Maine, 1820–1861.* University of Maine Press, Orono, Maine, 1935, reprinted 1961.

Zelz, Abigail Ewing, and Marilyn Zoidis. *Woodsmen and Whigs: Historic Images of Bangor, Maine.* Virginia Beach, Virginia: Donning Co., 1991.

Interviews

Sally A. Bates
Severin Beliveau
Douglas Brown
David Carlisle
P. James Dowe Jr.
G. Clifton Eames
David Fox
Mike Healy
Glen Hutchinson
James F. Jaffray
Malcolm E. Jones
Regina Jones
Alice McInnis
David Nealley
Christopher Pinkham
Howard Trotzky
C. Dexter Wilson Jr.
Francis J. Zelz

Manuscript Collections

Hamlin Family Papers, University of Maine, Orono
Peirce Family Papers, University of Maine, Orono
Stetson Family Papers, University of Maine, Orono
Vickery, James B., Collection of Manuscripts, and Research Collection, University of Maine, Orono
Muzzy Papers, Maine Historical Society
William D. Williamson Collection, Maine Historical Society

Newspapers and Journals

Bangor Daily Whig and Courier
Bangor Daily Commercial
Bangor Daily News
Bangor Historical Magazine
Board of Trade Journal
Biographical Directory of the United States Congress

Central Maine Newspapers

Chamber of Commerce Journal of Maine

The (Farmington) *Chronicle*

Oxford (Paris, Maine) *Democrat*

Eastern (Portland) *Argus*

Evening (Portland) *Express*

The (Bangor) *Industrial Journal*

Kennebec (Augusta) *Journal*

The Machias Union

Maine Times

Maine Sunday Telegram

Portland Advertiser

Portland Press Herald

Sprague's Journal of Maine History

Thomas Business Review

Miscellaneous Documents and Sources

American Heritage Encyclopedia of American History.

Bangor Savings Bank. Annual reports and self-produced reports, booklets and commemorative publications and internal documents.

Bangor/ Brewer City Directories

Bangor Death Records, 1800–1892, Church of Latter Day Saints

Bangor, City of. Mayor's address and annual reports of city departments.

Bangor, City of. Tax Inventories

Bangor, Maine Community & Economic Profile, Department of Community & Economic

Gale Encyclopedia of Native American Tribes

Grolier Multimedia Encyclopedia

Maine, State of. Report of the Bureau of Taxation.

Maine Register or Yearbook. Published annually or biennially by the State of Maine.

Maine, State of. Acts and Resolves. Annual reports of the acts and resolves passed by Maine legislature.

Maine, State of. Public Documents. Annual reports from state agencies.

Maine, State of. Annual Report of the Bank Commissioners of the State of Maine. Annual or biennial reports from the agency that oversees state banking.

Maine, State of. Superior Court records, Augusta

Maine, State of. District Court records, Augusta

Maine, State of. Augusta Insane Asylum register, Augusta

Maine, State of. Supreme Judicial Court records, Augusta.

Mount Hope Cemetery Interment Listings, September 14, 1861 – Bangor, Me. Mount Hope Corporation 1993

New Encyclopedia Britannica

Report of the Governor's Banking Study Advisory Committee, August 1974

Report of the Superintendent Bureau of Banking of the State of Maine for the Ten Year Period June 30, 1972–June 30, 1982.

United States. Federal census records. Manuscript and Industrial and Agricultural Schedules

World Book Encyclopedia

Selected Web Sites:

Finnegan, Pat. "The Twelve Days: January, 1880" in To the Limits of the Soul's Ideal. www.lenweaver.com/joshua/jlc12day.htm.

Maine State Archives, "Summary Unit Histories and Related Records," http://www.state.me.us/sos/arc/archives/military/civilwar/reghis.htm

WCTU organizational history, www.wctu.org/history.html

1918 Influenza Pandemic. www.stanford.edu/group/virus/uda/

Influenza Timeline,
www.pbs.org/wgbh/amex/influenza/timeline/index.html

Ten Hour Work Day Circular, published at
www.oberlin.edu/~gkornbl/Hist258/TenHourCirc.html

Encyclopedia.com

Index